# HIERARCHICAL ORGANIZATION IN SOCIETY

*With thanks, to Priscilla, as she travels with me.*

*With pride, to Sarah and David, as they journey into the future.*

# Hierarchical Organization in Society

A Canadian perspective

JAMES A. POOLER
*University of Saskatchewan*

Routledge
Taylor & Francis Group
LONDON AND NEW YORK

First published 2000 by Ashgate Publishing

Reissued 2018 by Routledge
2 Park Square, Milton Park, Abingdon, Oxon OX14 4RN
711 Third Avenue, New York, NY 10017, USA

*Routledge is an imprint of the Taylor & Francis Group, an informa business*

Copyright © James A. Pooler 2000

All rights reserved. No part of this book may be reprinted or reproduced or utilised in any form or by any electronic, mechanical, or other means, now known or hereafter invented, including photocopying and recording, or in any information storage or retrieval system, without permission in writing from the publishers.

Notice:
Product or corporate names may be trademarks or registered trademarks, and are used only for identification and explanation without intent to infringe.

Publisher's Note
The publisher has gone to great lengths to ensure the quality of this reprint but points out that some imperfections in the original copies may be apparent.

Disclaimer
The publisher has made every effort to trace copyright holders and welcomes correspondence from those they have been unable to contact.

A Library of Congress record exists under LC control number: 00132826

ISBN 13: 978-1-138-72468-6 (hbk)
ISBN 13: 978-1-138-72466-2 (pbk)
ISBN 13: 978-1-315-19233-8 (ebk)

# Contents

*List of Figures*      ix
*List of Tables*      xiii

**1 Introduction**      1
   Everyday Hierarchies      2
   The Importance of Hierarchies      10

**2 All about Hierarchies**      17
   Properties of Hierarchies      17
     *Physical Properties of Hierarchies*      17
     *Communications Properties of Hierarchies*      18
     *Geographical Properties of Hierarchies*      19
   Processes in Hierarchies      20
   Hierarchies within Hierarchies      24
   Hierarchies in Nature      25
   Hierarchies at Different Scales      26
   Conceptual Hierarchies      26
   Structured/Unstructured Hierarchies      27
   Dynamic/Static Hierarchies      27
   Open/Closed Hierarchies      28
   Democratic/Autocratic Hierarchies      28
   Political/Benign Hierarchies      29
   Formal/Informal Hierarchies      29
   Self-Organizing Hierarchies      30
   The Direction of Information Flow in Hierarchies      30
   Diffusion in Hierarchies      31
   Private/Public Hierarchies      31
   Competitive/Cooperative Hierarchies and "Coopetition"      32
   The Physical Form of Hierarchies      32
     *Symmetry*      32
     *Dimensionality*      33

|  |  |
|---|---|
| *Maturity* | 34 |
| Functional/Nonfunctional Hierarchies | 34 |

## 3  Up the Corporate Ladder — 37
| | |
|---|---|
| Canadian and Global Corporate Hierarchies | 38 |
| Corporate Mergers and Acquisitions in the Global Economy | 45 |
| A Contrarian Point of View | 49 |
| Evidence of Global Change | 50 |
| The United States of Europe? | 51 |
| The Evolution of the Internal Corporate Hierarchy | 53 |
| The Optimum Form of the Corporate Hierarchy | 57 |
| The Corporate Hierarchy - An Absolute Necessity or a Dinosaur? | 62 |

## 4  Education and Inequity — 65
| | |
|---|---|
| The Educational System in Canada - In Decline? | 66 |
| The Educational Hierarchy | 68 |
| Accounting for the School Hierarchy within Cities | 69 |
| The Educational Hierarchy in Rural Areas | 72 |
| Should Families in "Have-not" Towns be Reimbursed in Regard to the Extra Costs of Their Location? | 75 |

## 5  The Future of Communities — 79
| | |
|---|---|
| Why do People "Huddle Together" in Communities? | 80 |
| How Does a Hierarchy of Communities Emerge? | 81 |
| Corporate Hierarchies within Hierarchies of Communities | 84 |
| The Changing Face of the Hierarchy of Communities | 85 |
| The Canadian Population | 88 |
| The Canadian Hierarchy of Communities | 90 |
| The "Americanadian" Hierarchy of Cities | 93 |
| Toronto - World Class City? | 95 |

## 6  Travel, Transport and Continentalization — 99
| | |
|---|---|
| Transportation within Hierarchies | 100 |
| The National Transportation Hierarchy | 103 |
| Ongoing Changes in the National Transportation Hierarchy | 108 |
| The $49^{th}$ Parallel - Gateway to the U.S. | 111 |

## 7 Getting Around in the City — 117
  The Journey across Town — 118
  The Public Transit Hierarchy in the City — 120
  The Timing of Urban Flows — 122
  Urban Transportation and the Automobile — 123
  Planning for the Future of Urban Transport — 129
  Urban Evolution — 131

## 8 Retail in the City and the Countryside — 139
  Shopping and Travel — 141
  Retail Hierarchies in the City — 143
  Retail Hierarchies in the Countryside — 147
  Impacts of the Rural Retail Hierarchy — 148
  Rural Communities in Decline — 150
  Retail Strategies — 151
  Shopping Malls as Hierarchies — 153

## 9 Leaving Home — 157
  Canadians on the Move — 159
  The Hierarchy of Migration — 161
  Migration among Canadian Cities — 163
  Continental and International Migration among Cities — 165
  The Brain Drain - Canada as a Competitor in the International Jobs Hierarchy — 169
  Migration from Canada to the Rest of the World — 173
  Migration from the Rest of the World to Canada — 175

## 10 How Our Communities Shape the Quality of Our Lives — 181
  Sports Hierarchies — 181
  Information and News from the Media — 188
  Social and Cultural Facilities and "Critical Mass" — 192
  Goods and Services on the Move — 193
  Travelling Entertainment — 194
  Fads and Innovations — 195

| | |
|---|---:|
| **11 Canadian Medical Care - Equal Treatment for All?** | **197** |
| How Big is the Doctors' Bill? | 198 |
| Community Size and Health Care | 201 |
| Erosion at the Bottom of the Medical System | 204 |
| Calgary - The Best Place in Canada to Have a Stroke | 206 |
| How Far to the Nearest Doctor? | 207 |
| The Medical "Brain Drain" to the United States? | 209 |
| Health Care Funding in the United States and Canada | 211 |
| Should the United States Provide a Second Tier of Health Care for Canadians? | 215 |
| *Index* | *219* |

# List of Figures

| | | |
|---|---|---|
| Figure 1.1 | Basic Hierarchy or Corporate Ladder | 1 |
| Figure 1.2 | Typical, Simple Corporate Hierarchy | 3 |
| Figure 1.3 | Shopping Hierarchy | 4 |
| Figure 1.4 | Hardware Store Hierarchy | 4 |
| Figure 1.5 | Canada's Educational Hierarchy | 5 |
| Figure 1.6 | Typical Within-School Hierarchy | 5 |
| Figure 1.7 | Airline Hierarchy | 6 |
| Figure 1.8 | Canadian Stock Market Hierarchy | 7 |
| Figure 1.9 | The Hierarchy of Cities, Towns and Villages | 7 |
| Figure 1.10 | Sports Playoffs Elimination Hierarchy | 8 |
| Figure 1.11 | Street Address Hierarchy | 9 |
| Figure 1.12 | The Human Hierarchy | 14 |
| Figure 2.1 | Treelike Hierarchy | 18 |
| Figure 2.2 | Normal Triangular Shaped Hierarchy | 21 |
| Figure 2.3 | Bottom-Heavy Hierarchy | 22 |
| Figure 2.4 | Narrow-Bottomed Hierarchy | 23 |
| Figure 2.5 | Narrow-Waisted Hierarchy | 23 |
| Figure 2.6 | Top-Heavy Hierarchy | 24 |
| Figure 2.7 | A Conceptual Hierarchy | 27 |
| Figure 2.8 | Unbalanced or Nonsymmetrical Hierarchy | 33 |
| Figure 2.9 | The Fast-Food Hierarchy | 35 |
| Figure 3.1 | The Canadian Corporate Hierarchy Based on the TSE | 39 |
| Figure 3.2 | Canadian Corporate Hierarchy | 42 |
| Figure 3.3 | International Corporate Hierarchy | 43 |
| Figure 3.4 | Top 10 Companies by Market Capitalization - 1998 | 50 |
| Figure 3.5 | Top 10 Companies by Market Capitalization - 1990 | 51 |
| Figure 3.6 | Typical, Simple Corporate Hierarchy | 57 |
| Figure 4.1 | Educational Hierarchy | 68 |
| Figure 4.2 | Map of Educational Bussing Pattern | 73 |
| Figure 4.3 | Map of Educational Hierarchy | 74 |
| Figure 4.4 | Tree Diagram of Educational Hierarchy | 74 |
| Figure 5.1 | Map of a Simple Set of Communities | 81 |
| Figure 5.2 | Map of a Simple Hierarchy of Communities | 82 |

| Figure 5.3 | Map of a Hierarchy of Communities | 83 |
| Figure 5.4 | Treelike Hierarchy of Communities | 83 |
| Figure 5.5 | Map of Warehouse Hierarchy within Community Hierarchy | 84 |
| Figure 5.6 | "Hierarchy" of Provincial Populations | 90 |
| Figure 5.7 | The Canadian Urban Hierarchy | 93 |
| Figure 5.8 | The Canadian-American Hierarchy of Cities | 97 |
| Figure 6.1 | Map of Travel in an Urban Hierarchy | 101 |
| Figure 6.2 | Map of Size of Flows in an Urban Hierarchy | 102 |
| Figure 6.3 | Canada's Airport Hierarchy | 106 |
| Figure 6.4 | Map of Hub and Spoke Air Traffic Hierarchy | 106 |
| Figure 6.5 | Map of "Double" Hub and Spoke with Connecting Link | 107 |
| Figure 6.6 | Typical Road Classification Hierarchy | 110 |
| Figure 6.7 | CN Railway Acquires Illinois Central Railway | 114 |
| Figure 7.1 | Map of the Journey across Town in the Street Hierarchy | 119 |
| Figure 7.2 | The Endless Cycle of Road Improvement | 121 |
| Figure 7.3 | Map of Mass Transit Flows in a City | 122 |
| Figure 7.4 | The Timing of Flows in the City | 124 |
| Figure 7.5 | Daily Transit and Automobile Flows in Edmonton | 127 |
| Figure 7.6 | The Endless Cycle of Traffic and Development | 131 |
| Figure 8.1 | 1934 Map of Where Farmers Got Their Goods and Services | 142 |
| Figure 8.2 | Urban Shopping Hierarchy | 143 |
| Figure 8.3 | Map of the Retail Hierarchy in the City | 145 |
| Figure 8.4 | The Hierarchy of Roads in the City | 146 |
| Figure 8.5 | Shopping Hierarchy in a Rural Area | 147 |
| Figure 8.6 | Map of Rural Shopping Hierarchy | 149 |
| Figure 8.7 | Typical Shopping Mall | 155 |
| Figure 9.1 | The Hierarchy of Community Migration | 162 |
| Figure 9.2 | The Global Hierarchy of City Migration | 165 |
| Figure 9.3 | The Hierarchy of Major American and Canadian Cities | 168 |
| Figure 9.4 | Immigration to Canadian Provinces | 178 |
| Figure 10.1 | The Hockey Hierarchy within Canada | 182 |
| Figure 10.2 | The Canadian Urban Hierarchy and the NHL | 186 |
| Figure 10.3 | The Canadian-American Hierarchy of Cities and the NFL | 187 |
| Figure 10.4 | "Map" of Canadian Cities According to News Flows | 191 |
| Figure 10.5 | Flows of Fads and Innovations in the Hierarchy of Communities | 196 |

| | | |
|---|---|---|
| Figure 11.1 | Number of Physicians per 100,000 Population, 1996-1997 | 199 |
| Figure 11.2 | Total Health Expenditure by Province, 1998 - Dollars Per Person | 200 |
| Figure 11.3 | Number of Physicians by Age-Group and Gender, Canada, 1997 | 201 |
| Figure 11.4 | Medical Hierarchy within a Major City | 202 |
| Figure 11.5 | Medical Hierarchy in a Rural Area | 203 |
| Figure 11.6 | Map of Medical Hierarchy in an Area Surrounding a City | 204 |
| Figure 11.7 | 1997 Budgets for Cancer Research | 213 |
| Figure 11.8 | Average Budget of Research Projects in Canada and the U.S. | 214 |

# List of Tables

| Table 3.1 | The TSE 35 | 40 |
|---|---|---|
| Table 3.2 | The *Financial Post Magazine* Top 50 Canadian Companies, 1997 Revenue | 40 |
| Table 3.3 | The *Fortune* Top 50 Global Companies, 1998 Revenue | 44 |
| Table 3.4 | Top Five Canadian Mergers of 1998 | 52 |
| Table 3.5 | Comparison of the Economies of EMU and U.S. | 53 |
| Table 4.1 | Enrollment in Elementary and Secondary Schools | 66 |
| Table 5.1 | Farm Numbers and Size in Canada | 86 |
| Table 5.2 | Farm Income and Value in Canada | 88 |
| Table 5.3 | Provincial Population Sizes | 89 |
| Table 5.4 | Canadian Metropolitan Areas by Population and Rank | 91 |
| Table 5.5 | "Americanadian" Metropolitan Population | 94 |
| Table 6.1 | Canada's Busiest Airports | 105 |
| Table 6.2 | The Most Popular Types of Transport | 109 |
| Table 6.3 | Trade Patterns within Canada and with the U.S. and the World | 112 |
| Table 6.4 | The World's Top 10 Biggest Trading Partners, 1995 | 113 |
| Table 9.1 | Net Interprovincial Migration of Population, 1991-1996 | 160 |
| Table 9.2 | Net Migration for Canadian Cities, 1996-1997 | 164 |
| Table 9.3 | Percentage Rates of Growth of Major Canadian Cities | 166 |
| Table 9.4 | Fastest Rates of Growth for Canadian Municipalities | 167 |
| Table 10.1 | Newspapers by Community Size | 190 |
| Table 11.1 | Migration of Active Canadian Physicians, 1991-1996 | 209 |
| Table 11.2 | Health Spending - Select G-7 Countries, 1994 | 215 |

# 1 Introduction

Hierarchies are one of the most important concepts we have in order to understand the world around us. They affect us as individuals. They determine the nature of the social and economic systems in which we live. At the same time most of these hierarchies are almost invisible. People do not see them until their attention is drawn to them. But once they see them, it is hard for them to look at the world again without seeing it from the unique perspective that hierarchies provide.

A hierarchy is an organizational system that is structured in a treelike manner, with levels of status or authority stacked one above the other. The classical and best known example of a hierarchy is probably the typical diagram that describes the structure of a company or business, also known as The Corporate Ladder (see Figure 1.1). The essence of the inverted "tree" of a hierarchy is that it is typically broad at the bottom and narrow at the top.

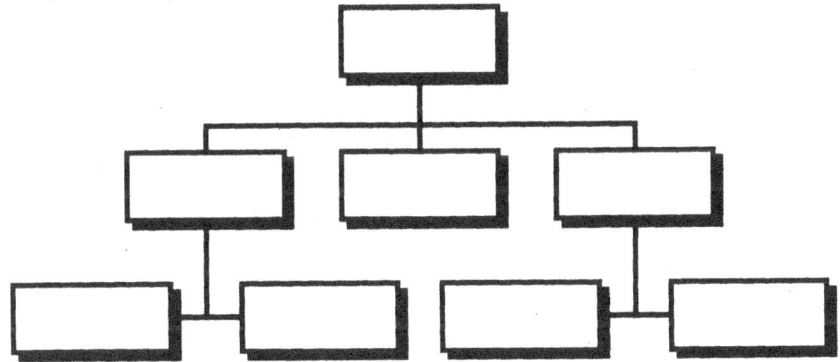

Figure 1.1 Basic Hierarchy or Corporate Ladder

All kinds of things of interest to human beings are organized as hierarchies. Companies, educational systems, transport systems, retail stores, corporations, communities, population migrations, medical systems, and all other sorts of real world phenomena can be thought of as being hierarchical.

This book is about all kinds of hierarchies and their effects at a variety of scales. It is about understanding the hierarchical systems around us, and the ones in which we are immersed every day. The central theme is that it is possible to get a better grip on the past, present, and future of the world, if it is viewed through the point of view of hierarchies.

Anyone who is interested in planning for the future needs to understand and appreciate the hierarchical nature of the systems around us. Schools, small businesses, large corporations, government and non-government organizations, and even individuals need to be cognizant of the hierarchies that surround us, and respectful of their significance in our society. Legitimate planning for the future recognizes hierarchies and gives due attention to their significant place in the planning process.

Hierarchical thinking is for all people. Appreciating the existence of hierarchies tells individuals a great deal about their place in their personal and professional lives. You, and the world around you, are positioned in, and defined by, a wide variety of hierarchical systems that are constantly shaping the form of your existence. Like invisible hands these forces work to determine the course of your life and the course of the world around you.

Unlike many other books, it is not the purpose of this one to forecast or predict social or economic trends. Instead, this book is intended to promote a new perspective; a new point of view; a new way of looking at things. Out of this comes a new way of solving problems or dealing with situations that are intrinsically hierarchical but that were not perceived that way in the past. In other words, this book presents a new way of looking at old problems. In the chapters that follow, the perspective of hierarchies is applied in greater detail to a multitude of topics, and it is through this diversity that readers will come to see the wide ranging applicability of hierarchical thinking.

**Everyday Hierarchies**

Every one of us is an everyday participant in a very large number of hierarchies. Hierarchies are employed to organize things, and almost every organized thing, from a tree leaf to a corporate structure, is a form of hierarchy. To understand how the world around us functions from day-to-day is to understand how virtually everything is organized hierarchically.

Most people think of themselves as living in an isolated world where they are masters of their own fate. Little are they aware of the fact that they are emerged in hierarchical organizations all day long, and that these organizations have a direct effect on guiding and organizing their daily lives and activities. Consider some examples. When you are at work you are normally part of a corporate or institutional work hierarchy (see Figure 1.2). A hierarchical organization will normally come into place whenever any business has more than a few employees. Hierarchies occur whenever there is a task to be accomplished that is too big for a few individuals to handle. When tasks are delegated to a number of people or employees, a hierarchical system of organization will tend to arise. Employees move from the bottom toward the top as they earn promotions.

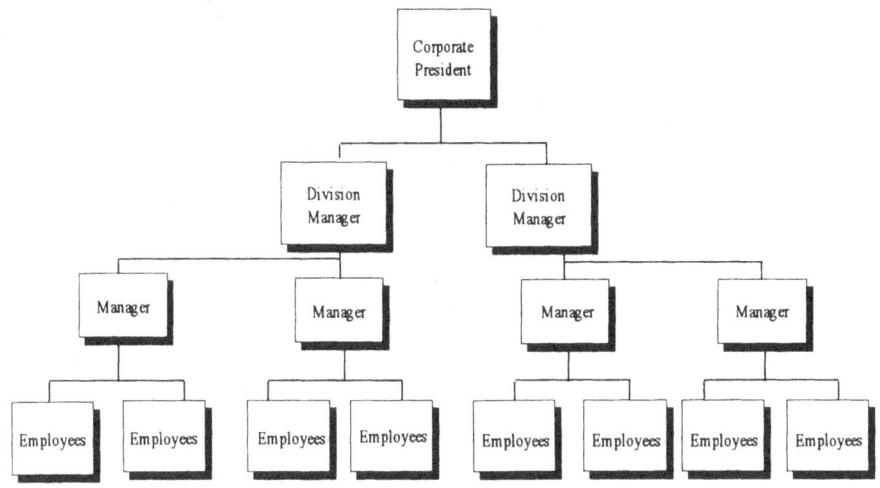

**Figure 1.2 Typical, Simple Corporate Hierarchy**

Regardless of whether you choose to shop at a convenience store, a mall, or in the downtown area, you are doing your shopping in a hierarchical retail system. Figure 1.3 indicates how stores, businesses, and shopping centres are organized as a hierarchy within a typical city. As is the case with all hierarchies, this is a shopping system that is broad at the bottom and narrow at the top. There is always a single large downtown shopping area, followed by a sprinkling of very large suburban malls, dozens and dozens of minor neighbourhood and strip malls, and hundreds of individual and neighbourhood convenience stores. Shoppers advance from the bottom toward the top as they seek out more specialized goods and services.

Not only do hierarchies exist all around us, but they are also rapidly changing the way we live. Consider the retail hierarchy of hardware stores, for example. Although the hardware retail hierarchy may still look somewhat like the pattern illustrated in Figure 1.4, it is apparent that the

4  *Hierarchical Organization in Society*

structure of this hierarchy is changing through time. In particular, we are all aware that the presence of the "big box" stores at the top is causing the smaller neighbourhood retailers, and even the other franchisees, to go out of business. In fact, the bottom levels of the hierarchy of Figure 1.4 may have already started to disappear. As we shall see, this ominous pattern of hierarchical shift is happening in several sectors of our economy.

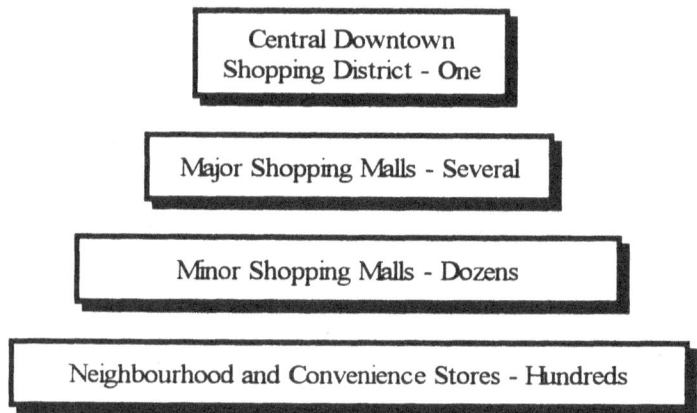

**Figure 1.3  Shopping Hierarchy**

If your kids go to school, the school system is organized as a hierarchy all the way from the elementary to the post-secondary level. Consider Figure 1.5, which illustrates the hierarchy of the national educational system. Once again there is the typical inverted treelike structure with fewer branches at the top and many branches at the bottom.

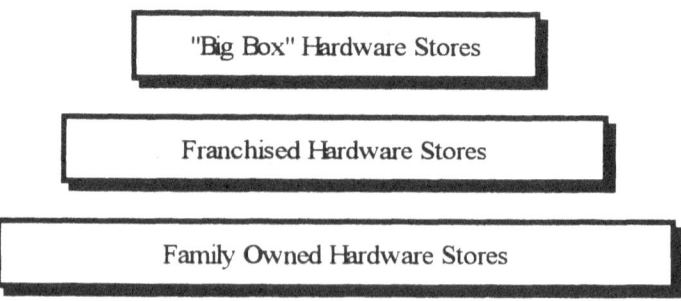

**Figure 1.4  Hardware Store Hierarchy**

There are good reasons why hierarchies have this characteristic pyramid shape, as will be discussed in the chapters that follow.

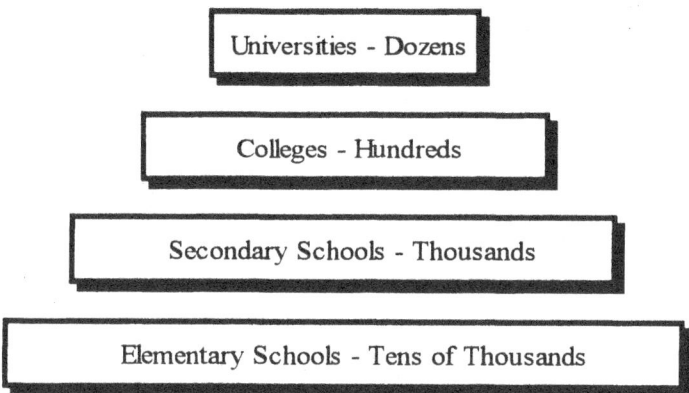

**Figure 1.5  Canada's Educational Hierarchy**

In addition to the classic educational hierarchy laid out in Figure 1.5, it is interesting to note that the organization *within* each school or institution can also be seen as being hierarchical, from the principal on down (see Figure 1.6). In most such hierarchies there is an element of "control" or authority that emanates from the top and spreads towards the bottom.

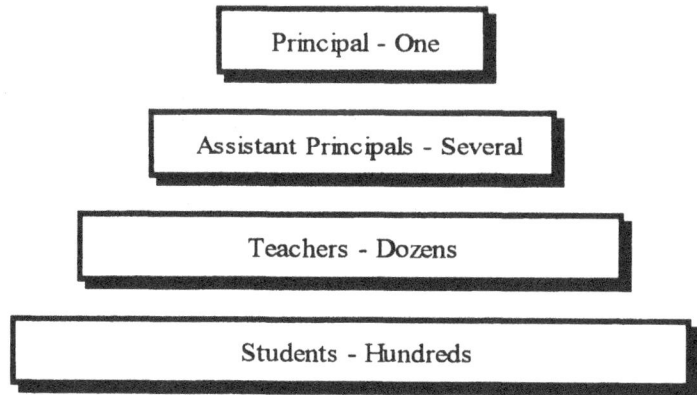

**Figure 1.6  Typical Within-School Hierarchy**

## 6  Hierarchical Organization in Society

Hierarchies are so prevalent in our lives that they not only literally dominate our day-to-day activities, but they also control the world around us. Most businesses and corporations can be considered as being parts of hierarchies. For example, consider airlines in Canada. Obviously the company atop the Canadian hierarchy is Air Canada. But below it there are other "levels" of other airlines in Canada (see Figure 1.7).

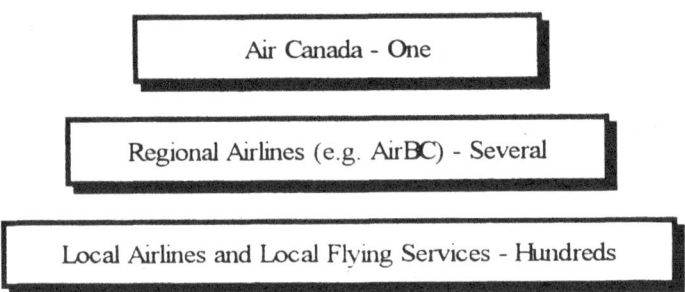

**Figure 1.7  Airline Hierarchy**

Are you following any of the big corporate mergers or acquisitions in the news? If so, you are watching the corporate system transform itself into a more efficient economic hierarchy. Are you interested in the changing face of Canada's industrial and economic future? For it to be truly understood, Canada's economy must be considered to be but a small part, a minor player, in the North American, and global, industrial hierarchy. Ever wonder why there are so many new trade agreements that are being pursued around the world? It is because the old borders and boundaries do not accurately reflect the new international trade hierarchy.

Do you follow the stock markets? Stocks sort themselves into a hierarchy by company size, where size is often measured as market capitalization (that is, number of stock shares multiplied by their value). There are Blue Chip stocks (really big companies), Large-Cap stocks (big companies), and Common stocks (average companies), (see Figure 1.8).

Interested in investing in mutual funds? You will be putting your money into a relatively young and immature hierarchy that has yet to evolve into its optimal form. There should be many more mergers to come as the youthful mutual fund industry sorts itself into clearer, separate hierarchical levels. What is clear at the moment is that the Fidelity Company is on top of the hierarchy, as the biggest mutual fund company in the world, with over 12 million investors and over $900 billion (U.S.) in assets.

Introduction 7

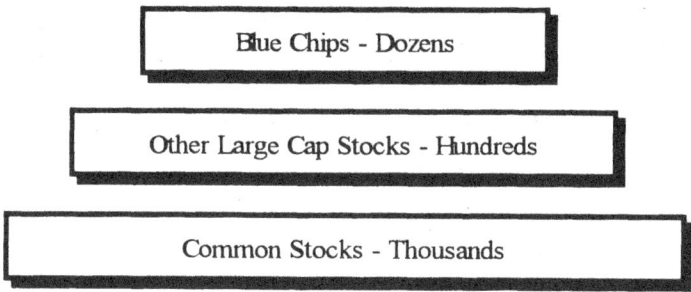

**Figure 1.8 Canadian Stock Market Hierarchy**

Villages, small towns, and cities, wherever they are located geographically, are all parts of a hierarchy of communities, shown in Figure 1.9. Consider a typical Canadian province. At the bottom level there are several hundred small communities, or villages. Next come hundreds of larger towns. The top level consists of dozens of still larger cities. We shall see later the importance of living within this hierarchy of communities and how it shapes our daily lives in innumerable and almost invisible ways. When you travel among these communities, whether on the road, by rail, or by air, you travel also within a transportation hierarchy.

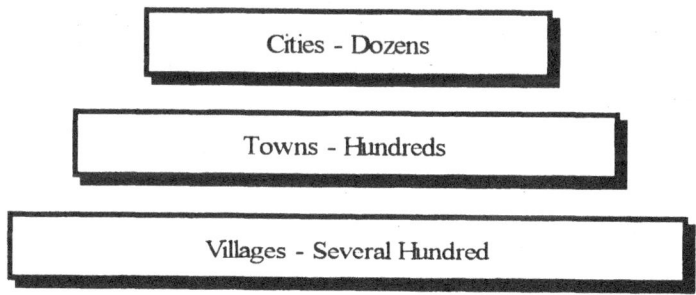

**Figure 1.9 The Hierarchy of Cities, Towns and Villages**

It becomes a challenge to think of activities and events that do *not* involve hierarchies. Almost all of them do. If you seek out medical treatment today you will participate in the medical hierarchy. If you watch professional sports on TV you are looking at one particular level of a sports hierarchy. In addition, sports event playoffs are usually organized as hierarchies. This type of elimination hierarchy will be familiar to most readers (see Figure 1.10). Going to church this week? You are participating

8  *Hierarchical Organization in Society*

in another organized system with a rigidly hierarchical framework. Are you part of a sports team? If you are, you are part of a team hierarchy. Hoping for a promotion at work? This is a desire on your part to move up in the hierarchy. Don't like your boss? Too bad. He or she is higher than you in the hierarchy. Do your kids play minor sports? If so, they're in a hierarchic system where control, just like most things in life, runs from the top down.

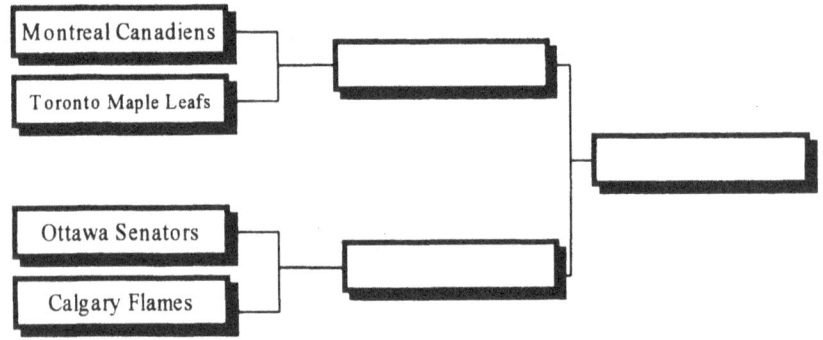

**Figure 1.10  Sports Playoffs Elimination Hierarchy**

When you travel around a city by automobile you are driving in a street hierarchy. At the bottom of this tree are the smallest lanes and alleys, and at the top are the major arteries and expressways. The street network serves as a conduit to direct traffic flows through a treelike hierarchy, like water through a funnel.

The postal address of every Canadian is also part of a hierarchical system of ordering information. Consider the address:

The Prime Minister
24 Sussex Drive
Ottawa
Ontario
Canada

What most people see here is a simple, traditional street address. What you should see instead is a system for organizing hierarchical information about the location of individuals (Figure 1.11).

This is a highly effective system; it enables us to locate a single individual from among the 30 million individuals in Canada in just five lines of text or levels in a hierarchy. That is very efficient. Think of the address as being part of the Windows program on a computer screen.

Canada is like the Start button. At the next level the user chooses a province, at the next level a city, at the next level a street, and finally an *individual* at that street address. To choose *one individual among the globe's 8 billion people* it would simply look like this:

Individual
Street Address
Community
Province or State
Country

Can you think of a more effective way for organizing such a complex set of information, more simply? Hierarchies are indeed powerful organizing systems.

The same line of reasoning applies to the very territorial organization of Canada. It too is organized as a hierarchy. In Canada, counties or municipalities are merged to form provinces and territories, while provinces and territories are merged to form the country. Like the pieces of a jigsaw puzzle, all of the pieces of one level fit neatly inside the next level. Similarly, the Government of Canada consists of Members of Parliament (MP's) representing geographical regions which are then ultimately represented in Ottawa where the Prime Minister, the first minister if you will, is at the top of the hierarchy.

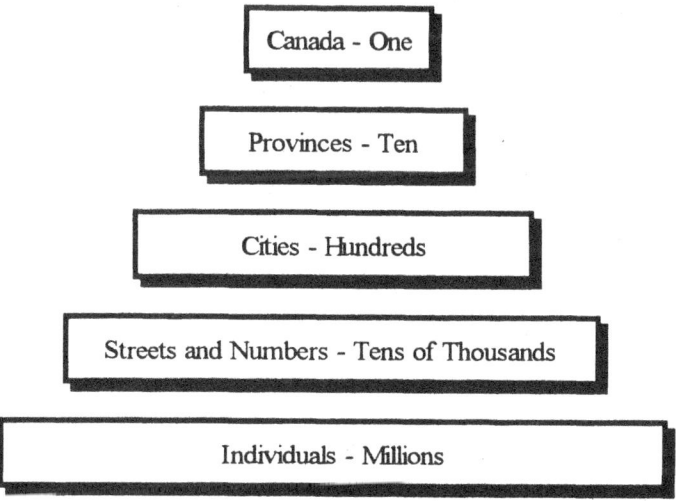

**Figure 1.11 Street Address Hierarchy**

Consider some of the other types of hierarchies around us: Labour unions. All businesses with more than a few employees. All large companies. Police services. Mall layouts. Water and sewer line systems. Your cardiovascular system. Natural gas and electrical distribution systems. Fire departments. Telephone networks. Parking lot and store aisle layouts. The military. All national and international government organizations such as the UN, NATO, WHO, UNICEF, NASA, etc. Newspapers. All government services, bureaucracies and agencies such as Revenue Canada, Statistics Canada, Canada Pension Plan, etc. Organized crime. Professional organizations. Committees. The legal system. The RCMP. The staff at every store at which you shop. Clubs. Universities. The local fund raising committee. And so on. The list is almost endless.

Does this roster of activities and organizations sound impressive? It should; it covers virtually every imaginable type of organized activity or system. But, at the same time, most of us are unaware of the presence of these hierarchies around us. Most people participate in them willingly, unknowingly and without the slightest awareness of their existence. Yet they have an enormous influence on almost everything we do including where we work, how we invest our money, where we spend our leisure time, where we travel, the services available to us, and many other facets of our lives.

## The Importance of Hierarchies

Hierarchies explain a lot of things. They enable us to make predictions. They tell us which cities should have sports franchises, or what towns should have specialized medical facilities, such as CAT scans. They allow us to forecast what geographical areas should have shopping centres or schools. They enable us to understand Canada's position as an industrial power, or to predict where the next corporate mergers should take place.

Hierarchies are important for individuals. It is not just a matter of seeing the world through the perspective of hierarchies but also a matter of dealing with the consequences of hierarchies from an everyday point of view. Suppose you live in a smaller town or city. What are the social and cultural services, and facilities, that you are giving up by not living in the big city? What are the medical and educational services and facilities that you must sacrifice by living in a small community? For example, suppose you live in a smaller community that does not have a university or community college, but your children wish to pursue education beyond high school. If your children *have* to live away from home to take advantage of higher education, what are the physical and emotional costs to your family? Should governments reimburse Canadians who live in smaller centres for costs like these?

Hierarchies are important for businesses. Businesses both small and large need to understand their place in the corporate hierarchy. Moreover, they need to maintain or advance their hierarchic positions if they wish to excel. Why, for example, are most of the major corporate entities in Canada located at the "top" of the Canadian urban hierarchy in Toronto? What are the implications for corporations that are located at "lower" levels in the hierarchy of communities? For smaller companies, it is important to consider "positioning" within the local retail hierarchy. What is the difference between a mall location or a plaza location? What is the difference between a mall location and a downtown location?

Planners need to have a thorough understanding of hierarchies. For instance, consider the hierarchy consisting of the elementary, secondary, and post-secondary school systems. Could the elementary educational system be made more cost efficient with fewer larger schools, and more bussing? Does every new neighbourhood or every small village need to have its own elementary school?

Hierarchies change throughout time. It is important to appreciate that a hierarchy is a dynamic, active entity that evolves through time. Corporate decision-makers should be acutely aware of this. In no case is this more evident than with respect to the Free Trade Agreement (FTA) with the United States, and later the North American Free Trade Agreement (NAFTA) with the United States and Mexico. Prior to these free trade agreements, Canada remained somewhat isolated as a distinct economic entity having its own corporate hierarchical structure. However, with the arrival of the free trade agreements, Canada's economic hierarchy became but a small part of the larger American and North American economic hierarchy. An identical line of reasoning applies to virtually all Canadian businesses and corporations. What was formerly east-west national thinking must now become north-south, bilateral and trilateral thinking. *Continentalization* has become a crucial corporate concept. More importantly it is essential to think hierarchically, to think of Canada as being a part of a number of international hierarchies.

A crucial issue in understanding the hierarchical structure of the Canadian economy is to appreciate the extent to which it is, and is not, integrated with the American economic hierarchy. A good example of the confusion Canada faces in understanding the positioning of its own hierarchies with respect to those of the United States is found in the case of Toronto and the Skydome. Here clearly is a city that is large enough to be considered as a part of the United States hierarchy of cities and participates in it with franchises in baseball (the Bluejays), hockey (the Leafs) and basketball (the Raptors). Yet when it comes to football, Toronto and the Skydome are still in the Canadian Football League. Everybody expects Toronto to get an NFL franchise because everybody implicitly understands Toronto's place in the North American urban system. Unfortunately we do not always extend this intuitive line of reasoning to other topics and especially other cities.

Corporate hierarchies are shifting and are adjusting to the new global economy. For example, recent news reports indicate that in just a few years, as a result of corporate restructuring, there may be only five or so automobile manufacturers left in the world. The recent merger of Chrysler and Mercedes-Benz is said to be just the tip of this corporate merger iceberg. In the *Financial Post*, David Olive suggests tongue-in-cheek, that we'll end up with FordVolvoMazda, GeneralMotorsNissanFiat, and VolkswagenPeugeoutRenaultBMW. Recently the German bank Deutsche Bank AG bought up New York based Bankers Trust (for $10.1 billion U.S.) to become the largest bank in the world. The deal puts Deutsche at the top of the international banking hierarchy. Similarly, rival Exxon Oil purchased Mobil Oil for $77 billion (U.S.) to make the new Exxon Mobil Corporation the largest Oil Company in the world. As such changes occur at the pinnacles of these international hierarchies, so too will shifts occur in the lower echelons as the hierarchies restructure themselves.

All of these market shifts are hierarchically driven. When there is a significant shift at one level in a hierarchy, other levels have to adjust until the structure rebalances itself. One purpose of this book is to help the reader gain an understanding of these shifts as an aid to achieving a greater awareness of the social and economic forces at work around us all. Hierarchies help to explain not only where things are, but also where they are going in the future.

Hierarchies are also about human and corporate mobility. It is not unusual to see news reports lamenting the loss of young educated Canadians to the United States. This is said to be especially true of graduates of science and engineering programs. The gist of the argument is usually that there is a so-called "brain-drain" occurring wherein the best and brightest young scholars are lured to jobs in the United States. Supporters of this point of view fail to point out that such mobility is simply a very natural part of the flow of human resources within a hierarchical system. The Canadian economy is a part of the North American economic hierarchy, and it is only natural that talented individuals will make their way upwards in the economic hierarchy to take advantage of the economic opportunities that exist at the top. The concept of hierarchies explains and accounts for the existence of such flows and makes them seem a natural part of the global economy.

Understanding one part of a hierarchy will help to illuminate other parts. While many people see the brain drain to the United States as a crisis to be resolved, the concept of hierarchies puts it in its proper perspective. When Newfoundlanders move to Ontario to seek out new employment opportunities we usually do not give it a second thought, even though it is a part of the same process of upward migration in the economic hierarchy. Newfoundlanders move to Alberta, Albertans move to British Columbia, and British Columbians move to the state of Washington in the Pacific Northwest. Meanwhile residents of Washington migrate to California or New York. It is all a part of the normal hierarchical flow. At the same time there is a counterbalancing process at work. In addition to the "brain drain," Canada also has a brain gain, that is an offsetting gain of highly educated persons from the rest of the world.

The concept of hierarchies helps us to understand our neighbours to the south. This is not to say that Canada is not distinctive from the United States. There are innumerable ways in which the countries remain unique. But at the same time there is an undeniable economic link between the countries that can only be understood by looking at them as being parts of the same, unified hierarchical system.

It becomes evident very quickly that hierarchies, and the concept of hierarchies, know no bounds. We have identified hierarchies as having influences on virtually every facet of life, some very obvious but others subtler. Yet we have barely touched upon the existence of hierarchies in the physical world. Biologists, for example, think of human beings themselves as being biological hierarchies. Our bodies are considered to be organized as in Figure 1.12.

As is typical of the pattern of hierarchies, there is just one organism at the top of the tree, and millions of cells at the bottom. So, just like the human hierarchical world of corporations, governments, countries and industries, nature is hierarchical as well.

When we analyze the world around us according to hierarchies, we gain the advantage of a unique perspective that provides new insights. Consider this industrial-automotive example from an article by Christine Tierney in the *Financial Post*. There are about 60,000 automobile dealerships in Europe and only about 22,000 in the United States. Both of the markets are about the same size, so clearly one of these regions is out of synch with respect to the number of dealers. A hierarchy perspective suggests to us that these markets should have about the same numbers of dealers. Moreover since we know from experience that the United States automakers are currently streamlining their dealership networks, it is understood that the European market is the one that is at odds with the prevailing market forces. Hierarchical systems have a tendency to optimize themselves to maximize efficiency.

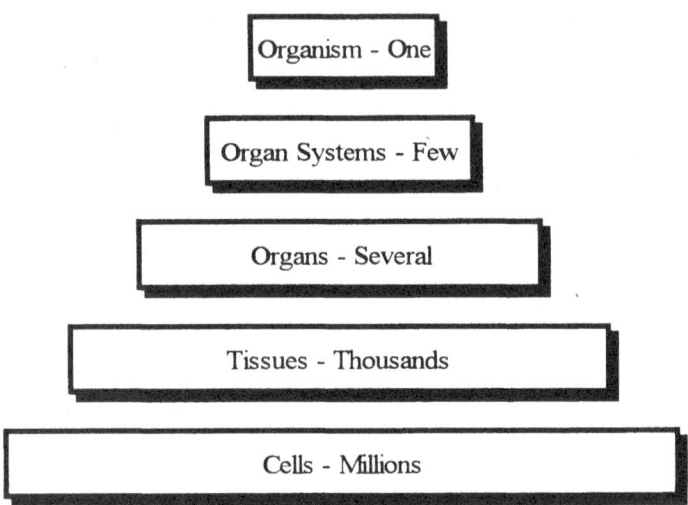

**Figure 1.12 The Human Hierarchy**

This book is about hierarchies at all levels. Your children's local soccer or hockey team is a part of a hierarchy, as are General Motors, IBM, and Microsoft. Yet, as hierarchies, there are principles and ideas that bind them together in spite of their differences in size. Similarly with respect to geographical extent, there are hierarchies that span the globe, such as the Coca-Cola international corporate hierarchy, and there are hierarchies that are purely local, such as the treelike emergency-phoning list of an elementary school class. In both cases these are hierarchies for organizing and handling complex information in an efficient manner.

The next chapter provides a basic look at what hierarchies are and how they are defined. After that, each chapter stands alone, with a look at hierarchies in particular contexts. Readers are encouraged to follow their own interests in reading beyond Chapter 2 since the order of chapters after the next is not of great significance.

This book, like most others, is organized as a hierarchy. This introductory chapter is the equivalent to the top of the tree. Chapter 2, with a number of sub-sections, is equivalent to the next level of the hierarchy. Choosing among the remaining chapters is analogous to choosing from the other levels of the hierarchy.

## References

Olive, D., 'Fearless forecasts for 1999', *Financial Post*, January 5, 1999.
Reguly, E., 'Ford deal an admission of weakness', *Globe and Mail*, January 30, 1999.
Tierney, C., 'Suppliers catch auto industry's merger mania', *Financial Post*, December 12, 1998.

# 2  All about Hierarchies

One thing that is truly fascinating about hierarchies is that they occur in nature, as well as in the human world. This is, however, perhaps not that surprising at all, given the usefulness of hierarchies as organizing systems for information and materials. Virtually every kind of complex system is organized hierarchically, and as we shall see in this chapter, there are a number of properties and characteristics that are common to all hierarchies.

A hierarchy was defined in the first chapter as an organizational system that is structured in a treelike manner, with levels of status or authority stacked one above the another. Let's take a look at just what this means in a little more detail.

**Properties of Hierarchies**

The treelike hierarchy in Figure 2.1 has several interesting properties. These can be divided into three basic categories: physical properties, communications properties, and geographical properties.

*Physical Properties of Hierarchies*

First of all, under the topic of physical or visible characteristics of hierarchies we can note that there is a clear direction to a hierarchy. There is a definitive top and a definitive bottom. Second, the treelike shape shows us a large number of small branches at the bottom and a small number of large branches at the top. Small branches merge together to form larger branches, or alternatively, large branches split into smaller ones. Most hierarchies culminate in a single, final large branch. Third, there is an interesting logic to the connections in a hierarchy. Most of the levels in the hierarchy, except for the very top and very bottom ones, connect to both a lower level and a higher level. Thus we could say that many of the internal levels in a hierarchy are bi-directional having one link looking upwards and another link looking downwards. This property can be very important for individuals or corporations in the middle levels of a hierarchy.

18  *Hierarchical Organization in Society*

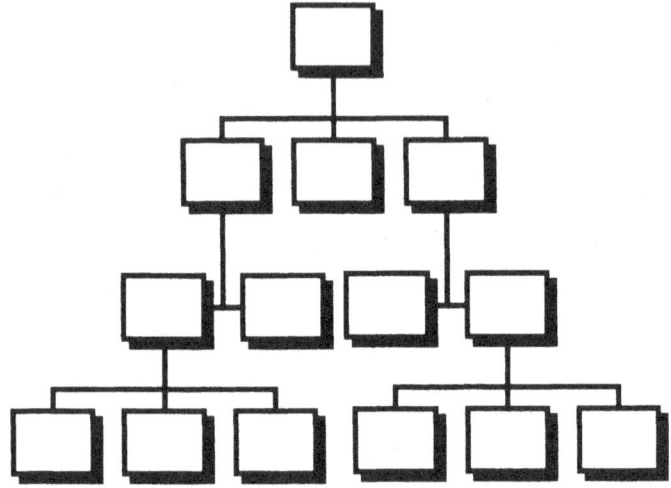

**Figure 2.1  Treelike Hierarchy**

Another physical feature of hierarchies is their so-called "branching properties" and other such mathematical features. There are scientists who study, for example, the mathematical properties of hierarchies such as the number of branches at each level. Although these properties are interesting, they are well beyond the scope of the present discussion.

*Communications Properties of Hierarchies*

Hierarchies often serve as conduits for information. This may be information flowing through a corporation, a minor hockey league, or through the hierarchy of communities in an area. Information flows are an essential part of a hierarchy. They are also bi-directional. Information that flows upward in a hierarchy may be as important as that flowing downward, and bi-directional flows are essential to the proper functioning of the hierarchy.

In many cases the information flowing through a hierarchy is neutral, and when it is neutral, whether it is flowing upward or downward in the hierarchy is of little or no consequence. However, more often than not, the information flow in a hierarchy is not neutral. Rather there is often a tendency for the information flowing from the top of the hierarchy to be of a significantly different nature than that flowing from the bottom.

As a basic principle we should state that there is often more power, control or authority located at the top of a hierarchy. Thus the content of information flowing downward in many hierarchies will be considerably different from that flowing upward. If there is power at the top there is usually information related to control or guidance flowing downward from the top. This might be in the form of new corporate guidelines from headquarters, or in new penalty rules from the local minor soccer association. In either case this information is usually intended to be obeyed with little or no recourse to appeal. From this situation emerges one of the most important properties of hierarchies; they are often very focused on power and control.

In contrast to the commanding and controlling role of the top level of most hierarchies, there is the typical subservient role of the lowest level. As examples consider the students at the bottom of an educational hierarchy or the soldiers at the bottom of a military hierarchy. Both groups have little or no input into the nature and structure of command and control that comes from the top. The bottom level of a hierarchy usually has the least input into decision making in the hierarchy.

In the middle ranks of the hierarchy the story is different. Here members of the hierarchy play a double role, wherein they obey commands from the level above, but at the same time issue orders to the next level below. This presents an interesting dilemma because middle level members of a hierarchy serve as both master and slave. In many cases this can be taken to indicate that their job is the most difficult of all. Sometimes they must play the role of the domineering boss, or person "in charge," while at other times they must play the role of the subservient employee. Not only must they deal with two types of information, that from above and that from below, but they must also be capable of acting on two types of information that may be self-contradictory. For example, it may be necessary to reconcile employee complaints from below with demands from above for greater productivity. Surely this type of tension filled environment puts middle level participants or managers, in any type of hierarchy, into one of the most difficult roles of all. For people in such positions it is crucial not only to appreciate and understand the dualistic nature of the role that needs to be played, but also to be able to function in either role successfully, while maintaining an awareness of the sometimes self-contradictory nature of the roles.

*Geographical Properties of Hierarchies*

An interesting aspect of many hierarchies is that they have important geographical characteristics that cannot be ignored if they are to be understood. There are four types of geographical situations. First, there are hierarchies where geography is not at all an issue of importance. An example of this type would be for typical Internet chat groups. These are usually organized hierarchically, by users' topics of interest, but the members of the chat groups may be scattered all over the world. The geography of the hierarchy does not matter. Second, there are hierarchies where geographical closeness of the members is not acute but is nevertheless of importance. A good example is the typical corporate hierarchy where it is usually assumed that most powerful members of the group are in the same geographical area (e.g., headquarters) though it is not crucial. Third, there are hierarchies where the geography is important to understanding the nature of the hierarchy. An example of this type would be the hierarchy of cities, towns and villages wherein the location of a community may play a role in determining its position in the hierarchy of communities. Fourth and finally, there are those types of hierarchies where geography is a necessary part of the system. An example is found in the case where counties merge together to make-up provinces and, in turn, provinces merge together to make-up a country. This kind of hierarchy is, of course, inseparable from its geographical components.

**Processes in Hierarchies**

It is possible to detect "processes" at work in the shape of hierarchies. By analyzing the general shape of a hierarchy it may be possible to come to conclusions regarding the effectiveness of processes at work within that hierarchy. In hierarchies that are not functioning adequately, or efficiently, it may be possible to take corrective actions in order to create a pattern that more adequately reflects the goals or purpose of that particular hierarchy.

Hierarchies can be characterized as being of five general types and shapes. First there is the *normal* or regular hierarchy which approximates a normal triangular shape (Figure 2.2). This triangular shape sets the standard to which the others are compared and is considered to be especially typical of the "normal" corporate hierarchy. Why is the shape triangular? A triangular shape is representative of an efficient and well organized structure. As jobs or tasks are delegated downward in the organization, they cascade naturally into a triangular shape as the most effective way of handling complex information. It is simply an excellent way to delegate tasks when information flows from the top down. Consider as an analogy the usual emergency "phoning tree" that is used in elementary schools. This is set-up typically so that in the event of an emergency, where the children all have to leave the school (e.g., blizzard), the "top parent" phones three others, the next three phone three others, and so on. With this "triangular" type of tree it takes only four levels to contact twenty-seven families. It is fast and efficient because it instantly spreads or delegates the workload fairly and *evenly* among the participants. Responsibilities are clear. In spite of whatever "emergency" is at hand, any individual need only phone the next three names on the list to cover off his or her duties. The phoning tree imposes order on what would otherwise be a very chaotic situation, with everyone trying to phone everyone else, all at the same time.

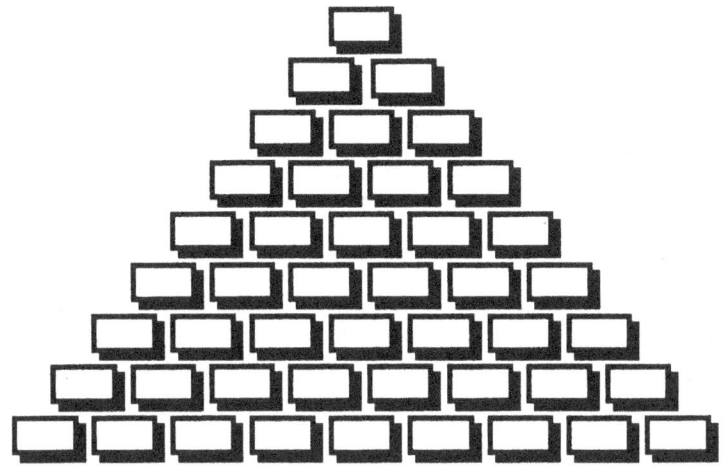

**Figure 2.2 Normal Triangular Shaped Hierarchy**

An identical and equally efficient delegation of tasks takes place in any efficient corporation or organization. A triangular shaped hierarchy implies an even and equitable delegation of tasks to those "down the line." In any organizational task that is too big for one individual to handle efficiently, a triangular hierarchy delegates responsibilities and imposes order. Each individual in the tree has unique duties and it is the sum of all of these individual efforts that produces success. Anyone in any position of authority, or aspiring to one, needs to understand this important characteristic of organizations and hierarchies. The triangular shape in Figure 2.2 represents a hierarchy where information flows assume a normal, balanced form and where responsibilities are assigned clearly.

A second type of shape for a hierarchy is the *bottom-heavy* hierarchy which, as the name implies, may have too broad a base given the size of the infrastructure at the top (Figure 2.3).

Here the wide base implies a lack of functionality, with either inadequate or overloaded communications between the wide bottom and next higher level. In other words there may be too much information moving from the bottom up, or too little moving from the top down. In such a situation there may be an overlap or duplication of duties at the bottom level, because it is out of proportion to the size of the top. If we return to the analogy of the phoning tree it can be seen in this hierarchy that those at the fifth level from the top suddenly have more duties, or more subordinates, than those at other levels. The wide bottom pattern leads to an inequitable assignment of tasks within the hierarchy.

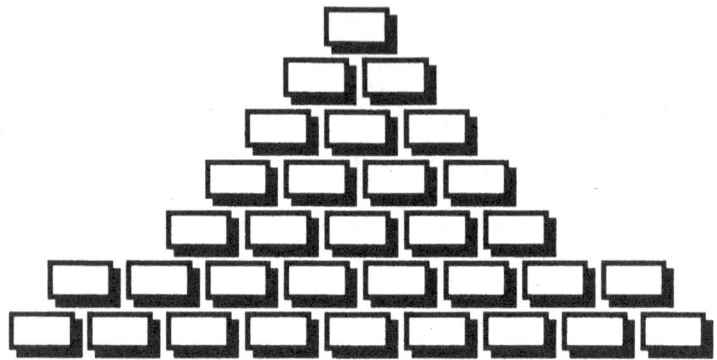

**Figure 2.3 Bottom-Heavy Hierarchy**

As a third general form of hierarchy there is the complement to the bottom-heavy shape, in the form of a *narrow-bottomed* hierarchy, which has the pattern of an inadequately developed base (Figure 2.4).

This shape may lead to inadequate information emanating from the base or, alternatively, too much information coming down from the top. Once again, in the analogy to the phoning tree, there may be an inequitable distribution of duties within such a hierarchy. In this particular hierarchy, those at the bottom three levels have fewer subordinates, and fewer duties, than those above them. In effect, in the bottom three layers, there may be more "bosses" than there are "employees" at all levels. The suggestion is that this represents an inefficient and inappropriate pattern for a hierarchy wherein there is a specific task to be accomplished.

Another possibility is the *narrow-waisted* hierarchy, which, with its concave sides, is too narrow in the middle (Figure 2.5). This shape implies a constriction of information flows in the middle ranges of the hierarchy and hence a lack of communication between the top and the bottom. If this were a phoning tree there would be a clearly uneven distribution of responsibilities. In particular, those at level "A" would have fewer duties than those below them, while those at level "B" would be swamped by their extra duties given the larger number of subordinates they have. There are probably a lot of employees, in companies and organizations, who are swamped by their duties as a result of being stuck in the middle of a narrow-waisted hierarchy. At the same time there are probably a lot of managers of hierarchies who, in the efforts of "downsizing" or intended efficiencies, do not appreciate that they are managing constricted, dysfunctional, narrow-waisted hierarchies.

**Figure 2.4  Narrow-Bottomed Hierarchy**

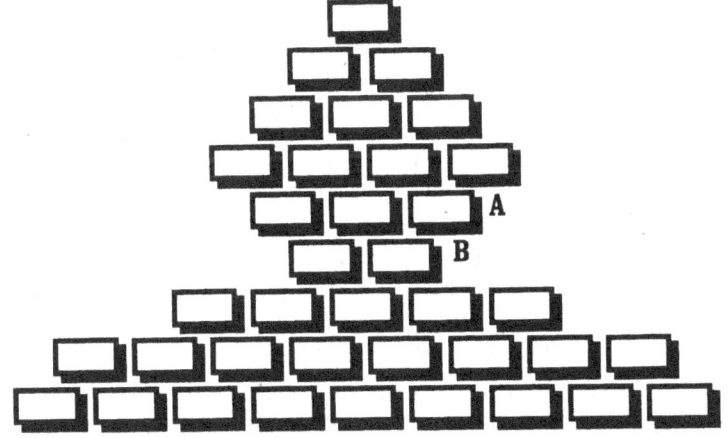

**Figure 2.5  Narrow-Waisted Hierarchy**

As a final pattern to consider, there is also the *top-heavy* hierarchy, which has too much infrastructure at the top (Figure 2.6). This shape may result in information congestion, confusion, and indecision at the top of the decision-making tree. If this were an emergency-phoning tree, for example, we might expect to find confusion or disagreement at the top. Is there an emergency or isn't there? Who makes the decision? Who is in charge? And who calls whom? The lines of command and information flow are more ambiguous in this top-heavy pattern, as is the role of decision-makers.

Figure 2.6 Top-Heavy Hierarchy

**Hierarchies within Hierarchies**

In addition to the four distinct properties discussed above it is also important to realize that there is an interesting category of hierarchies where different types are mixed together. These make up some of the most interesting hierarchies of all. Consider as an example of this, the mixing together of a shopping hierarchy, for example groceries, together with the community hierarchy of cities, towns, and villages (see Figure 1.9). In order to appreciate this type of mixed hierarchy, consider that while the hierarchy of communities consists of different sized communities, the grocery shopping hierarchy consists of different sizes of stores. In a *village* we might expect to find a small convenience type store selling groceries. In a *town* we would expect to see a small grocery store, perhaps a family business. In a large *city*, however, we count on finding a major "chain" grocery store of immense proportions.

The point is that there exists a one-to-one correspondence between the grocery shopping hierarchy and the hierarchy of communities. *The two hierarchies co-exist.* In addition, the two types of hierarchies are closely related; obviously there is a connection between the size of a community and its ability to support a grocery store. This is just one among many possible examples of hierarchies within hierarchies. We shall see as we go along that ultimately *most* hierarchies are of this mixed type, with one embedded in another. Interestingly, many business and corporate hierarchies exhibit this pattern.

**Hierarchies in Nature**

As with hierarchies in the human world, there are hierarchies in nature. Consider the following fascinating examples of hierarchies that exist in nature:

- Tree branches
- Tree roots
- The surfaces of leaves
- The human circulatory system of veins and arteries
- Blood vessels in the lungs and other organs
- Streams and rivers.

What all of these seemingly disparate systems have in common is that they are distinct hierarchies. Clearly such natural hierarchies will have many of the properties of human hierarchies. The principal difference is that while human hierarchies are concerned often with information and control, such physical hierarchies are concerned most often with flow and circulation. Consider that in each of the physical systems above there is a common concern with getting a *liquid* to flow over, or through a *surface* via a flow through *lines*. For example, the *veins* in the surface of a leaf are designed to efficiently circulate liquid over the *surface* of the leaf.

Another example of a hierarchy in nature is the one listed in the introductory chapter, namely the one consisting of the set of levels: Organism, Organ Systems, Organs, Tissues, and Cells. Here again there are properties in common with human hierarchies, but the most notable is that the systems at each level combine together to make-up the next level above. The final result is a unified whole, made-up of a series of hierarchical levels. Similarly ecologists, at their level of study, would look at a hierarchy consisting of these levels: Community, Population, and

Organism. Hierarchies are of interest to almost all sciences at some level of analysis.

What are we to make of the fact that *nature is hierarchical?* Primarily that when something works well, it works well across a variety of systems of different types and scales. The existence of hierarchies in nature is testament to the fact that hierarchic systems are effective and efficient, whether it comes to organizing the flow of information in a corporation or the flow of liquid in a leaf. We have many things to learn from nature in the design and understanding of human systems of organization.

## Hierarchies at Different Scales

One hierarchy can sometimes be seen in existence, at the top of another, at a different scale. Consider the simple examples of a tree and a leaf. At one scale of analysis we can examine the tree as a stand-alone hierarchy. But consider what happens as we zoom in on a tree and follow a branch right to the end. There we find *another complete hierarchy* at the end of the branch, in the form of a leaf of the tree. The leaf is considered a separate hierarchy by virtue of the fact that it has its own stem. It is a distinct hierarchical system, but is literally on top of the hierarchical tree below it. Human systems can have the same features. Consider the city of Lethbridge, Alberta as a member of the Canadian hierarchy of communities. At one scale of analysis we see Lethbridge as a whole entity, as one branch of the Canadian tree of communities. But we can also zoom in again and see the details of the street map of Lethbridge as consisting of yet another distinct hierarchical level unto itself, just like the leaf on the tree branch.

## Conceptual Hierarchies

An important topic that should be considered in any discussion of hierarchies is the use of a visual device called a conceptual hierarchy. These represent one way to put into action the ideas implicit in the hierarchical perspective. The best way to illustrate a conceptual hierarchy is with an example. Consider Figure 2.7, which illustrates a conceptual hierarchy of agriculture. In the figure it can be seen that as one moves downward in the hierarchy, the information becomes more specific, but remains consistent with the levels above. This line of thought describes another interesting property of hierarchies.

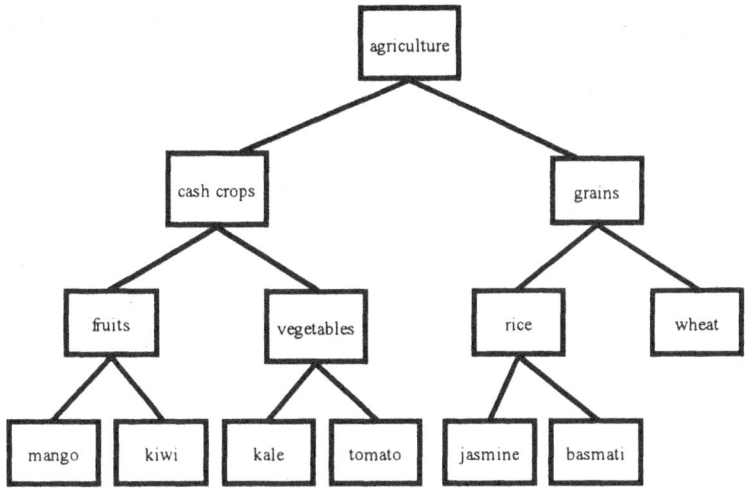

Source: Reprinted with permission from an Internet article by Krzysztof Koperski, Junas Adhikary, Jiawei Han, 'Spatial Data Mining: Progress and Challenges', 1996.

**Figure 2.7  A Conceptual Hierarchy**


**Structured/Unstructured Hierarchies**

Although all hierarchies evolve and change over time, when we look at them in the present, a basic distinction we can make is whether they are currently rigid, structured and unchanging, or whether they are unstructured and loosely organized. A case in point might be to compare a structured hierarchy, such as that of a religion in a church, to an unstructured hierarchy, such as that which might exist in a non-formal organization, such as a temporary committee formed to achieve a specific purpose, for example, fund raising or a task within a corporation. In the former, the "rules" of ascension in the hierarchy are formally laid out, while in the latter most duties typically are relegated either to those who "step-up" to take them on voluntarily or to those to whom they are assigned.

**Dynamic/Static Hierarchies**

Regardless of whether a hierarchy is structured or unstructured we can also distinguish between those that are dynamic or static. An example of interest here might be the case of a military organization. Certainly a military unit is one of the most rigid or static of all types of hierarchies. "Command" comes from the top down and is strictly enforced. Rank, or level in the hierarchy is very clearly defined and regimented. Yet compare this with the performance of a military unit in the field, as in the case of a ground attack. In this situation "leadership" revolves from soldier to soldier as the unit makes its way over the battlefield. It is a very fluid hierarchy, redefining itself as it goes along. The distinction between these static and dynamic hierarchies may provide a role model for certain corporate, and other similar hierarchies.

## Open/Closed Hierarchies

Another way to examine a hierarchy is to ask whether it has an open or closed form. A hierarchical organization that is "open" to innovation will go out of its way to allow for the creation of new branches, or even new levels, in the existing hierarchy. A flexible and open corporation might create a new level of "assistant" vice-president or add an extra, new associate vice president. Such moves may be permanent or ad hoc, depending on the task to be accomplished.

A closed firm will tend to keep the existing hierarchy closed, delegating new tasks and responsibilities to existing members of the hierarchy. This may be a less effective, and less innovative, approach to task management.

## Democratic/Autocratic Hierarchies

Sometimes it is useful to consider the issue of whether a hierarchy is democratic or autocratic. This topic can get somewhat complex given that it applies in different ways to different hierarchies. Consider first, government electoral hierarchies. In a democratic hierarchy, voting is undertaken by the masses at the bottom to elect officials at the top, but then governance is accepted from the top, by those at the bottom. In an autocracy, there is no voting, there is simply a single person that has absolute power at the top. In both cases, then, power or control comes from the top down, but in a democracy there is an opportunity to elect new leaders from time-to-time.

But how do we distinguish between democracies and autocracies when it comes to other non-governmental forms of hierarchies? It seems that most hierarchies can simply be classified into democratic or autocratic in the same manner as governmental ones. For instance, as examples of autocratic hierarchies we might think of churches, the military, organized crime, the police force, and so on. In these cases there is usually a single leader who has absolute power. As examples of democratic hierarchies consider trade unions, corporations formed of stockholders, or volunteer organizations. In these cases voting procedures are often employed as a means of decision making. There will also be instances in hierarchies wherein power and control are somewhat unclear and ambiguous as, for example, in the hierarchy of communities, or in relations among educational systems at different levels.

## Political/Benign Hierarchies

Closely related to the issue of democracy in hierarchies is the subtler question of whether or not there is a "political" element to a particular hierarchy. What is meant here of course is "political" in the sense that there may be some hierarchies where some members have a political agenda while others do not. The classic example is probably with respect to school boards, for instance, where religious or other groups may have some political motive for achieving a degree of control of the hierarchy. The same ideas would sometimes apply to corporate and other hierarchies.

## Formal/Informal Hierarchies

Many of the hierarchies we have discussed or mentioned to this point have been formal ones; the military, the church, the police and so on. It is important; however, to sometimes recognize that some hierarchies may be very informal. For instance, a group of people may elect to carry out some task (e.g., organize a block party, organize an office function) and immediately an entirely informal and unofficial hierarchy will emerge, wherein various "leaders" will simply "assume" positions of command and control. In some cases, the other participants in the hierarchy are relieved to be free of the duties involved, while in other cases, participants may feel that they have been imposed upon, or even put into an inferior position of having to obey a self-appointed "leader." Such hierarchical subtleties are a common part of everyday and corporate life.

More importantly such informal hierarchies can also break-out in the work place, forcing feelings of antagonism and resentment against self-appointed leaders. Imagine a company meeting, where some new task needs to be accomplished, and where certain people, by appearing to "volunteer," actually put themselves into positions of authority and control. Not only will they probably generate feelings of resentment from co-workers, but also the resulting environment of antagonism will probably result in a less productive work environment. Managers at all levels of hierarchies should be aware of these "stealth volunteers."

**Self-Organizing Hierarchies**

Discussions of hierarchies in nature often refer to self-organizing hierarchies that are generally those which "organize by themselves," that is, they do not require human intervention. A good example is the hierarchy formed by the series of tributaries and streams that ultimately join together to form a river. Such a hierarchy "organizes itself," in the sense that it requires no human input. Moreover, and this is important, it evolves into a *naturally* best form of efficiency. For a parallel process, in the content of human hierarchies, consider any task, large or small, which people challenge themselves to achieve. Whether we are talking about a science fair at the local elementary school, or the setting-up of a brand new corporation, there are usually enough tasks involved that specialization is necessary. Any such complex undertaking usually devolves into separate components, and individuals usually relegate themselves to areas where they have strengths. Thus, *even under the lack of an explicit source of control*, when there is a task to be completed, a self-organizing hierarchy will tend to emerge. If managers are aware of this tendency to self-organization, they will be better able to manage and control its emergence and direction.

Self-organizing hierarchies should be viewed in contrast to formally organized and *deliberate* hierarchies wherein the form and function of the hierarchy is carefully laid-out in advance. Although there is a planning advantage in following this type of approach, there is a disadvantage in the degree of flexibility or adaptability that is given-up with a pre-planned structure.

**The Direction of Information Flow in Hierarchies**

Managers of hierarchies should be aware of information flows in the hierarchies that they manage. They should be aware that there are three possible directions for information flows. First, there are *lateral* flows across a given level of the hierarchy. Second, there are information flows that *percolate* from the top of the hierarchy downward. Third, there is information that *floats* from the bottom of the hierarchy upward. In all three cases it is necessary not only to understand where the information flows are, but also to manage and control them to achieve the results desired. Furthermore, information flows should always be considered in the context of control and authority in the hierarchy, as discussed earlier.

**Diffusion in Hierarchies**

In the study of hierarchies at the national and regional scales an important consideration is in the diffusion of new concepts, innovations, or ideas. For example, suppose there arrives in Canada a new medical, agricultural, or industrial innovation from elsewhere in the world. In the study of hierarchies there is an interest to see where the new innovation is first adopted, and then to see how it spreads and diffuses through the hierarchies of which it is a part. The general line of thought is that innovations are usually first introduced in the top of hierarchies and then tend to diffuse downward through them. This concept might apply to a new medical innovation being adopted first in Toronto, or a new corporate innovation being employed at corporate headquarters in Montreal. In both cases it is theorized that innovations, inventions or new ideas or concepts follow a general downward pattern of diffusion in a hierarchy. This idea may be of particular interest to those whose job it is to "stay on top" of the latest developments in a particular field, or line of work.

**Private/Public Hierarchies**

A further distinction can be made between hierarchies that exist in the public domain and those that exist in the private domain. As an example of the former we might consider the typical hierarchy that defines an urban or municipal government, with a mayor at the top and a variety of positions and departments below. As an example of the latter we might again consider the typical corporate hierarchy, with a CEO or president at the top and a number of associates and managers below. An issue of compelling interest here is in the extent to which public and private hierarchies differ in their structures. It is of interest, for example, to compare public and private hierarchies with respect to their size and relative efficiencies. It is also of interest to determine whether the shape or general form of these two types of hierarchies varies significantly and, if so, how.

## Competitive/Cooperative Hierarchies and "Coopetition"

A critical issue of relevance is in the extent to which particular hierarchies can be classified as being either competitive or cooperative in nature. The concern here is not with the extent to which one hierarchy competes with another. We know, for example, that the General Motors corporate hierarchy competes with the Ford corporate hierarchy. Rather the interest is in the degree to which there is competition or cooperation *within* a given hierarchy. Consider as an example of this distinction, the difference between a hierarchy of volunteers where everyone is working toward a common goal, and a hierarchy of competitors who are obliged to cooperate with one another, within the hierarchical structure, but at the same time are actually competing with one another. A typical example of the latter type would be in the situation where employees in sales are working for commissions, or where competing employees are working for promotions. In these situations a contradiction exists in the purpose of the hierarchy. Although hierarchies are intended usually to foster cooperation and teamwork, in this particular case the hierarchical structure may be working at cross-purposes with itself. This presents an interesting dilemma for managers of hierarchies.

A new word has emerged to describe situations in which there exists simultaneously cooperation and competition, namely, *coopetition*. This word emerged in the computer business where companies see a need to compete with each other, but at the same time find it in their own best interests to cooperate on *standards* in the industry. The word applies well to many organizations that are organized hierarchically.

## The Physical Form of Hierarchies

One of the appealing characteristics of hierarchies is that they can be expressed visually, thus providing the reader with a simple "picture" or "snapshot" of what can be a very complex organization. Clearly the possibility of visualization is partly responsible for the popularity of the everyday use of hierarchies. There are a number of aspects of the visual form of hierarchies that can be discussed.

*Symmetry*

One basic aspect of a hierarchy relates to the question of whether the hierarchy is visually symmetrical or "balanced." Figure 2.8 provides an indication of what is meant by the distinction between a symmetrical and an irregular (or nonsymmetrical) hierarchy. Although there is no theoretical reason why a particular organization should have a "balanced" hierarchy, it seems intuitively clear that it is probably desirable, from a decision-making point of view, to maintain a fundamental level of balance in an organizational structure.

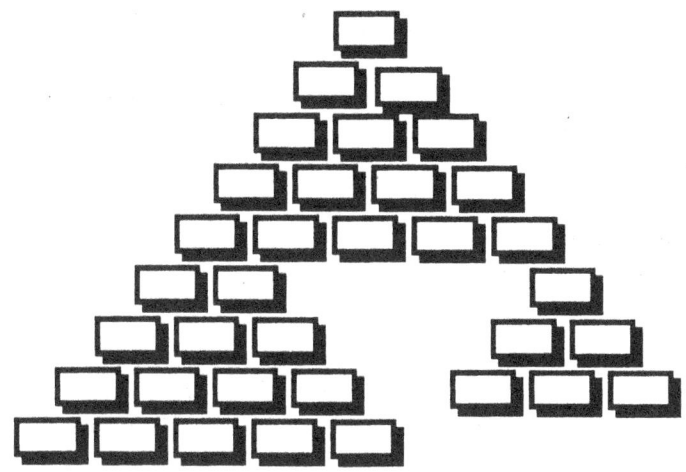

**Figure 2.8 Unbalanced or Nonsymmetrical Hierarchy**

*Dimensionality*

Although several examples of three-dimensional hierarchies have been discussed already, we have not pointed out explicitly that they have this unusual dimensionality. Typically, when we look at corporate and other such hierarchies we are looking at two-dimensional or "flat" hierarchies that can be drawn on a flat piece of paper. These can be distinguished from hierarchies, such as trees, or the human circulatory system, which exist in three dimensions. Although we may draw a real tree on a flat piece of paper, it is really a three-dimensional entity. This distinction is important because it shows us that hierarchies in nature are more complex and richer, than we usually imagine. Given their extra dimension it means that they have far more, smaller branches than does the typical human, two-dimensional hierarchy. There may be a lesson in human design implicit in this difference, perhaps in the possibility for the creation of three-dimensional hierarchies for human systems.

## Maturity

It is possible to classify hierarchies by their relative age or maturity. In the first instance, we might imagine a "youthful" hierarchy characterized by a relatively small size, incomplete connections, and lack of a fully developed, integrated structure. Secondly, we can define a "mature" hierarchy consisting of a moderate size, adequate links and connections, and a fairly well developed structure. Finally, it is possible to consider the "old age" hierarchy, having a large size, full connections, and a fully developed structure. These three stages might, for example, characterize the stages of development of a corporation. They might also aid as a guide in establishing the relative maturity of an existing corporation or hierarchical organization, especially in relation to others.

## Functional/Nonfunctional Hierarchies

A final but very important distinction needs to be made between functional and nonfunctional hierarchies. By the former we mean those hierarchies wherein there is a *direct* functional link or connection between the levels of the hierarchy, while in the latter case we refer to those hierarchies where the parts of the hierarchy are not linked, but are independent. Consider two examples. If we were to examine the hierarchy that exists within a fire department we would find a chain of command consisting of a chief, division commanders, assistant chiefs, and firefighters. In such a hierarchy there is a direct *functional* connection among the members. Orders are issued and information is conveyed among the levels of the hierarchy. Compare this type of functional hierarchy to that that would be found in, say, the corporate hierarchy of fast-food franchises. Here we would find McDonald's and Wendy's at the top levels of the hierarchy, followed by KFC, Pizza Hut, Burger King and Taco Bell at the third level. According to the *Financial Post* these six companies control 39 percent of sales in the industry. These top *levels* in the fast-food hierarchy would be followed by a larger number of smaller and/or regional fast-food companies at the fourth level (see Figure 2.9).

What we have here is a quite distinct corporate hierarchy, but one that is *nonfunctional*, that is, the companies within the hierarchy share no communications and have nothing to do directly with each other. This is quite different from a functional hierarchy. Readers may be interested to know, by the way, that KFC, Taco Bell, and Pizza Hut are all operated by a single company, Tricon Global Restaurants.

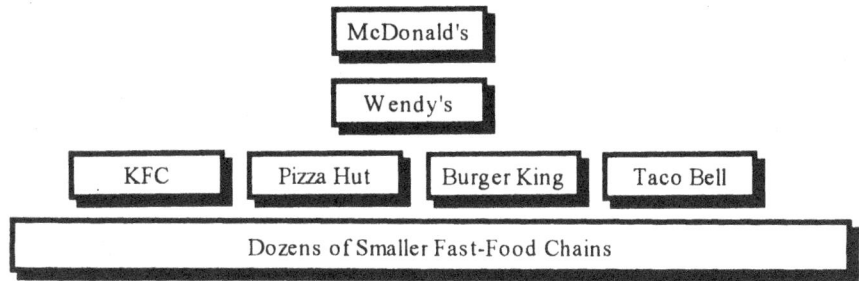

**Figure 2.9 The Fast-Food Hierarchy**

## References

Koperski, K., Adhikary, J. and Han, J, (1996), 'Spatial Data Mining: Progress and Challenges', Internet address: http://fas.sfu.ca//cs/people/GradStudents...1/research/survey.html/survey/survey.html.

Thomas, D., 'Fast-food heydays given over to mature markets', *Financial Post*, January 13, 1999.

# 3 Up the Corporate Ladder

Have you ever thought about the height of the buildings in a city? Think about it. If we were to classify the buildings in a big city according to their heights we would find the following general pattern:

| *Height of Building* | *Number of Buildings in a City* |
|---|---|
| Really tall buildings | Just one, or a few |
| Tall buildings | Dozens |
| Moderately tall buildings | Hundreds |
| Shorter buildings | Thousands |
| One-story buildings | Tens of thousands |

What you can see here is that we have the makings of a classical hierarchical pattern. In Toronto, for example, the CN Tower is the king of the building height hierarchy while, at the other end of the scale, there are tens of thousands of single family homes and businesses that are one story in height. The remaining buildings, at various other heights, form the other levels of the hierarchy.

One thing that is important to point out at this time is that the "categories" for building heights, and many other hierarchies, are somewhat arbitrary. In other words, the heights of buildings do not fall automatically into nice neat groups. Rather there is a "continuum" of heights, and the placing of the buildings into distinct height categories is at our discretion. This creation of arbitrary categories is a necessity for many of the hierarchies that we consider.

Corporations' sizes are just like building heights. There is a continuum of corporate sizes, stretching all the way from the largest corporations down to the smallest businesses. When the corporations are classified into groups, according to their size, these corporations can be considered to make up corporate hierarchies.

We can explore corporate hierarchies at a number of different scales where, at every scale, one hierarchy forms part of another hierarchy. For example, we could examine the corporate hierarchy in Toronto. In turn, the Toronto hierarchy could be considered a part of the Ontario corporate hierarchy. At the next level, the Ontario hierarchy is but a part of the Canadian corporate hierarchy. It follows that the Canadian corporate hierarchy is then a part of the North American hierarchy, which, in turn, is a part of the global hierarchy. Once again, all of the levels fit neatly inside one another like the parts of a puzzle.

For the purposes of this chapter it is important to make a distinction between two types of corporate hierarchies. On the one hand we can examine hierarchies *within* corporations, for example the corporate hierarchy within Coca-Cola Canada or within the Royal Bank. On the other hand we can also think about *hierarchies of corporations*, for example the hierarchy of Canadian airline service industries, with Air Canada at the top and local carriers at the bottom. The first part of this chapter looks at *hierarchies of corporations* in Canada and the world. The second part presents an examination of hierarchies within corporations.

## Canadian and Global Corporate Hierarchies

An important property of hierarchies is that they allow us to express the structure of a collection of things in visual form. There are a number of ways in which we can identify the structure of corporations in Canada. It is important not just to identify Canadian corporate hierarchies, but also to appreciate that they have evolved over time. Any given hierarchy is a "snapshot" in time and reflects the result of a history of corporate evolution, including mergers and acquisitions. It is crucial to understand the processes involved as corporate hierarchies change through time and as new forms emerge. As mergers and acquisitions take place it is also essential to distinguish between lateral moves and vertical moves in the corporate hierarchy.

So just what is the Canadian corporate hierarchy? In the first instance a helpful guide is provided by the Toronto Stock Exchange (TSE). The TSE lists more than 1300 Canadian corporations, including most of the largest ones, and accounts for over eighty percent of the value of shares traded in Canadian stock exchanges.

The TSE does more than just list the largest corporations however. It also creates a hierarchy of its own. The TSE subdivides the companies that it lists into subgroups, namely the TSE 300 Composite Index, the TSE 100 Index and The Toronto 35 Index.

The TSE 300 Composite Index is a broad benchmark used to measure the general performance of the Canadian equity stock market. It does not focus exclusively on the largest companies, although it contains most of them. The TSE 100 Index does focus on the largest capitalized stocks of the TSE 300, and therefore sets out the basis of a hierarchy. Furthermore the Toronto 35 Index focuses, in turn, on the larger, heavily traded companies within the TSE 100 Index, and so represents the top 35 corporations of the hierarchy. So we have a rough hierarchy consisting of the 35 corporations at the top of the TSE, the 100 and the 300 in between, and the remaining 1000 other corporations that are not in the indices (Figure 3.1).

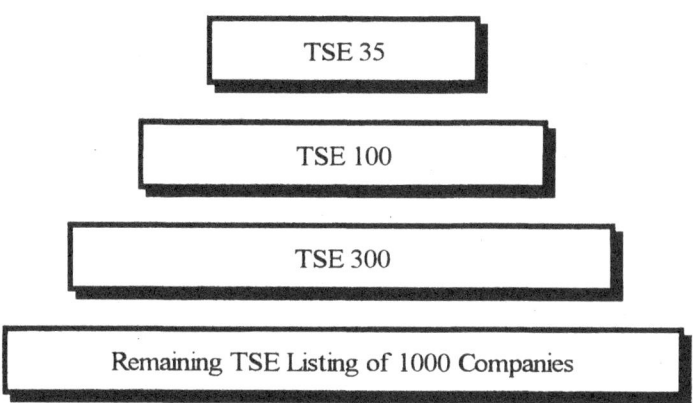

**Figure 3.1 The Canadian Corporate Hierarchy Based on the TSE**

Who are the companies that make-up the TSE 35? Who is at the top of the hierarchy? Table 3.1 presents a listing of the members of the group as of February 1999. It can be seen that it is a very diverse group with companies from a variety of economic sectors. It represents many of the best known and most respected Canadian corporations.

Interestingly, the TSE itself is part of the global hierarchy of stock exchanges in North America and the world. In size, the TSE is the second largest stock exchange in North America (the New York Stock Exchange, (NYSE), is the biggest) and the TSE ranks among the top ten in the world. So the TSE not only creates a hierarchy of Canadian corporations, but is itself a part of a larger hierarchy of stock exchanges.

A second way in which to identify the basis of a Canadian corporate hierarchy is to look at the ranked lists of corporations that the media produce annually in their examinations of the corporate world. A popular one of these in Canada is *The Financial Post* Top 500 Companies. As the creators of the *Financial Post*'s listing state, "Our overriding goal is always to make the FP500 the most timely, accurate and complete source of information on the performance of corporate Canada."

## Table 3.1 The TSE 35

Abitibi Consolidated Inc.
Alcan Aluminum Ltd.
Bank of Montreal
Bank of Nova Scotia
Barrick Gold Corp.
BCE Inc.
Bombardier Inc.
Canadian Imperial Bank of Commerce
Canadian National Railway Co.
Canadian Occidental Petroleum Ltd.
Canadian Pacific Ltd.
Canadian Tire Corp.
Dofasco Inc.
Imasco Ltd.
Inco Ltd.
Laidlaw Inc.
MacMillan Bloedel Ltd.
Magna International Inc.
Moore Corporation Ltd.
National Bank of Canada
Noranda Inc.
Northern Telecom Ltd.
Nova Chemicals Corp.
Petro-Canada Common
Placer Dome Inc.
Renaissance Energy Ltd.
Royal Bank of Canada
Seagram Company Ltd.
Suncor Energy Inc.
Talisman Energy Inc.
Teck Corp.
Thomson Corp.
Toronto-Dominion Bank
Transalta Corp.
Transcanada Pipelines Ltd.

A source of many debates is the issue of how to measure accurately the size of a company. A common approach is to use the "market capitalization" of companies. The market capitalization is the number of shares of stock of a company multiplied by the share value. This gives an indication of the overall, total value of a company. In addition to market capitalization we could look at revenues, assets, numbers of employees, return on investment or other indices. One of the leading indicators, and one that the *Financial Post* uses, is gross revenue. Looking at annual revenues in Canadian dollars, the top fifty corporations in Canada in 1997 were as listed in Table 3.2.

## Table 3.2 The *Financial Post Magazine* Top 50 Canadian Companies, 1997 Revenue

| Rank | Company | City | 1997 Revenue $millions |
|---|---|---|---|
| 1 | General Motors | Oshawa, ON | 34,249,489 |
| 2 | BCE | Montreal | 33,191,000 |
| 3 | Ford Motor Co. | Oakville, ON | 27,911,591 |
| 4 | The Seagram Co. | Montreal | 17,160,728 |
| 5 | Chrysler Canada | Windsor, ON | 16,688,000 |
| 6 | TransCanada Pipelines | Calgary | 14,242,800 |
| 7 | George Weston | Toronto | 13,921,000 |

| | | | |
|---|---|---|---|
| 8 | The Thomson Corp. | Toronto | 12,137,404 |
| 9 | Onex Corp. | Toronto | 11,212,384 |
| 10 | Alcan Aluminum | Montreal | 10,768,034 |
| 11 | Imasco Ltd. | Montreal | 10,008,000 |
| 12 | Canadian Pacific | Calgary | 9,560,000 |
| 13 | Imperial Oil | Toronto | 9,512,000 |
| 14 | Power Corp. of Canada | Montreal | 8,615,000 |
| 15 | Bombardier | Montreal | 8,508,900 |
| 16 | Magna International | Aurora, ON | 7,691,800 |
| 17 | IBM Canada | Markham, ON | 7,400,000 |
| 18 | Westcoast Energy | Vancouver | 7,312,000 |
| 19 | Quebecor | Montreal | 7,013,346 |
| 20 | The Oshawa Group | Etobicoke, ON | 6,813,100 |
| 21 | Hudson's Bay Co. | Toronto | 6,446,652 |
| 22 | Noranda | Toronto | 6,407,000 |
| 23 | Amoco Canada Petroleum | Calgary | 6,176,701 |
| 24 | Petro-Canada | Calgary | 6,017,000 |
| 25 | Provigo | Montreal | 5,956,200 |
| 26 | EdperBrascan | Toronto | 5,886,000 |
| 27 | Air Canada | Dorval, QC | 5,572,000 |
| 28 | Shell Canada | Calgary | 5,445,000 |
| 29 | NOVA | Calgary | 4,840,000 |
| 30 | Canada Safeway | Calgary | 4,719,500 |
| 31 | Sears Canada | Toronto | 4,583,479 |
| 32 | MacMillan Bloedel | Vancouver | 4,521,000 |
| 33 | Canadian National Railway | Montreal | 4,352,000 |
| 34 | Saskatchewan Wheat Pool | Regina | 4,229,325 |
| 35 | Canadian Ultramar | Montreal | 4,175,400 |
| 36 | McCain Foods | Florenceville, NB | 4,150,639 |
| 37 | Laidlaw | Burlington, ON | 4,147,513 |
| 38 | Canadian Tire | Toronto | 4,057,197 |
| 39 | Jim Pattison Group | Vancouver | 4,000,000 |
| 40 | Honda Canada | Scarborough, ON | 3,794,562 |
| 41 | Abitibi Consolidated | Montreal | 3,747,000 |
| 42 | Maple Leaf Foods | Toronto | 3,678,419 |
| 43 | Moore Corp. | Toronto | 3,642,902 |
| 44 | Mitsui & Co. | Toronto | 3,581,714 |
| 45 | Metro-Richelieu | Montreal | 3,432,300 |
| 46 | Mobil Oil Canada | Calgary | 3,307,485 |
| 47 | Inco | Toronto | 3,277,348 |
| 48 | Potash Corp. of Sask. | Saskatoon | 3,220,481 |
| 49 | Empire | Stellarton, NS | 3,149,773 |
| 50 | Stelco | Hamilton, ON | 3,149,000 |

Any listing like this should be viewed, not just as a "list," but as a potential corporate hierarchy, by looking at its different levels. The three largest companies in Canada, as measured by revenues, are General Motors, Bell Canada and the Ford Motor Company. An obvious break occurs after the first three corporations; the difference between Ford and The Seagram Company is over 10 billion dollars. Another natural break seems to occur between Alcan and Imasco with a difference of nearly one billion dollars. This means that from these fifty corporations we can identify a hierarchy where the first three companies comprise the top level, the next seven make-up the second level and the bottom forty make up the third level (Figure 3.2).

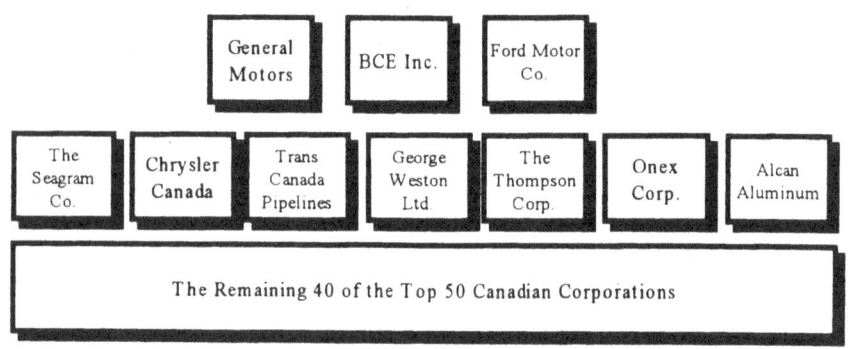

**Figure 3.2 Canadian Corporate Hierarchy**

Of course, we could examine also the entire list of 500 corporations and identify another much larger Canadian corporate hierarchy.

Looking beyond Canada, we can also identify the top corporations at the global level. *Fortune Magazine* makes available "The Global 500" which lists the largest companies in the world in 1998, again according to their revenues. The top fifty from the list (Table 3.3) include some of the best known brand names in the world, as well as many companies, especially foreign, of which readers will never have heard. Interestingly, there are no Canadian companies listed in the Global Top 50.

Once again it is possible to reconfigure this "list" as a corporate hierarchy in order to provide a better indication of the "structure" of the corporations that dominate the globe (Figure 3.3). First of all it is clear that General Motors dominates the Fortune Global 50 list with revenues far in excess of the next nearest competitor. At the next level, the Ford Motor Company, and Mitsui & Company, stand head and shoulders above the competitors that follow. Mitsui is a trading company. The third level of the hierarchy consists of the seven companies with revenues in excess of 100 billion dollars (U.S.). They, in turn, are followed by the remaining 40 companies that make up this particular global hierarchy.

All three of the corporate hierarchies illustrated have one important property in common. None of them distinguish between the *types* of companies that are listed. We have grouped together corporations with diverse interests. Automobile manufacturers, oil companies, computer companies, and food companies, among others, have all been mixed in the same pot.

What would be of greater interest, perhaps especially to the leaders of the corporations themselves, would be to see the hierarchies that occur within *sectors* of the economy. For example, we might look at the corporate hierarchy of just global energy companies, or just Canadian food and grocery companies. Such detailed analysis, on a case by case basis, is not within the scope of this book. Our interest, instead, is to consider hierarchies from a broader perspective. In particular, the concern here is to focus on the significance of the changes ongoing in these corporate hierarchies.

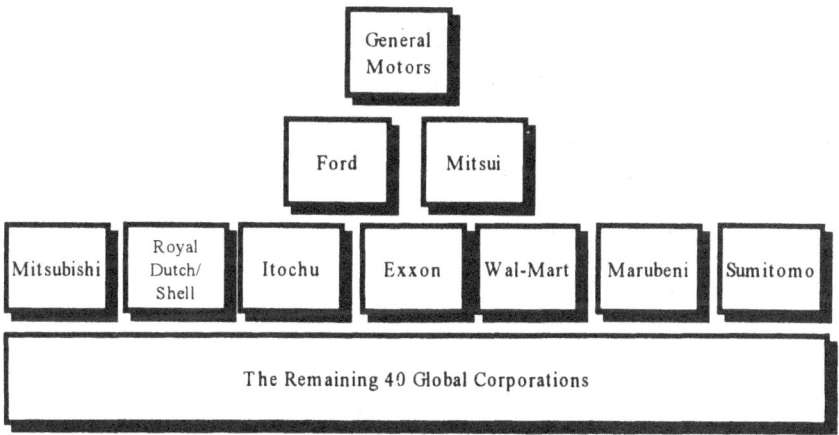

**Figure 3.3 International Corporate Hierarchy**

## Table 3.3 The *Fortune* Top 50 Global Companies, 1998 Revenue

| Global 500 Rank | Company | 1998 Revenues $millions |
|---|---|---|
| 1 | General Motors Corp. | 178,174 |
| 2 | Ford Motor Co. | 153,627 |
| 3 | Mitsui & Co. | 142,688 |
| 4 | Mitsubishi Corp. | 128,922 |
| 5 | Royal Dutch/Shell Group | 128,142 |
| 6 | Itochu Corp. | 126,632 |
| 7 | Exxon Corp. | 122,379 |
| 8 | Wal-Mart Stores Inc. | 119,299 |
| 9 | Marubeni Corp. | 111,121 |
| 10 | Sumitomo Corp. | 102,395 |
| 11 | Toyota Motor Corp. | 95,137 |
| 12 | General Electric Co. | 90,840 |
| 13 | Nissho Iwai Corp. | 81,894 |
| 14 | International Business Machines | 78,508 |
| 15 | Nippon Telegraph & Telephone | 76,984 |
| 16 | AXA | 76,874 |
| 17 | Daimler-Benz AG | 71,561 |
| 18 | Daewoo Group | 71,526 |
| 19 | Nippon Life Insurance Co. | 71,388 |
| 20 | The British Petroleum p.l.c. | 71,193 |
| 21 | Hitachi, Ltd. | 68,567 |
| 22 | Volkswagen AG | 65,328 |
| 23 | Matsushita Electric Industrial Co. | 64,281 |
| 24 | Siemens AG | 63,755 |
| 25 | Chrysler Corp. | 61,147 |
| 26 | Mobil Corp. | 59,978 |
| 27 | United States Postal Service | 58,216 |
| 28 | Allianz AG | 56,785 |
| 29 | Philip Morris Companies Inc. | 56,114 |
| 30 | Sony Corp. | 55,033 |
| 31 | Nissan Motor Co. Ltd. | 53,478 |
| 32 | AT&T Corp. | 53,261 |
| 33 | Fiat S.p.A. | 52,569 |
| 34 | Honda Motor Co. Ltd. | 48,876 |
| 35 | Unilever N.V./Unilever p.l.c. | 48.761 |
| 36 | Nestl S.A. | 48,254 |
| 37 | Credit Suisse Group | 48,242 |
| 38 | Dai-ichi Mutual Life Insurance | 47,442 |
| 39 | The Boeing Co. | 45,800 |
| 40 | Texaco Inc. | 45,187 |

| | | |
|---|---|---|
| 41 | Toshiba Corp. | 44,467 |
| 42 | State Farm Insurance Co. | 43,957 |
| 43 | Veba AG | 43,881 |
| 44 | Elf Aquitaine | 43,572 |
| 45 | Tomen Corp. | 43,400 |
| 46 | The Tokyo Electric Power Co., Inc. | 42,997 |
| 47 | Hewlett-Packard Co. | 42,895 |
| 48 | Sumitomo Life Insurance Co. | 42,279 |
| 49 | E.I. du Pont de Nemours and Co., Inc. | 41,304 |
| 50 | Sears, Roebuck and Co. | 41,296 |

**Corporate Mergers and Acquisitions in the Global Economy**

We've all seen the cartoons where a bigger fish eats a smaller fish, only to then be eaten itself by a still larger fish. Such is the nature of corporate mergers and acquisitions. In recent times, mergers and acquisitions (M&A's) are the two hottest topics in the business news. A merger is the joining together of two companies, most likely where the two are about equal in size. An acquisition, on the other hand, normally involves the taking over of one company by another. In this situation usually one company is significantly larger than the other is.

The newspapers are filled almost every day with discussions of the latest corporate M&A's. Mergers and acquisitions are taking place in the corporate world at a pace that has never been witnessed before. In the January 1999 *Globe and Mail* Eric Reguly reports that "In 1998, according to CIBC, a record $1.9 trillion of mergers took place in the United States while Canada saw deals worth a record $88 billion." Why is all of this activity happening? What is it that is occurring in the corporate world that is driving the number of M&A's to unprecedented heights?

Corporate M&A's are driven by the competitive desire of corporations to reposition themselves within their own corporate hierarchies. There is a good reason for this. As a company moves upward in a corporate hierarchy it is able to take advantage of *economies of scale*. In other words a larger company can spread costs over a wider base, and thereby reduce operating expenditures. As a result, when companies become larger than their competitors they acquire the ability to drive up profit margins and to become winners in the corporate battle for performance. There are a number of reasons why M&A's take place. Consider some corporate examples.

It was indicated in Chapter 1 that in 1998 the German bank Deutsche Bank merged with New York based Bankers Trust Corporation to create the world's biggest bank with combined assets of $800 billion (U.S.). The deal will result in cost savings; it was reported in the *National Post* in 1998 that as many as 5,500 jobs will be lost, primarily in London and New York. In addition to cost savings there were expected to be tax advantages. As well the companies claim that they will be better able to manage their assets. But the primary reason for the merger was to allow Deutsche to gain a foothold in the large U.S. market. This is a good example of "globalization" in action. A large successful European bank makes a move into the North American market.

Another merger described in Chapter 1 was that of Exxon Oil and Mobil Oil to create Exxon Mobil Corporation. The new company will have a larger market capitalization than General Motors and thus will become one of the largest companies in the world. It was reported in the 1998 *National Post* that one of the principal reasons for such a merger is that "...only the biggest firms can afford to explore for oil that's increasingly difficult to find." Thus economies of scale in exploration play a large role in this huge merger.

A recent example of an acquisition by a Canadian company was in the attempted takeover of a smaller Vancouver resource company Argentina Gold Corporation, by the huge Canadian company Barrick Gold Corporation. Argentina, the company, has a mining project called Veladero underway in Argentina, the country. Barrick also has a project underway in neighbouring Chile, that is only six kilometres away from Veladero, and wanted to gain control of both projects for the economies of scale the combined operation will produce. As company spokesman Vince Borg was quoted in the *Post* as saying "It's not clear whether Veladero is at all economic on a stand alone basis. Pasqua, with its infrastructure, brings that value to Veladero by virtue of being next door." The implication is that in this particular case the economies of scale that result from the acquisition are a result of the geography of the gold mining sites. Ultimately, the acquisition did not take place.

Canadian advertising agencies are being forced into U.S. mergers or relocations as a result of the relatively small size of the Canadian advertising market. A news report in the *National Post* indicates that as the Canadian market shrinks, some Canadian advertisers are buying up or acquiring American advertising agencies so as to enable them to expand into the U.S. market. The irony of the situation is that it is corporate mergers and acquisitions *within the Canadian advertising business* that is driving the mergers and relocations in the first place. So here we have a situation where mergers and acquisitions, and a subsequent tightening of the market, are forcing still more mergers and acquisitions, but in a different market.

Sometimes mergers and acquisitions result from conditions that are beyond the control of companies. Consider, for example, the position of Canadian energy companies in the 1990's. As a result of a surplus of oil supplies around the world, and the accompanying decline in oil prices, many oil companies will find that their stock prices are depressed. This in turn makes them vulnerable to M&A activity. The same logic applies to any sector where stock prices are at a low level.

"Win-win" mergers can result when two companies have common interests and when they each have something that the other needs. A case in point is reflected in the merger of Excel Communications Inc. and Teleglobe Inc. These two companies shared mutual interests that made a merger natural for them. Excel is a *retailer* of long-distance service, while Teleglobe provides the *hardware and technology* that makes global communications possible. It's a big merger. A 1998 *National Post* report by Andy Riga indicates that Excel is the world's fourth largest long-distance provider, behind AT&T, Sprint and MCI. Meanwhile, Teleglobe has the world's second biggest telephone/satellite network, second only to AT&T, and reaching 240 countries worldwide. The merger took place in late 1998.

If all of the examples above have one thing in common it is that these mergers and acquisitions alter the position of the companies in their respective corporate hierarchies. In every case the new, and usually larger, corporate entity should be seen as striving to move upward in its hierarchy to a position of greater strength, power, and stability.

The shared element is globalization. As trade barriers fall, and technology makes the world smaller, more companies have come to realize that there will be fewer and fewer, but larger and larger players, in the global economy of the future. In turn, this means that global corporate hierarchies will undergo a major transition. More mergers can only mean that hierarchies will get leaner, and their elements will get relatively stronger. This is a trend we should anticipate in the future structure of corporate hierarchics, that is, fewer but larger elements. In many cases the smaller players at the bottoms of the hierarchies are being eliminated, as they merge and move upward to higher levels.

These changes mirror a general trend we see ongoing elsewhere in society. In several sectors of the economy there is an ever-present trend towards fewer things, but larger things. For example, in the farm economy in Canada and the United States there is a definitive, long-term trend towards the existence of fewer farms, but those that remain are larger. Similarly, in the retailing industry, fewer and larger "big-box" stores replace smaller sales outlets. Across the Canadian landscape, small rural towns stagnate or decline in size, while their big urban cousins continue to grow at their expense. In the retail food business, a dozen fast-food chains have replaced tens of thousands of individually owned restaurants. In all of these cases, there is a common trend towards fewer, but larger entities. The hierarchies are changing and evolving. The same processes are at work at the corporate scale. Fewer but larger corporations seem to be an inevitable consequence of globalization and continentalization.

From the Canadian perspective we need also to consider not just globalization, but also continentalization. The point is made again in Chapter 4 on education, in Chapter 6 on transportation and in Chapters 9 and 11 on migration and medicine that it is crucial for Canadians to start to think on the continental scale. The Free Trade Agreement (1989) and the North American Free Trade Agreement (1994) both changed the face of North America forever. They opened the doors for Canada to the bright new marketing opportunities that exist in the huge American market. From the perspective of corporate mergers and acquisitions, Canadian companies should be actively looking south of the border as a means of tapping into the new continental economy. Many have done so already.

Is so-called "merger-frenzy" a real phenomenon? Consider this statement by Harvey Schachter in an article from *Profit 100 Magazine*:

> Historically viewed as a Bay Street affectation, acquisition fever has now infected Main Street. And nowhere is the trend more evident than among the PROFIT 100. Fully 38 of Canada's 100 Fastest-Growing Companies have acquired other firms in the past five years. Of those, 22 firms can attribute more than 20% of their growth to mergers and buyouts. ... As these bold and aggressive firms are proving, acquisitions can be a quick way to cut costs and crack new markets. By carefully acquiring complementary skills and resources, venturesome firms are exploiting real synergies and reaching new heights. The boom is now overtaking entrepreneurial business in general. Comprehensive figures are difficult to obtain, but a report by Toronto-based investment banker Crosbie & Co. shows that for public companies in the past two years, mergers and acquisitions valued at less than $10 million jumped by 38%, from 164 in 1995 to 226 in 1997. Crosbie partner Glenn Bowman says the merger frenzy is being driven in part by macroeconomic factors such as low interest rates, which make debt financing cheap, and a stable economy, which reduces apprehension among would-be buyers. But Bowman also contends that many companies are finding internal growth sluggish these days. For these businesses, the quickest way to grow may be by acquisition. By combining operations, companies can spread out their fixed costs and increase profitability. Mergers also beget mergers, he adds. If everyone is gobbling up competitors and you don't, you'll soon be in trouble.

The trend toward M&A in the corporate world is a strong one. And as has been emphasized all along in this discussion, an excellent way to study and understand the M&A activity is to look at it from the point of view of the restructuring of hierarchies. In particular, it is not always enough to just merge or acquire another company. A more fundamental question is whether a merger or acquisition leads to a *lateral* or *vertical* move within the corporation's hierarchy. It is crucial to distinguish between the two. A merger or acquisition may result in a *lateral* move within a corporation's hierarchy, but this may do little to enhance the relative success or profitability of the corporation. Its relative position as a competitor will remain largely unchanged. Rather a firm should aspire to achieve a *vertical* move in its corporate hierarchy. In so doing it will advance to the next higher level of the playing field. This represents a true advance within the corporation's domain.

## A Contrarian Point of View

In spite of the "lets all get on board" bandwagon effect of the M&A trend, there are those that argue that a merger or acquisition is sometimes a sign of weakness and should sometimes be avoided. In the January 1999 *Globe and Mail*, Eric Reguly examines Ford's 1999 purchase of Volvo and takes the position that:

> A merger is usually a last-resort option, a way of buying yourself out of a hole that was dug when a new product didn't catch on, growth faltered or government regulations threw up an obstacle. Mergers expose these shortcomings.

Reguly goes on to argue that mergers tend to fail when companies pay too much in a takeover, only to find that the market does not grow as expected or else that new competitors enter the field. The mergers that do seem to work are those where the goal is primarily to cut costs by eliminating redundancies. For those contemplating M&A activity, Reguly sends up a warning flag:

> Continuing studies done by Mercer Management Consulting of New York show that almost two-thirds of all U.S. and Canadian mergers fail, that is, the new company underperforms the industry in the years after the deal is sealed.

Caveat emptor — let the buyer beware.

## Evidence of Global Change

There is no better way to illustrate the significance of corporate change ongoing in the world than to look at some of the dramatic changes that have taken place over time. Figures 3.4 and 3.5 indicate the reorganization that has taken place in the top ten global corporations between 1998 and 1990. These numbers represent the market capitalization (U.S. $billion) of the largest corporations in the world and therefore they differ from the list given in Table 3.3, which was based on revenues.

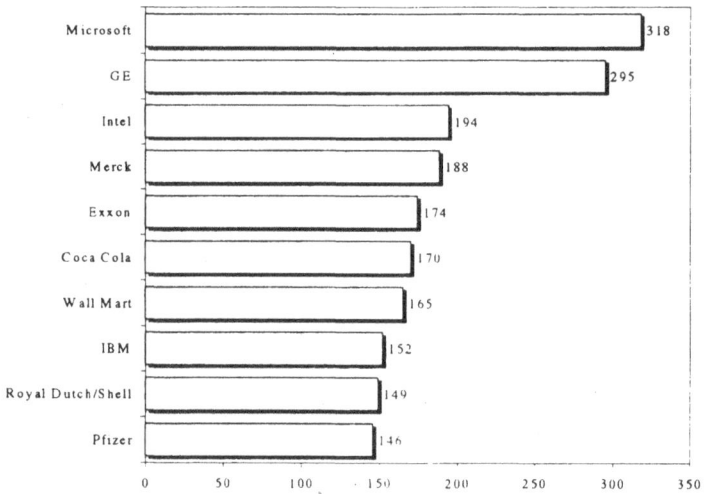

Source: *Financial Post*, 'Appraising corporate gigantism', 1998.

**Figure 3.4 Top 10 Companies by Market Capitalization - 1998**

There are some interesting differences between the two time periods in Figures 3.4 and 3.5. Microsoft, with the largest market-cap in the world in 1998, was not even on the list in 1990. The same goes for Intel, in third place overall in 1998. Notably, there were four Japanese banks in the top ten in 1990, and by 1998 there are none. Another remarkable feature of the two lists is that only four companies, GE, Exxon, IBM and Royal Dutch/Shell Group remain on the lists through both time periods. What better evidence could there be of the dynamic and ever changing nature of the global economic hierarchy?

Another indicator of the magnitude of corporate change in Canada is illustrated in Table 3.4, which shows the largest five mergers in Canada in

1998. It is evident that Canada has become a major player in M&A as indicated by the size of the deals that are taking place. In both the first and fourth deals it can be seen that The Seagram Company has moved beyond the boundaries of Canada to become an international corporation, it having become a major company in the global entertainment business by acquiring the record and entertainment company PolyGram. Other major deals in Canada include those in the energy and telecommunications sectors. Such deals may be only the tip of the iceberg in Canadian corporate mergers yet to materialize.

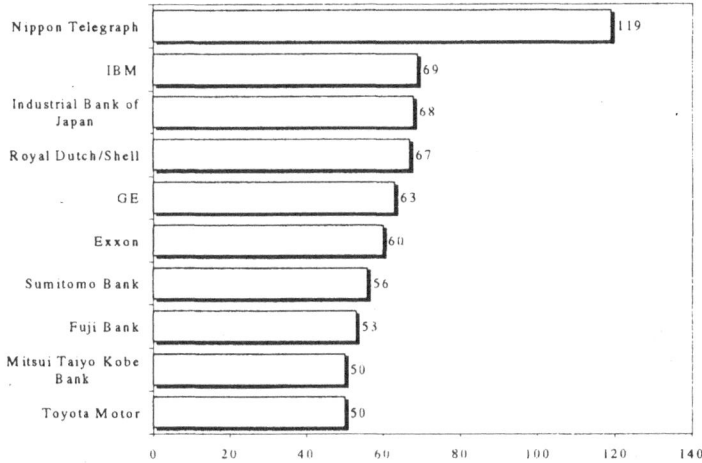

Source: *Financial Post*, 'Appraising corporate gigantism', 1998.

**Figure 3.5 Top 10 Companies by Market Capitalization - 1990**

**The United States of Europe?**

Another important global hierarchical shift that is underway is the one occurring in Europe. As part of an attempt to improve the economic unity of Europe, the "Euro" became the official new currency of Europe in January 1999. Eleven countries joined together in the European Monetary Union (EMU) to create a new and powerful global economic power. The countries include Finland, Ireland, the Netherlands, Belgium, Germany, Luxembourg, France, Austria, Italy, Spain, and Portugal. As of January 1999 the Euro became the official currency for *business* of these countries, and in January 2002 the currency will go into common circulation. This new union creates an economic powerhouse that rivals the United States in scope and wealth. Table 3.5 sets out the numbers comparing the size of the EMU with the United States.

The new union creates a market that provides head-to-head competition with the United States in terms of international investment. As Guy Dixon notes in a December 1998 *Globe and Mail* report:

> Investing in Europe has meant first picking a country, and then choosing a stock market sector or bond market niche. But now, with currency risks eliminated within the new eurozone, country risks fall by the wayside. This is expected to allow a much freer flow of investments in a capital market that already matches the United States in size.

### Table 3.4 Top Five Canadian Mergers of 1998

| Estimated value | Name | Role | Announced |
| --- | --- | --- | --- |
| $15.1-billion | Seagram Co. Ltd. | Acquiror | May 21, 1998 |
| | PolyGram NV | Target | |
| $11.0-billion | TransCanada Pipelines Ltd. | Target | Jan. 22, 1998 |
| | Nova Corp. | Target | |
| $ 9.9-billion | Northern Telecom Ltd. | Acquiror | May 13, 1998 |
| | Bay Networks Inc. | Target | |
| $ 4.9-billion | PepsiCo Inc. | Acquiror | July 20, 1998 |
| | Tropicanca Products Inc. | Target | |
| | Seagram Co. Ltd. | Vendor | |
| $ 4.6-billion | BC Telecom Inc. | Target | Oct. 19, 1998 |
| | Telus Corp. | Target | |

Source: *Globe & Mail*, 'Value of mergers soars 47% in 1998', 1999.

Media speculation is that the Euro, and the eurozone, may be just the first steps toward the creation of a political union of European countries to be known as the United States of Europe. This "new country" may be able to supplant the United States as the world's leading economic power. Significantly, the change suggests a massive shift in the form of the world's economic hierarchies. As the result of a simple economic and perhaps political union, the United States will suddenly have a new competitor along side it, atop the global economic hierarchy.

### Table 3.5 Comparison of the Economies of EMU and U.S.

|  | EMU | U.S. |
|---|---|---|
| Population | 289 million | 263 million |
| GDP | U.S.$6.3-trillion | U.S.$7.8-trillion |
| Outstanding debt | US$6.5-trillion | US$13.6-trillion |
| Exports | US$823-billion | US$689-billion |
| Imports | US$768-billion | US$899-billion |

Source: *Financial Post*, December, 1998.

In Canada the creation of the Euro has prompted a call for a unified North American currency. In particular it has been suggested by some that Canada and Mexico should adopt the United States dollar as a common currency. The idea is that this would enable the North American "economic union" to better compete with Europe. As might be expected, there has been some strong opposition to this idea in Canada, especially as it is seen as another blow to Canadian independence from the United States. At the same time however, global economic forces are pushing in the opposite direction and towards the creation of larger and more unified economic unions. Ultimately, it is not difficult to imagine a day when there will be a single currency for the whole world. This seems to be the way in which the economic winds are blowing.

## The Evolution of the Internal Corporate Hierarchy

Having looked at some hierarchies *of* corporations, we turn our attention now to the form of hierarchies *within* corporations. GE, Exxon and IBM will all, of necessity, have internal organizations that are in the form of hierarchies or "corporate ladders." Our interest is in looking more closely at what it is that constitutes an efficient and effective form of ladder. What is it about the form of internal organization that gives one firm an advantage over another? Moreover, how can firms change and adjust their internal hierarchies to enable themselves to better compete?

Several books have gone to lengths over the years to discredit the notion of the corporate hierarchy. In this line of thought, the corporate hierarchy is likened to a dinosaur from the ancient past. It is argued that the traditional corporate ladder dates from the stone ages of the industrial revolution and that it is no longer appropriate to the modern corporation. The present book argues that the corporate ladder is an *essential* and *necessary* part of any modern corporate structure. It argues that *all* companies are of necessity organized hierarchically and as a consequence it is imperative: (1) to examine hierarchical structures critically, (2) to understand hierarchical structures, and (3) to be able to respond to, monitor, and effectively manipulate hierarchical structures.

In order to gain an understanding of the organizational evolution of the modern firm, it is necessary to take a look back in time. In particular it will be useful to examine the origins of our current methods of production and how they came to be managed. Not surprisingly, Ford and General Motors were key players in this history.

The process of breaking complex tasks into a series of small jobs is known more formally as the "division of labour." It was pioneered as long ago as 1776 by Adam Smith who wrote about the idea in his book entitled *The Wealth of Nations*. The idea is a simple one and is repeated here from *Reengineering the Corporation*. Suppose you were going to open a factory to manufacture standard household pins. There are two basic ways in which you can organize your factory. On the one hand, you can have each employee work on a single pin from start to finish. On the other hand, you can break the pin manufacturing process down into a series of steps and have each employee carry out a single step. Smith argued that the latter approach, where the "labour is divided" into steps is far more efficient at producing a product. Smith visited a small factory where there were just ten employees involved in carrying out the eighteen steps in the manufacture of pins. Smith wrote that:

> One man draws out the wire, another straightens it, a third cuts it, a fourth points it, a fifth grinds it at the top for receiving the head; to make the head requires two or three distinct operations; to put it on is a peculiar business, to whiten the pins is another; it is even a trade by itself to put them into the paper. These ten persons could make among them upwards of forty-eight thousand pins in a day. But if they had all wrought separately and independently, and without any of them having been educated to this peculiar business, they certainly could not each of them have made twenty, perhaps not one pin in a day.

The simple yet elegant observation that Smith makes is a profound idea for increasing the productivity of a workforce. In fact, it can be said that it is this simple idea that is at the heart of the success of the industrial revolution.

## Up the Corporate Ladder 55

There are a number of reasons why the division of labour leads to efficient production. As Smith himself noted, the benefit of splitting a complex task into small pieces is:

> owing to three different circumstances; first, to the increase of dexterity in every particular workman; secondly, to the saving of the time which is commonly lost in passing from one species of work to another; and lastly, to the invention of a great number of machines which facilitate and abridge labor, and enable one man to do the work of many.

What Smith fails to mention is that splitting a task into simple steps also makes it much easier and less expensive to train workers for jobs, and also makes it easier to replace employees, or to shift them to new positions. In addition, it also makes it easier to automate the steps of the process. The better known example of the division of labour is, of course, found in the assembly line methods used by Henry Ford. This was "mass production" for a more complex product, but the same line of reasoning — giving each worker a single task which he did repeatedly until it was automatic — was exactly the same.

Lest the reader be misled into believing that these arguments apply only to the manufacture of products, it should be made clear that mass production and the division of labour are ideas that apply to any sort of business. For example, in an insurance firm, a salesman takes an order and passes it to a secretary, who in turn passes it to clerk, who passes it to another clerk, and so on. In the grocery store, the clerk scans your purchase, then the bagger bags it. Business tasks of all sorts are broken down into small steps with an individual working on each step. The idea of the division of labour applies to almost every kind of organized activity.

So far the "division of labour" has described the division of *manual* labour. We have yet to examine the *management style* that goes hand in hand with Adam Smith's approach to production.

When a complex task is broken down into a series of simple and uncomplicated steps it becomes obvious that *coordination* of the workers "along the pin line" becomes a matter of crucial importance. Supplies or parts must arrive at an appropriate pace, the timing of steps along the line must be in sync, bottlenecks need to be identified, and so on. Clearly it becomes necessary to have a *manager* to oversee the operation of the whole production line. If you were running the pin factory, a "line manager" would be essential. That's the first step towards the creation of a management structure.

Imagine now that you wish to expand your pin factory to include a new line, say safety pins. In order to accomplish this, we set up an entirely new and separate production line and, of course, the new line will need a new manager. If expansion were to continue along these lines it is apparent that before long you will have a company with the beginnings of a hierarchically organized management, that is, hundreds of employees, several managers, and one boss. That's step two.

Suppose now that this company continues to grow and expand as more and more new product lines are added. At some point the number of managers will become unwieldy and it will become apparent that further re-organization is necessary. The obvious solution is to create a new level of managers to oversee the existing "line managers." A convenient way to keep track of the whole thing is to create a *division* for each new manager to oversee. There will be fewer of these new "division managers," each one overseeing several line managers. Thus each new division becomes equivalent to a small company like the one with which we started. That's the final step (see Figure 3.6).

It becomes obvious very quickly that as the company grows, a hierarchical form of *management tree* emerges naturally as a form of organization. As was said previously, an efficient delegation of tasks takes place in any efficient corporation or organization. A hierarchy implies an even and equitable delegation of tasks to those "down the line." If a task is too big for one individual to handle efficiently, a hierarchy delegates responsibilities clearly. Each individual in the tree has particular duties and the sum of these individual efforts produces a functional hierarchy. To repeat, anyone in any position of authority, or aspiring to one, needs to understand this important characteristic of organizations and hierarchies.

There is an interesting historical analogy to the evolution of the "divisions" in a hierarchy just described. In an article in *Forbes ASAP*, Tom Peters describes the competition between Henry Ford at the Ford Motor Company and his counterpart, Alfred P. Sloan, at General Motors in the 1920's:

> Henry Ford's little outfit was walloping Alfred Sloan's little outfit. Ford, creator of the first effective system of mass production, was giving every man the chance to own a car for several hundred dollars — the Model T— and, as Ford apparently bragged, 'in any color you want...as long as it's black.' Then Sloan had a profound — and profoundly simple — idea: to reorganize his company, General Motors, into divisions...the Chevrolet Division...the Buick Division...the Pontiac Division...and so on. Each division was an enterprise within an enterprise, with its own personality and character. Each attracted a different type of customer and captured a different segment of the market. Sloan's tactic worked so well that, by the dawning of World War II, he had accelerated past Ford.

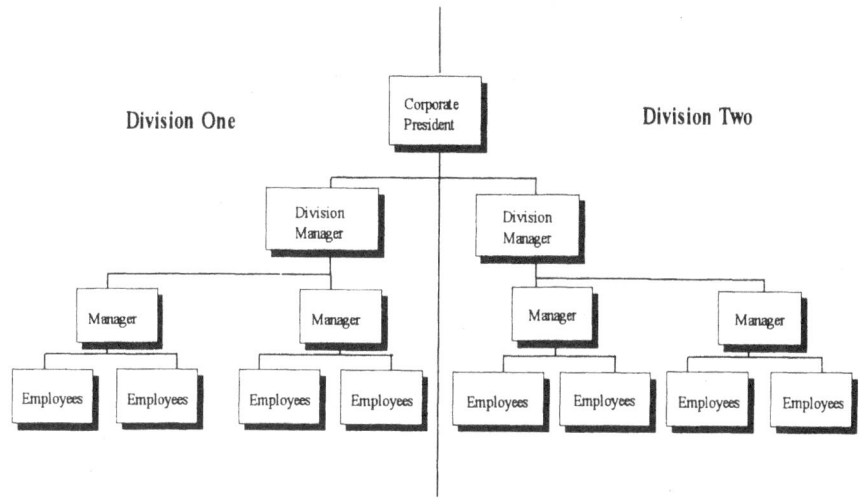

**Figure 3.6 Typical, Simple Corporate Hierarchy**

It can be argued that Sloan's pioneering efforts in the restructuring of management at General Motors set the tone for the general form of management in the modern North American firm. Smith had promoted the *division of labour*. Sloan pioneered the *division of management*. In fact, this is implied in the very use of the word *division*. As Michael Hammer and James Champy note in *Reengineering the Corporation*, "Sloan was applying Adam Smith's principle of the division of labor to management just as Ford had applied it to production."

## The Optimum Form of the Corporate Hierarchy

Given the idea of the division of management, how then do we arrive at the optimum form for the corporate hierarchy? What is there to guide us? How is a firm to know if it has a corporate hierarchy that is appropriate to its goals?

In the simple firm which evolved in the preceding section it was easy to see how the firm split into two divisions, each with a manager of its own. In so simple an example, the optimum form of organization is obvious. But how are we to apply these ideas to a larger firm? Clearly the modern firm is a far more complex entity than that given in the example, and it becomes necessary to consider more sophisticated forms of corporate organization.

The over-riding principle is one of balance or equilibrium. As in any other aspect of a business environment, a balance must be struck between costs and effectiveness. In this particular case we are looking at the balance between the *costs* of adding extra management, against the *benefits* resulting from adding extra management. At what point are we ahead of the game? At what point do the benefits exceed the costs?

In order to gauge the effectiveness of a corporate hierarchy it is necessary to look at it as a conduit for information flows. It is only in this manner that we are able to judge accurately the effectiveness of a corporate hierarchy. We usually think of a hierarchy as a static picture, as a diagram at a single point in time. In order to appreciate better the purpose of the corporate hierarchy, it is essential to think of it instead as an active and dynamic entity with information flowing through it. Imagine, in other words, if we could "see" the information flows coursing through a corporate hierarchy, like blood running through arteries. Clearly what would be of interest to us in such an image would be two main things. First, we would be concerned with the restrictions or blockages to flow in the system. Secondly, we would be interested in the places where the capacity of the system was in excess: where the elements are too big for the flows they handle. It is important to clarify here that we are not focusing on the "links" or "lines" in the hierarchy, but rather on the flows through the "boxes." It is only by doing such a "cardiovascular check-up" on the information flows in a hierarchy that we will be able to diagnose accurately the "health" of the corporate hierarchy.

Let us return to our simple example of the growing pin factory. Suppose the firm continues to grow well beyond the boundaries discussed earlier. Expansion, merger and acquisition lead to the development of the General Pin Corporation which has dozens of *divisions*, hundreds of managers, and thousands of employees. Of course, the company will now also have assistant managers, a sales division, an accounting division, a human resources division, a strategic planning division, and so on. The corporate hierarchy will be very large and perhaps difficult to sort out. It might be so large, in fact, to be almost incomprehensible. How are we to do our "diagnosis" on such a cumbersome system?

The answer is simple: it is not an easy task. Yet it is not impossible either. An effective corporate hierarchy will be characterized by vigorous information flows, where the managers at all levels in the system will be working, not at "overload" but at peak capacity. A thorough internal examination of the system should reveal links, lines of communication, bottlenecks, and "surplus capacities." It is necessary not only to look at the status quo, that is, the *existing* lines of flow, but also at the possibility for opening new lines of information flow, and for deleting existing, redundant ones. All the while, the goal is to emphasize the balance between the costs of maintaining the hierarchy, as against the benefits that accrue from the elements of the hierarchy. As is the case in any "medical diagnosis," outside, and expert opinion, should be consulted.

What are some of the approaches that can be employed in order to make a corporate hierarchy more effective and efficient? Any gardener knows that a successful garden requires a lot of diverse work. Most gardening operations are not carried out on the basis of any high ideals. Rather, the prosperous garden responds to the environment as circumstances see fit. Every year brings a new set of challenges that are unique to that season's conditions. Just like a garden, the modern corporation is not static. Rather it is an ongoing *process* that adjusts and responds to the never-ending changes in the conditions that it faces.

Given that hierarchies take on a treelike form, a useful analogy is to be found in looking at the techniques that are employed in the proper care, growth, maintenance, and propagation of natural trees and vegetation.

- Trimming — Trimming a tree implies working at the edges, creating a desired shape or outer form. In the case of a corporate hierarchy, this might mean trimming peripheral or marginal branches that are superfluous to the successful management of the core of the firm. We would look here especially for small, outlying branches that have become outdated or just plain redundant.
- Pruning — Pruning implies a much deeper kind of cutting, where it may be necessary to eliminate major branches or arteries now, to ensure the future success of the tree. In the interim the tree may even look awkward or "hacked-up," but that is the price that is paid for future prosperity. In a corporate environment this may suggest the gutting or cutting of entire divisions or units in order to secure the future of the company as a whole. Some dramatic cuts may be needed to ensure success. It is interesting to note that when a real tree is pruned, most of the cutting is done on "inside" branches, that is, on those that are growing upward "inside" the tree and interfering with other "main" structural branches. Thus it may be necessary for a firm to determine which large branches are the "main" ones and which are the "suckers" that contribute little to the overall health of the hierarchy. There may be a lesson to be learned from a leader of one of the largest corporations in the world. Arie de Geus, Royal Dutch Shell's former head of strategic planning, compared corporate performance with pruning roses as follows (quoted in a 1998 article by Tom Peters in *Forbes ASAP*): "If you prune long — if you are tolerant — you will certainly not be the best performer in the industry with highest return

on investment. You may not have this year's largest roses," he said. "But you have considerably increased the chances that you will have roses every year. Tolerant pruning...gradually renews the plant over time and is more effective in a world you cannot control."
- Thinning — Another approach to ensuring the health of a tree is by thinning out the branches. Unlike "trimming," this operation takes place all over the tree, both inside and outside, and strives to give the remaining branches "room to grow." In a corporation, one can imagine thinning out every branch or division by doing a little bit of cutting everywhere. Although each small cut seems insignificant, they all add up.
- Fertilizing — Although it may sound demeaning when used in the corporate analogy there is nothing more favourable towards the healthy growth of a tree than a good application of manure. In the corporate domain, of course, we are talking about the application of systems of rewards or incentives. The most obvious reward in the corporate hierarchy is in *advancing upward in the hierarchy itself*, through promotion. Expanding the hierarchy, by adding *new branches*, or even levels, might provide the incentive needed to produce greater productivity. Of course, there are many other systems of reward that might lead to a more productive corporate hierarchy as well.
- Watering — Water is the lifeblood of the tree, in the same way that salary and bonus is the lifeblood of the corporation. Does anyone ever think to examine the corporate hierarchy according to the *levels of salary or bonus* that are associated with each level and station of the tree? This would represent an innovative way to examine the hierarchy and to restructure it in more appropriate ways. If the creation of a hierarchy of *promotion* is out of the question, why not create a *hierarchy of salary or especially a hierarchy of bonuses* as a system of incentive?
- Propagating — Propagation is a method whereby a new plant is reproduced from the parent stock. In the corporate context this is equivalent to taking an existing healthy division, management team, or group and "culling" from it a new smaller team, or teams, in order to head up a new project or unit. Success breeds success, and the effectiveness of the propagation approach lies in the idea that a successful team or unit should "give birth" to additional units headed up by those who were responsible for the success of the original unit.
- Dismantling and Reassembling — One of the advantages of a corporate tree over a real tree is that the corporate tree is virtual; it can be completely disassembled and reassembled countless times over. This provides the opportunity to *simulate* changes to the tree and look

at the implications. Major branches can be cut, divisions can be reorganized, and in fact the whole operation can be turned on its head, just to get some new ideas or innovative perspectives. Managers tend to resist change. This is a way to look at change without necessarily making the final plunge.

Often it will be discovered through diagnosis that it is necessary to cut the size of management. Hierarchical structures that are "top down" are often said to be notorious, perhaps often wrongly so, for breeding inefficiency in organizations and corporations. When cutting is necessary there are a number of well-known approaches. One of these, known as *delayering*, eliminates an entire layer of the management hierarchy. A similar and related approach, called *teaming*, combines two layers of the management hierarchy into one, in order to achieve efficiencies. As John Kersell and Peter Heimler note in a website article:

> Observers and doers alike have come to realize that managers (as distinct from leaders) add little to production or services. They pass problems down to the operations level and solutions up to decision-makers, adding mostly distortions, delays and costs. The barriers to good information flow and decision making can be overcome by delayering and teaming the organization. This delayering process can be supported by utilizing information and communication technology to aid decision-making. This general pattern of eliminating an entire layer of senior management has been effectively tried in conjunction with team leadership of geographically large and politically diverse municipal governments in Ontario.

Either of these approaches, delayering or teaming, leads to the "flattening" of hierarchies. This may be an effective cost cutting strategy so long as the cuts are not so deep as to significantly interfere with the functional structure of the hierarchy. There are numerous case studies where hierarchical cutting has led to greater efficiencies. A case in point is described by Kersell and Heimler as follows:

> Organizations such as General Motors, which was to pare-to-the-bone its management staffs by 1996, and Swiss machinery manufacturer, Asea Brown Boveri Ltd. (ABB), which has already reduced its corporate head office from 4,000 to 100 managers supported by 50 hi-tech personnel, obviously agree. ABB found that about 30 percent of the too contented disappeared through attrition and other layoffs; another 30 percent relocated elsewhere in the organization where they began to add to productivity; and 30 percent found useful positions in related organizations. Ten percent remained at the corporate centre for the initial period of transition, more than half to be

reassigned as needs evolved. Perhaps less reported, if at all, are cases of corporate cutting where the results have backfired.

## The Corporate Hierarchy - An Absolute Necessity or a Dinosaur?

In the end, the ultimate question is whether the hierarchy, as a method of structuring the corporation, is obsolete. There are those that would have us believe that the idea of the corporate hierarchy has outlived its usefulness. Chief among these detractors are the authors of, *Reengineering the Corporation,* Michael Hammer and James Champy. These authors argue that the very idea of the corporate hierarchy is out-of-date. By their reasoning:

> The reality that organizations have to confront, however, is that the old ways of doing business — the division of labor around which companies have been organized since Adam Smith first articulated the principle — simply don't work anymore. ...Adam Smith's world and its way of doing business are yesterday's paradigm.

It is difficult, if not impossible to imagine any firm, anytime, anywhere that could operate in the absence of a hierarchical structure. Hammer and Champy go on to state that:

> It is no longer necessary or desirable for companies to organize their work around Adam Smith's division of labor. Task-oriented jobs in today's world of customers, competition, and change are obsolete. Instead, companies must work around *process.*

The present book argues, in contrast, that any effective *process* must of necessity be organized in a hierarchical manner. Indeed, though Hammer and Champy go on to describe examples of this so-called "process" approach, they fail to convince the reader that it can be accomplished without using hierarchical structures as its basis.

In fact, in a second book entitled *Reengineering Management,* Champy reverses himself and goes to lengths to justify the use and usefulness of corporate hierarchies. As he argues in the second book, in regard to the corporate "shift" that is ongoing:

> It doesn't mean that hierarchical chains of command or detailed job descriptions are completely vanishing from corporate life. There are some enterprises (small service companies, perhaps) whose goods or services are produced and brought to market by so few people that no arrangements have to be made to coordinate the work of production and marketing. In such an

enterprise, all of the players can fit into a room (real or virtual) to make decisions together. Anything larger, more dispersed, or more work specialized usually requires an 'elevated' or 'centralized' platform from which it's possible to see what's going on. Somebody has to answer for the coordination of the whole enterprise. Hierarchy grows out of that brute fact...

Furthermore, Champy goes on in greater detail to explain the important role of the hierarchy in the corporation:

All those layers of bureaucracy and narrow job descriptions cannot merely be jettisoned. This stuff is the life of a corporation. Where it exists, a hierarchical, bureaucratic structure doesn't simply support an organization, like the girders in a skyscraper. It is the armature of our deepest on-the-job feelings and attachments as well. Just think, for example, how hierarchy structures what is for many of us our most creative impulse, our ambition. Not everyone can be an entrepreneur, determined to make something out of nothing. Most of us, if we want to rise in the world, must have something to *climb*. Without a hierarchy (or with a very flat one), how are ambitious people going to measure their climb? How do you go up a ladder with only a few rungs...?

Exactly. How does flattening or teaming the corporate hierarchy act in any way as an incentive to those managers that remain? As was said earlier, one of the key rewards in the corporate hierarchy is in the prospect of *advancing upward in the hierarchy itself*. Detractors of the corporate hierarchy tend to overlook this fundamental fact.

The division of labour, and the division of management, have proven themselves over the long haul to be the most effective means of achieving complex tasks. To suggest that they, and the associated corporate hierarchy, can be eliminated from modern business methods is akin to suggesting that a task can be accomplished without any organizing framework whatsoever. What is the more efficient, more effective, and more logical alternative to the *hierarchical* organization of the corporation? There is none.

## References

Brent, P., 'Ad agencies seeking presence in the U.S.', *National Post*, December 21, 1998.
Champy, J. (1995), *Reengineering Management*, Harper Collins: New York.
Damsell, K., 'Barrick Gold makes $421M bid for Argentina Gold', *National Post*, December 10, 1998.
Dixon, G., 'Adventures in Euroland', *Globe and Mail*, December 19, 1998.
Hammer, M. and Champy, J. (1993), *Reengineering the Corporation*, Harper Collins: New York.

Kersell, J.E. and Heimler, P.C. (1997), 'Restructuring Management: in order to reduce costs and enhance effectiveness'. Internet site: http://www.golden.net/~kerse/fraser.htm.
Morton, P., 'Deutsche deal creates world's biggest bank', *National Post*, December 1, 1998.
Olive, D., 'Exxon-Mobil deal creates world's biggest company', *National Post*, December 2, 1998.
Peters, T., 'Destruction is Cool', *Forbes ASAP*, February 23, 1998.
Plender, J., 'Appraising corporate gigantism', *Financial Post*, December 11, 1998.
Reguly, E., 'Ford deal an admission of weakness', *Globe and Mail*, January 30, 1999.
Riga, A., 'A marriage of opposites', *Financial Post*, December 19, 1998.
Schacter, H., 'Don't grow it, buy it: Why more growth leaders are finding acquisitions the fastest route to market dominance', 1998. Internet site: www.profit100.com/ S98_dont.html.
Smith, A. (1776), *The Wealth of Nations*, Clarendon Press: Oxford.
*The Financial Post Magazine*, 'Financial Post Top 500 Companies: Ground rules, definitions & highlights', July, 1998.
Thomas, D., 'The debate begins: will euro be a dud, or will it be the currency of choice', *Financial Post*, December 19, 1998.
Waldie, P., 'Value of mergers soars 47% in 1998', *Globe and Mail*, January 9, 1999.

# 4 Education and Inequity

Consider this curious fact. Ask yourself whether the city in which you live, or live near, has more elementary schools or more secondary schools. Every reader should come up with the same answer; that the number of elementary schools exceeds the number of secondaries by a longshot. In fact, every city in Canada has far more elementary schools than it does secondary schools. Saskatoon, for example, with a population of about 220,000, has roughly eighty elementary schools but only thirteen secondary schools. One might wonder why this state of affairs exists. If school systems are efficient and well organized why is there such a disparity between the number of elementary and secondary schools? Are there too many elementary schools? Are there not enough secondary schools? Is there needless duplication in elementary schools? Is the high number of elementary schools inefficient and wasteful?

What about the other levels of the educational system? Is there unnecessary duplication? Do we have too many universities? Are there not enough technical colleges? How should the educational system be structured if it is to be economically efficient?

One of the best examples of a hierarchical system that is of enormous significance to people in their everyday lives is found in our educational systems. From the elementary level to the post-secondary level, the school system forms a quite precise hierarchy. It is difficult to really understand the educational system without appreciating its treelike nature. More importantly, it is impossible to examine the efficiency and economy of the school system without taking into account the fact that it must be structured as a top-to-bottom, national hierarchy.

The educational system is a hierarchy in which geographical distance plays a crucial role. Because there are limitations on the distances that students are willing to travel, at all levels in the system, a distinct hierarchy emerges. There are limits also on the distance or amount of time that parents wish to see spent on travel to school for young children. For secondary and post-secondary students travel *costs* can become a major source of concern. These travel time and cost factors are crucial in causing this interesting hierarchical system to evolve.

## The Educational System in Canada - In Decline?

Education in Canada is big. Consider that Canada has over five million students enrolled in elementary and secondary schools. Table 4.1 shows the enrollment trends over the five years ending in 1996. Clearly there is a pattern of constantly increasing enrollments over this period of time. In 1990-91 there were just over five million enrolled but by 1996 this number had grown to nearly five and a half million.

**Table 4.1  Enrollment in Elementary and Secondary Schools**

|  | Canada* | Public | Private | Federal | Other |
|---|---|---|---|---|---|
| 1990-1991 | 5,141,003 | 4,845,308 | 240,968 | 52,285 | 2,442 |
| 1991-1992 | 5,218,237 | 4,915,630 | 245,255 | 55,221 | 2,131 |
| 1992-1993 | 5,284,145 | 4,967,848 | 257,605 | 56,416 | 2,276 |
| 1993-1994 | 5,327,826 | 5,002,834 | 265,275 | 57,378 | 2,339 |
| 1994-1995 | 5,362,799 | 5,029,114 | 271,974 | 59,383 | 2,328 |
| 1995-1996 | 5,440,334 | 5,095,901 | 277,704 | 64,268 | 2,461 |

\* Canada total also includes Department of National Defence schools overseas.

Source: Statistics Canada, Catalogue no. 81-229-XPB, 1998.

In his book, *Boom, Bust and Echo,* David Foot argues that, as a result of the considerable demographic influence of the baby-boom generation, enrollment will soon start to decline in the Canadian school system. In particular he predicts that after 1999, elementary enrollments will start to drop and, after 2006, secondary enrollments will do the same. Unfortunately his analysis ignores three very important factors.

Consider first the issue of elementary enrollments. Even though elementary enrollments are the easiest to predict, because elementary students *must* attend school, it is still difficult to predict the future composition of the Canadian population. Canada's population is growing more as a result of immigration from other countries, than from natural population growth. In fact, according to Statistics Canada, as of 1996, 53 percent of Canada's population growth came from immigration while only 47 percent came from natural increase (births minus deaths). In the future we can anticipate an ever more significant influx to Canada of educated young migrants who either have young children, or else are in the child bearing years. These immigrants can only add more children to the elementary system.

Added to the trend described above is the fact that immigrants appear to place a premium value on education. The Statistics Canada report indicates:

> In 1996, recent immigrants (defined as those who arrived in Canada between 1991 and 1996) had higher levels of education than the Canadian-born population. About 34% of recent immigrants aged 25 to 44 had completed university, compared with 19% of the Canadian-born population in the same age group.

Presumably these immigrants will pass the high value they place on education on to their children.

Thirdly, consider that the participation rate of secondary students is on the increase. Foot's forecast is based on existing or past rates of retention in the secondary school system. Is it not reasonable to suggest, however, that as the economy gets tighter, and the job market gets more competitive, the number of students who choose to attend or finish secondary school will increase? Consider this statement from Statistics Canada:

> Consistent with higher levels of educational attainment, school attendance rates for young adults have increased. In 1996, 79% of young people aged 15 to 19 were attending school on a full time basis, up from 66% in 1981.

Given these trends, how can Foot predict confidently that secondary enrollments will drop after 2006? Furthermore, according to a recent survey, more and more teens find the thought of going on to university to be a desirable goal for themselves in the future.

The Canadian educational system is a wonderful but expensive endeavour. Some authors try to describe it as inefficient and over-expensive. Foot, for example, argues that the Canadian education system is simultaneously one of the most expensive yet least efficient educational systems in the world:

> ... Our spending on education, at more than 7% of gross national product, is the highest per capita among the G-7 leading industrialized countries, according to the Organization for Economic Co-operation and Development. We are spending more on education than other countries and getting less in return.

## 68  Hierarchical Organization in Society

It could be stated, in contrast, that Canada has one of the world's best educational systems and is willing to pay the price to achieve success. Teachers in Canada are paid a respectable wage for their work. And why not? This is society's way of giving due recognition to the important work that teachers do.

### The Educational Hierarchy

The Canadian educational hierarchy is shown in Figure 4.1, which is repeated here for convenience from the first chapter. The smallest branches of the educational hierarchy are formed by the elementary system. Elementary schools have the appropriate characteristics of their place in the hierarchy: there are more of them and they are smaller. At the second level, we find the secondary schools. There are fewer of them and they are usually quite a bit larger than the elementary schools. Third up from the base come the colleges and technical institutes. Once again there are still fewer of these, and once again the size becomes larger. Finally, at the top of the educational hierarchy, we find the universities. As expected we see that there are fewer of them and that they are the largest educational institutions in the land.

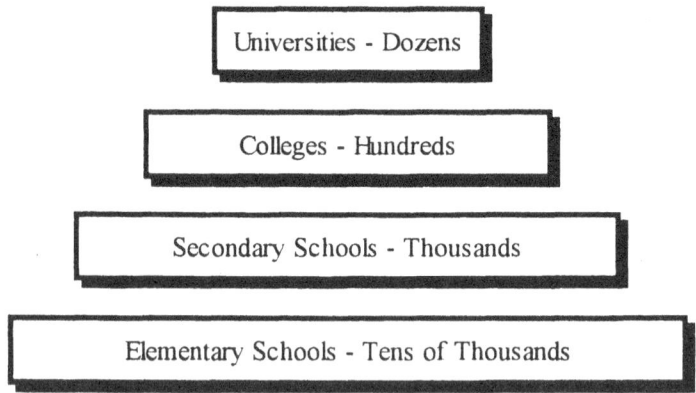

**Figure 4.1  Educational Hierarchy**

Significantly, what is missing is a single, stand-alone 'trunk' to the tree. There should perhaps be a recognized, distinct large institution that stands alone at the top of the hierarchy. The question is whether this should be considered a weakness of the Canadian educational system. What is most significant about the hierarchy is not so much that it exists, but rather that it has an effect on the daily lives of people, especially with respect to their travel patterns and the travel costs incurred by them. A more general, but equally important issue, is the extent to which the hierarchy of schools impedes *access* to the educational system for those taxpayers that happen to live in the "wrong" place in the hierarchy.

How do we explain the differences in the Canadian educational system? It is clear that schools at all levels form themselves into a quite distinct hierarchy. But why? Why are elementary schools so numerous? Why are universities so few and far between? There are obvious impacts on "consumers" of these institutions. University students often have to travel greater distances to get to their institutions. Secondary students usually are forced to travel farther than their siblings in elementary school. Why? How do we account for these significant differences? In the sections that follow we examine each of the levels of the educational system in an attempt to answer these questions.

## Accounting for the School Hierarchy within Cities

Young children, simply because they are smaller, cannot walk as far as older kids. A toddler literally "toddles," that is, walks with short, unsteady steps. A preschooler or a kindergartner is much the same. For such young children, walking is confined to relatively short distances. Teenagers, on the other hand, can walk as far as adults, if not farther. They are little constrained by distances when it comes to covering territory. Moreover, teens are able to ride bikes over great distances, ride public transit on their own, and even drive cars when they hit the magic age of sixteen.

The elementary and secondary school systems are designed with this subtle difference in mind. Most parents of elementary school children would prefer that their children *walk* to and from school if at all possible. When buying a house, parents often ensure that the local school is safely "within the neighbourhood," and a short walk away. City planners and school boards acknowledge this preference when they build smaller, more plentiful neighbourhood schools in our cities.

As children reach high school age they become more independent and better able to make their own way around over greater distances. As a consequence, fewer but larger secondary schools get built in our cities in recognition of the greater mobility and personal responsibility of teens.

But why don't we just build a small high school beside every elementary school, if only for the sake of the convenience of parents and students alike? The answer is simply because it's more expensive. Just as we saw within the chapter on corporate hierarchies, there are *economies of scale* at work within hierarchies. This includes the school hierarchy. Fewer, larger schools mean that the costs of infrastructure and management can be spread over larger numbers of students. Why pay the salaries of a hundred school principals when you can get the job done with a dozen of them? Similarly, why build a hundred high schools when a dozen larger ones will accommodate the same number of students, at a lower cost per student?

In many communities we find only a single college or university. Why not follow this lead and build just one, single elementary school in a city, and one single secondary school? Better yet, why not just build one single school *building* for everyone? After all, this would be the *least expensive* plan to implement. The answer is that there is clearly more involved here than just minimizing costs.

The school system is designed to serve a geographically spread-out market, or disbursed "customer base." As such it represents a balance between the two extremes of (a) spending the maximum amount of money on building schools, or (b) spending the least. Consider the two possibilities. At one extreme, we could build a multitude of schools, putting one on every city block. This would achieve the greatest convenience for students and parents. On the other extreme, we could build one single school for a whole city. This would keep construction costs to a minimum but cause the greatest *inconvenience* for students and parents. Obviously the trade-off solution is somewhere between these two extremes and it is in that compromising way that we, as a society, choose to build our schools.

There is an economy of scale to the construction of schools. We try to build the fewest schools possible, but subject to the realization that the *needs of users* must be taken into account. It is this compromise between minimizing costs and satisfying geographical needs of users that ultimately results in the creation of the hierarchy of schools. At the bottom of the hierarchy we find the elementary schools. Not only are there more of them, and they're smaller, but because there are more of them, they are also closer together on the average. At the second level in the hierarchy we find the secondary schools. They are larger, there are fewer of them than the elementaries, *and* they are farther apart from each other, on the average. It becomes evident that there is a pattern to the hierarchy.

One thing that has yet to be mentioned is that school attendance is mandatory for elementary students but is optional for secondary students over sixteen years of age. Perhaps it would be more accurate to say that secondary school attendance is "optional," subject to the desires and wishes of parents. In any case, as we proceed through each of the hierarchical levels of the educational system, the number of participants will decline with each level. This is a further stimulus to the pattern of the hierarchy of schools, since there are fewer seats needed at every step upward.

What about the colleges and technical institutes? How do they fit into the scheme of things? As we move from the level of secondary schools upward in the hierarchy to colleges and institutes, the same patterns observed in the elementaries and secondaries will repeat themselves. There are fewer colleges and technical institutes than there are secondary schools. Consider the typical Canadian community or small city that has anywhere from a few, to a few dozen, secondary schools, but only one "community" college. Given the higher value placed on a college education, and the potential financial rewards that will accrue to the graduates, there is a question of whether it is acceptable to expect students to travel farther to attain this higher level of education. But do we all agree that more of the costs of attaining this higher level of education should be born by the attendees? Perhaps those living in smaller communities would tend to disagree. Once again there is a simultaneous attempt to find a balance — to minimize construction and operating costs, but also to reasonably meet the geographical needs of users. The very name "community college" implies that there is agreement in society that any fairly sized community should have its own college. But usually just one. The larger cities, of course, will have more.

Last, come the largest and most expensive post-secondary educational institutions — the universities. As a society we agree that universities and the education they provide are desirable things. But once again there is a desire to minimize costs while providing *reasonable* geographical access. It is useful to look again at the extremes that are possible. At one end of the scale, we could build a university in every small town and community all across the country. This would be very costly but would be convenient to students and less costly to parents. At the other end of the scale we could build a single, national university in a single location. This would cut down greatly on construction and operating costs but would be very inconvenient and expensive to students and their families. The compromise solution is the one that we see in existence — a network of universities across the country existing in every larger community from coast-to-coast. Here again, one can ask, on the one hand, whether there is a societal consensus that some of the costs of travel should be born by those who ultimately will benefit from the education received. Alternatively, and on the other hand, one can ask whether there is an unfair advantage that accrues to those who happen to be fortunate enough to live in a university city.

There is one other subtle difference about colleges and especially universities that should be addressed. This is the idea that, with respect to their size, such large institutions usually need a so-called "critical mass" in order to function effectively. It is difficult, in other words, to imagine a "university" in the traditional sense of the word, made-up of just 500 students. This is another economy of scale issue that is typically taken into account when universities and colleges are considered.

At every level, whether it is elementary school or university, we see the same principles at work. In every case there is a balance between the convenience of users, and the costs of construction and operation. We do not build an elementary school on every block. We make the children walk what society judges to be a reasonable distance. We do not build a university in every small community. We make post-secondary students travel what society accepts as a reasonable distance. The end result is the hierarchy of educational institutions stretching all the way from the smallest elementary schools up to the largest universities.

## The Educational Hierarchy in Rural Areas

The hierarchical relationship that was just outlined describes the typical pattern of educational institutions in larger cities and communities. A somewhat similar hierarchical pattern exists in rural areas, but with a slight twist. The principal difference is that many small rural communities are usually not large enough to support schools at all of the different levels of the hierarchy. Nevertheless, there emerges a hierarchical pattern, which is just as strong, if not more so, as that found in larger communities.

Imagine a very small rural community, say a *hamlet*, and ask yourself what kind of school you will expect to find there. In keeping with the arguments made above, about the desire of parents to have very small children attend school near to home, we would probably expect to find that small communities would tend to have at least an elementary school. This idea is probably fitting with most peoples' expectations. Even if the community is not large enough itself to support an elementary school we might expect to find that there may be children being bussed in from rural and farm houses.

Now imagine a slightly larger, neighbouring, rural community, say a *village*, and consider again the question of the type of school system you would expect to find. In this case, with a larger population base, we might discover that the community is nearly large enough to support an elementary school *and* a high school. These may or may not be housed in separate buildings. The interesting question concerns the make-up of the student body at the secondary school. What we will expect to see now is that those high school age students from the nearby hamlets — those that only have elementary schools — will be bussed to the larger village for their secondary education. Figure 4.2 illustrates the idea.

What is evident on the map in Figure 4.2 is the beginning of a hierarchical pattern of communities. There are five small hamlets and one larger village. In addition, we have the beginnings of a *flow* of students within the hierarchy. Secondary students from the small hamlets, where there are no secondary schools, are bussed "upward" in the hierarchy of communities. This is just the start of a typical instance of the effect of the hierarchy on the everyday lives of people, in this case, high school students. They are travelling to a larger community in order to be able to attend school.

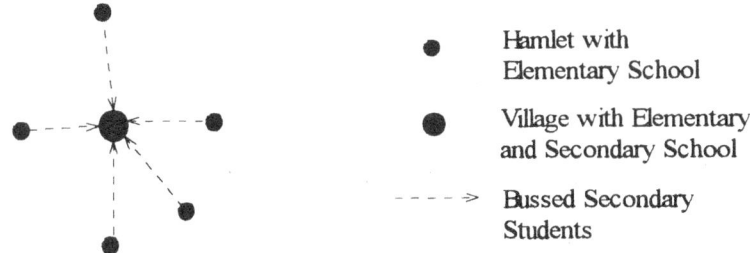

**Figure 4.2 Map of Educational Bussing Pattern**

Consider now the next level of the hierarchy. Imagine that in the vicinity of Figure 4.2 there exists also a single, larger *town*. In fact the town is so large that it is able to support a community college. Figure 4.3 illustrates what happens when we expand our scope to include the larger town *and, now, several new villages surrounding the town.* In this map we now have one town, five villages, and twenty-five hamlets. And therein you can see a clearly defined hierarchy of communities together with its educational system. In this final stage of the hierarchy, not only will secondary students be bussed from hamlets to villages, but also community college students will find it necessary to travel from *hamlets and villages* to attend the larger community college facility that is located in the town.

In the end, we have a set of communities that form a classic hierarchy pattern. There are lots of small hamlets (Figure 4.4), several larger villages and, at the top of the hierarchy, just one larger town. More interestingly, there is a one-to-one correspondence between the hierarchy of towns and the hierarchy of schools. Hamlets have only elementary schools, villages have elementaries and secondaries, but the town has elementaries, secondaries, *and* a community college.

74  *Hierarchical Organization in Society*

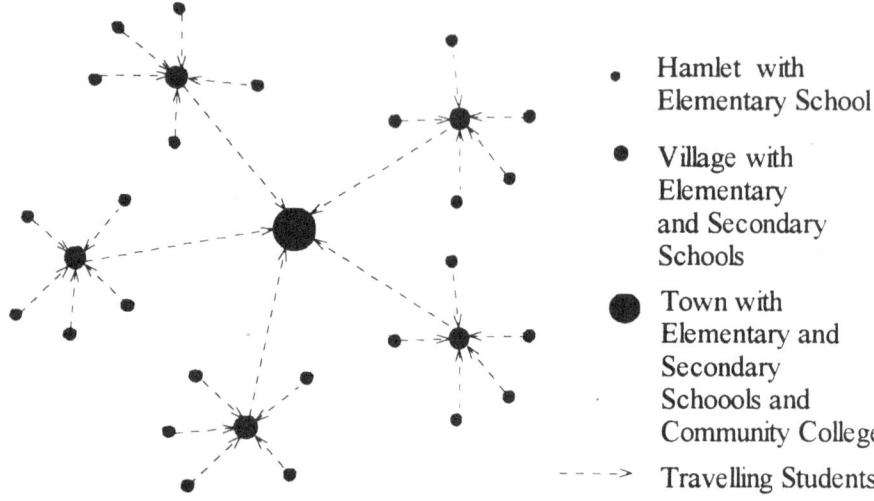

**Figure 4.3  Map of Educational Hierarchy**

Why is this important? Consider the situation of the family that lives in a hamlet. When their children are very young they can attend school at a *local* facility. They can walk to school. But, once they graduate from elementary school, they are "sentenced" by their location, to a life wherein it is necessary to *travel* in order to attend school thereafter. Similarly, for those who are lucky enough to live in a *village*, in addition to an elementary school, there will be a local high school within walking distance. But when it comes time to attend college, it will also be necessary for them to travel to, or even take up residence in, the town. So for anyone who does not live in the town there is extra inconvenience, and a cost to be paid, for living in a smaller place, farther down the hierarchy. At the same time for those people lucky enough to be able to live in the town, there is an advantage and a big cost saving that results merely from living in the town.

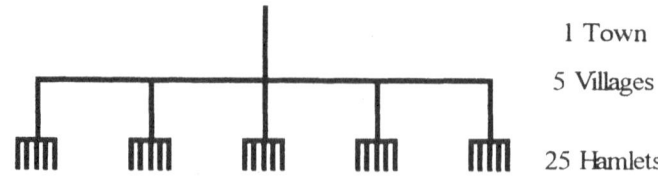

**Figure 4.4  Tree Diagram of Educational Hierarchy**

## Should Families in "Have-not" Towns be Reimbursed in Regard to the Extra Costs of Their Location?

If there is a general unfairness to living in any smaller community, does it not make sense that governments should financially reimburse families that suffer the financial and other consequences of their location? If families have children that have to travel daily by car or public transport in order to attend school, does it not seem fair that they be treated as equal to those families where travel to school is free or inconsequential?

There are examples of governments in Canada being willing to reimburse people for travel. For example, Revenue Canada is sometimes willing to reimburse people for moving expenses. If someone is moving to take up employment, and if they are moving at least forty kilometres, they are eligible to count moving expenses as a deduction. Similarly if college students are moving at least 40 kilometres to attend a *post-secondary* institution they are also eligible to claim a deduction of moving expenses. Why can't there be a similar deduction for travel for educational purposes for the elementary and secondary levels of the educational system? In particular, why can't there be a more substantial type of "location hardship" deduction for those people who live in communities that do not have a full set of educational institutions. There is more than just moving expenses to be taken into consideration. Residents of educational "have-not" communities also pay a price in terms of time and inconvenience. Moreover there is the added burden of everyday costs that are not covered by bussing, such as extra-curricular and other activities that are outside of regular school days or hours.

Oftentimes the costs of travel to school are in fact subsidized, that is, when they are covered by the taxpayer. In many cases, buses that are paid for by the taxpayer, for instance, carry secondary students from hamlets to villages. In these situations, taxpayers do actually partially reimburse those who are disadvantaged by their location. But what about that travel that does not take place at taxpayer expense? Should not travel to school by public transport or automobile also be recognized as a legitimate financial hardship by those who live in smaller, less advantaged, "have-not" communities?

At a more significant level consider the problem that exists in regard to those families who are not lucky enough to live in a community that includes a community college or university. Such families can face very extreme *extra* expenses when it comes to post-secondary education. Over and above the high cost of tuition the "geographically disadvantaged" community may face not only the costs of travel to and from the post-secondary institution but also conceivably the extra burden of *paying for living costs* for the student who finds it necessary to live away from home. Clearly in this situation there is latitude for allowing tax deductions in order to compensate families that are not lucky enough to happen to live in one of the communities that houses a community college or university. As was indicated above, there is currently a deduction for *moving expenses* for post-secondary students. But obviously this does not cover even a small fraction of costs for the student who finds it necessary to live away from home to attend university or college. Once again there is a definite need for a substantial location hardship deduction for citizens who live in "have-not" communities. If all taxpayers contribute equally towards post-secondary education, why should some be forced to carry the additional burden of paying extra for their sons' or daughters' costs of living away from home? As it stands at the moment, most people who live in communities without post-secondary facilities seem to take it for granted that a college or university education for their children will cost them more than their big city neighbours. However, this kind of "geographical discrimination" should not be allowed to continue.

In conclusion, the bottom line is that Canada and the provinces have developed highly effective and efficient hierarchies of school systems. There is logic and a rationale to the number, size and spacing of educational institutions, whether they are at the elementary level or at the post-secondary level. It is an orderly and highly structured system that has evolved on its own as a result of the collective wishes of the population, school boards, and planners. It has geographical features and size characteristics that are entirely appropriate to its purpose, but that are all but invisible to the average observer. It is only through the perspective of hierarchies that many of these interesting features become more apparent. What remains is to ask the question of whether there is a certain degree of geographical "unfairness" in the system that should be recognized by all Canadians and, in turn, by governments. I believe that residents of educational "have-not" communities should be given tax advantages that will offset the costs to them of their disadvantaged location. This is especially true in those cases wherein *access* to post-secondary education for those less well off is threatened by geographical disadvantage. One thinks particularly of potential students in Northern or remote locations.

As was indicated in the preceding chapter, a common thread that weaves throughout this book is in the idea of continentalization that results from Canada's ever growing closeness to the United States. As the Canada - United States border gets more open, given our free trade agreements with our neighbours, one wonders to what extent this should have an impact on post-secondary education. Most people would expect that, as the border becomes less of an obstacle, that more and more Canadian students will head south to pursue their degrees. However, in spite of this expectation, it would appear that the *cost* of post-secondary education in the United States is enough of a deterrent to curtail the flow of students' southward. Many states in the U.S. impose very high fees for "out-of-state" students, often double those for state residents. As a result we can forecast that the migration of Canadian students for post-secondary education in the United States is not an area that will be greatly affected by the existence of free trade. This pattern is much in contrast with the situation that exists in other areas of international relations with the United States, especially with respect to trade and transportation (Chapter 6) and medicine (Chapter 11).

As for hierarchies *within* the educational system there is little to be said that was not covered in Chapter 3. Most of the ideas that apply to corporations apply to educational organizations as well. The reader who is interested in the issue of hierarchies within schools is urged to consult Chapter 3.

## References

Foot, D.K. (1996), *Boom Bust & Echo*, Macfarlane Walter & Ross: Toronto.
Statistics Canada, 'Enrolment in elementary and secondary schools', Catalogue no. 81-229-XPB, 1998.
Statistics Canada, '1996 Census: Education, mobility and migration', *The Daily*, April 14, 1998.

# 5 The Future of Communities

Imagine yourself flying over Canada in a jetliner. It is nighttime, pitch black outside, but the skies are clear. As you make your way across the country, time and again you see beautiful, sparkling towns and cities passing by on the land below. You are left with an image of vast empty spaces punctuated every so often by clusters of people huddled together in shimmering communities that occasionally dot the landscape.

Why do people cluster themselves together so much, whether it is in little towns or in large cities? Why isn't the population of Canada spread out evenly over the land, instead of bunched together in tight-knit little communities? Why do three-quarters of all Canadians choose to live in communities, rather than in rural areas.

As they fly over the glittering communities of the nation, most people admire the beauty, but do not give the distribution of places a second thought. To the uninformed observer it would appear that the distribution of communities across Canada is almost random. But to the trained eye, there is logic and a pattern to the arrangement of Canadian settlements. In particular, there is a hierarchy of communities stretching all the way from the smallest hamlets up to the largest cities.

The hierarchy of places is evolving. The bottom layers of the hierarchy of communities is being eroded away, while the top levels of the hierarchy are getting larger, stronger, and more important. This has implications for urban and regional planners, for business people, for retailers, for corporations, for schools and educators, and especially for those people who live in small communities. Anyone who plans for the future needs to be aware of the hierarchical processes that are under way in the Canadian urban system.

Changes are occurring in the communities in which Canadians live. The big cities are not only getting bigger, but they are doing it at the expense of small communities. Just like the retail, corporate, agricultural, and other sectors, the "community sector" is undergoing an evolution of shape and function. It is being forced to face up to the realities of the New World economy. The pressures of that global economy are reaching right into our own backyards, altering the face of urban Canada forever. Small towns, big cities — no communities are immune from the forces of change.

## Why do People "Huddle Together" in Communities?

Imagine a rural, agricultural area in a time before cities and towns exist. Nothing but farmers, living on farms, as far as the eye can see. How would a "community" emerge out of this landscape? The key to the answer is to realize that farmers are producing goods *for sale or trade*, and they need a focal point at which to meet to carry out these activities. Farmers will gather together at a convenient, agreed upon "marketplace" to trade and sell their goods. The modern farmers' market is a close approximation to this event. Not only will farmers bring their produce and animals, but the more enterprising among them will bring processed and manufactured goods, for example sausage, apple cider, pies, bread, etc. Before long, other entrepreneurial people will see an opportunity, and will also take-up a site at the marketplace. They'll see the economic opportunity afforded by the gathering of people. In addition, successful farmers will produce more goods than they are willing to sell themselves, and will be glad to have someone else take over the job of storing and selling their products. Along come retailers who will buy and re-sell the goods for a small profit. The retailers, and other entrepreneurs, will no doubt take-up a permanent residence at the marketplace, and in this way a community will have begun to form. Other retailers will move in, and before long, still other entrepreneurs will come to see the economic potential of the marketplace. Taverns, restaurants and other such businesses and services will come to be established in the marketplace, and a true community will have begun to be established.

The same line of thought is true of the modern community, regardless of its size. It is first and foremost a place where goods are bought and sold. It is secondarily a place where businesses and services are established to serve those who are buying and selling those goods. This is why towns and villages exist. This is why cities exist. In the modern city, General Motors builds cars while the photocopy serviceperson fixes the GM photocopier. Steelworkers make steel, while mechanics fix their cars. In both cases, the basic nature of the economic activities in communities remains the same.

It may be worthwhile to note that the people of the newly founded community will invariably set up some system of governing themselves, with the primary motive to provide services for the common good. Water supplies, sewage systems, police, fire protection, garbage collection and so on, will all become essential in the new community. Taxes, a small contribution from every resident, will pay for these, and other, necessities. At the same time, other public needs will be served with the building of schools, libraries, and so on. What is interesting is that because these people are living in close proximity to one another, the *per person* cost of providing such services will be relatively small. Thus there are also *economies of scale* at work in communities and urban places.

Depending on the local geography of the area, and the travel propensities of farmers, soon the landscape will be dotted with marketplaces that will turn eventually into small communities. This is the beginning of the emergence of the hierarchy of communities. But we are left with the question of why some places grow so much larger than others do.

## How Does a Hierarchy of Communities Emerge?

Consider the collection of small communities in Figure 5.1. Let's call them hamlets. In this area, six farmers' marketplaces have arisen and have, in due time, grown into hamlets. Suppose now that a new entrepreneur arrives on the scene. He is planning to sell beer to the residents in this area, where previously the residents had to travel a large distance, outside the local area, to acquire their beer. The new entrepreneur plans to open only one sales outlet (six of them do not make economic sense to him). In which one of the hamlets do you imagine that the beer vendor will locate? If there is no other reason to distinguish between the hamlets, the obvious answer is to locate in hamlet A. Hamlet A is more centrally located with respect to all customers than are the other hamlets. The point is that hamlet A has an advantage over the other hamlets in the area simply due to its *central location*. If other entrepreneurs think like our beer vendor, they too will tend to locate in the most accessible hamlet, A. The community will grow. Thus it becomes apparent how some communities will grow faster than others will, and a collection of communities of different sizes will begin to emerge. As a consequence, hamlet A will ultimately turn into a larger *village* as illustrated in Figure 5.2.

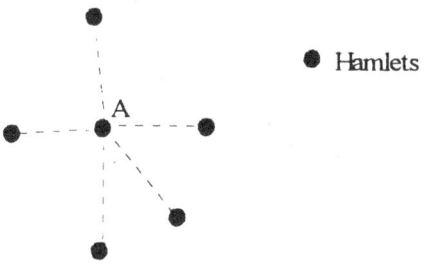

**Figure 5.1 Map of a Simple Set of Communities**

## 82  Hierarchical Organization in Society

Of course, it is also important to note that communities will grow at different rates for a variety of other reasons. For example, if we examine the history of most communities, we will see also that different rates of growth result from factors like the original placing of road or rail lines, the availability of a natural harbour, military or political history and so on. But a central location keeps the engines of growth going even after such factors have lost their original significance.

As this process repeats itself, we can imagine that communities will begin to sort themselves into different size categories. We will not only have hamlets and villages, but towns and cities will develop as well. How will this happen? You will want to imagine a very large area that, in the first place, is blanketed with nothing but hamlets. We saw that every collection of five or six *hamlets* will spawn a centrally located village. So eventually the area we are looking at will also be blanketed by a series of villages, one for every five or six hamlets. At the same time, as the process repeats itself, every set of five or six *villages* will spawn a centrally located town. So the area will also be covered by a series of towns, one for every five or six villages. And so on. A series of towns, in turn, will result in the emergence of a centrally located city (not illustrated here). Ultimately the collection of communities will come to look like that in Figure 5.3.

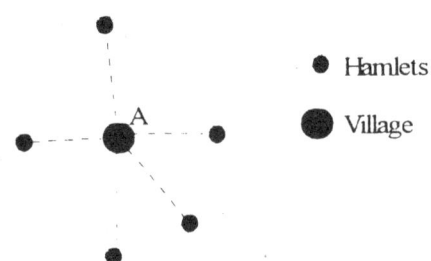

**Figure 5.2  Map of a Simple Hierarchy of Communities**

It is clear that a settlement structure has emerged that has all of the properties of a hierarchy. There is one town in the area, five villages, and 25 hamlets. Each *village* is surrounded by five or six hamlets. Five or six villages surround each *town*. Not only are there more hamlets, but they are closer together to each other, on the average, than the other communities. In turn, the villages will be closer together, on the average, than the towns. The mapped pattern of communities can be placed in the form of Figure 5.4, where the hierarchy on the map takes on the more familiar treelike form.

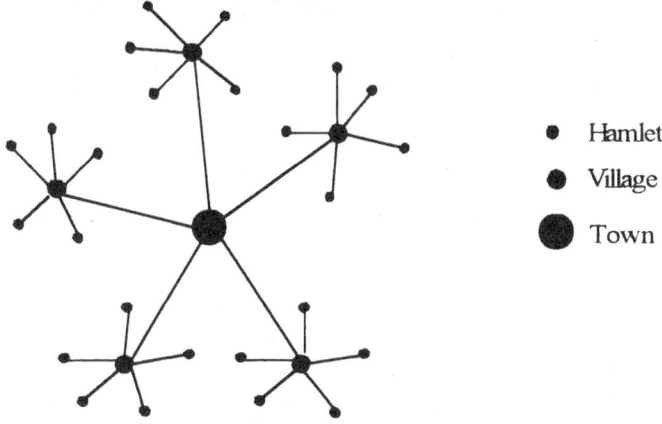

**Figure 5.3 Map of a Hierarchy of Communities**

What is really fascinating is that it has been discovered that communities all over the world, in every type of country, sort and arrange themselves *automatically* into the sort of hierarchy pictured in Figures 5.3 and 5.4. Whether we are looking at an advanced economy like that of Canada's, or an emerging economy like that of China's, the same pattern asserts itself, again and again. It is universal.

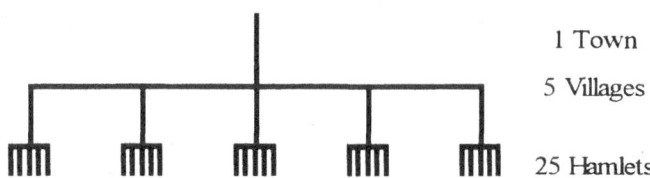

**Figure 5.4 Treelike Hierarchy of Communities**

When you are flying over the country looking at the shimmering communities that make-up the landscape of Canada, you are looking at a *system* of cities, towns, villages, and hamlets that, for the most part, has this definitive hierarchical form. And it shares these properties with all other urban systems everywhere in the world.

## Corporate Hierarchies within Hierarchies of Communities

The second chapter introduced the idea of hierarchies within hierarchies, that is that one hierarchy (e.g., grocery stores) will co-exist with another hierarchy (e.g., communities). The suggestion is that there is often a natural link between such co-existing hierarchies, especially in terms of "market size" and the types of activities that are related to market size.

We talked about corporate hierarchies earlier and we have spoken here of hierarchies of communities. What has not been mentioned is the idea that very often we may expect to find corporate hierarchies *within* hierarchies of communities. In other words, it would not be surprising to see that corporations might develop a size distribution that parallels the distribution of city sizes. There are two ways in which we can think about this occurring.

First, imagine *a single corporation* that has a series of branch plants or regional manufacturing centres, where the size of these centres mirrors the sizes of the urban places in which they occur. For example, an automobile manufacturer may have its main plant in a large city, and sub- and branch plants in smaller communities. Similarly, a company may maintain a multi-tiered distribution system, with a central distribution warehouse augmented by regional distribution warehouses, where the regional centres are normally smaller then the central one. Such a method of warehousing would suggest that the pattern of the warehouses match the size of the communities in which the warehouses exist (see Figure 5.5).

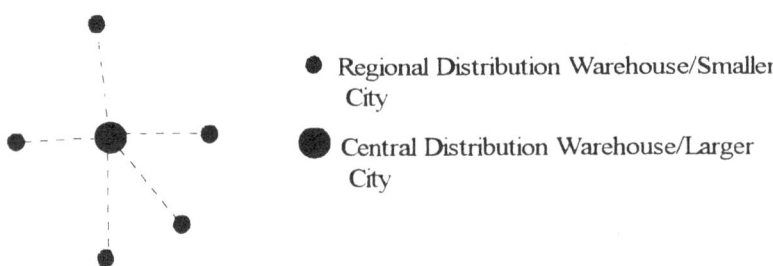

Figure 5.5  Map of Warehouse Hierarchy within Community Hierarchy

A second way to consider corporate hierarchies within urban hierarchies is to expect that, *within a given industry*, competing firms will be of different sizes, and that these sizes too will reflect the sizes of the communities in which they exist. This pattern would be expected because, as the local market size of the firm gets larger, so too does the firm. For example, we may expect to find larger bottlers of soft drinks, in larger markets.

The occurrence of these co-existing hierarchies has important implications for corporations with respect to transportation (see Chapter 6). In particular it suggests that for the single firm that is spread throughout a hierarchy of communities, that the firm's transportation and distribution procedures will mirror the flow of goods and services in the hierarchy of communities. This means those firms with central distribution warehouses and regional distribution warehouses will themselves have hierarchical distribution systems. Flows of goods *and information* will proceed both upwards and downwards in these warehousing hierarchies.

The co-existence of corporate and urban hierarchies-within-hierarchies is not surprising. It simply reflects the inter-connectedness of the corporate world and the world of communities.

## The Changing Face of the Hierarchy of Communities

Although it is of interest just to recognize that there exists a hierarchy of communities, it is more important to appreciate that there are immense challenges ongoing in the system of communities that should be of interest to all Canadians. In particular, there are changes taking place in the rural economy that are having profound effects on the lives of rural residents.

Imagine once again, our rural landscape peopled with farms and farmers, and dotted with towns, villages and hamlets. Imagine further that, over time, the farmers have become better and better at what they do. They become more efficient at raising crops and animals. As a result, the number of farms in the area starts to decline. More efficient farmers are able to buy out those who are not as productive. There is not less land being farmed, it is just that those farms that remain have become larger and stronger. What will be the impact on the small communities in the area? Obviously as the number of farmer customers starts to decline, the businesses in the communities will start to suffer economically as well. Fewer farmers mean fewer customers for everyone. As a consequence, the small communities will start to decline in population size and economic vitality.

The process described above is exactly what has happened to most rural areas across Canada. It is a documented fact that there are fewer, larger farms all across the country. As a result, there is a smaller rural population base. As the numbers of rural dwellers decreases, there is a smaller number of customers for local small towns and villages and, as a

86  *Hierarchical Organization in Society*

consequence, many of those small communities are in decline. The bottom levels of the hierarchy of communities are being eroded away.

Table 5.1 illustrates the patterns of change. It can be seen that between 1991 and 1996 the number of farms in Canada decreased from about 280 thousand to about 275 thousand. At the same time, the number of large farms (farms with gross receipts of more than $100,000) increased nearly eleven percent from about 75 to 83 thousand. What is interesting is that even as the number of farms *decreases* (in the first row of Table 5.1) the amount of land in crops *increases* by over four percent (in the fourth row). This is in spite of the fact that land in pasture remains about the same. So a smaller number of farms is putting more land in crops, even though the total amount of land on farms remains about the same. Finally, and most tellingly, the last row in Table 5.1 indicates the average size of the Canadian farm and here it can be seen, as expected, that the average size is increasing. Fewer, larger farms are the trend from the past, and into the future. A 1996 Statistics Canada report indicates that "the number of farms in Canada has declined steadily since the 1940's." More significantly:

> Larger farms also made up a growing proportion of all farms in Canada. Farms with gross farm receipts of $100,000 or more accounted for 30.2 percent of all farms in 1996, double the level of 15.3 percent reported in 1981.

**Table 5.1 Farm Numbers and Size in Canada**

| Variable | 1991 | 1996 | % Change |
| --- | --- | --- | --- |
| Total census farms | 280,043 | 274,955 | -1.8 |
| Farms with gross farm receipts of $100,000 or more | 74,905 | 83,090 | 10.9 |
| Land in crops (acres) | 82,799,535 | 86,286,077 | 4.2 |
| TOTAL land on census farms (acres) | 167,423,057 | 167,936,279 | 0.3 |
| Average census farm size (acres) | 598 | 611 | 2.2 |

Source: Statistics Canada, Census of Agriculture, *Canada Highlights*, 1997.

What is happening in the farm and agricultural sectors is, of course, happening in other sectors as well. We see a few, larger fast-food franchises taking the place of thousands of individually owned restaurants. We see mergers and acquisitions taking place in all sectors of the corporate world, all of it leading to fewer, larger corporations. We see fewer, larger "big-box" retail stores, pushing small independents out of business. As our free-enterprise economy advances, players in the game have to become more and more efficient. Farmers are under the same pressures to improve the bottom line as are the captains of the corporate world.

The magnitude of farming as a business in Canada is illustrated in Table 5.2. It can be seen that gross farm receipts grew from $26 billion dollars in 1991 to over $32 billion dollars in 1996. The average gross farm receipts increased from about $95 to $117 thousand dollars while total farm capital value had grown to $156 billion dollars in 1996. Clearly, farming is big business in Canada.

The point to make, however, is that as farmers pursue the bottom line, through no fault of their own, they are having a profound effect on the Canadian hierarchy of communities. As the bottom layers of the hierarchy erode, the top layers are growing. The entrepreneurs and other people that are forced to vacate small communities, re-establish themselves in the middle and upper levels of the hierarchy of communities. The top will grow and prosper, while the bottom withers.

This process is all but a part of the natural evolution of the system of communities in a modern, competitive economy. The downside of it is in the impact it has on the lives of those who live in the affected communities. Small town residents can usually do little but stand-by and watch as the competitive forces of the global economy wreak havoc on their local communities. The lucky towns and villages may have an industry, government-supported enterprise, or some other "extra" economic activity that keeps them afloat. For many communities though, it means the end of an era, as the farm economy retrenches itself for the continued onslaught of global competition.

There are important exceptions to the pattern of rural decline, of which readers should be aware. Many small towns are bucking the trends described above and are growing in population size. There are two main types of growth. One includes those communities that are near to large cities and serve as "commuter suburbs" for residents of those cities. The second includes those small communities that are "retirement destinations" for residents of large cities. These usually are found in "cottage country" in areas such as those immediately to the north of Toronto and Montreal. For developers and planners, these trends are noteworthy indicators of future population trends in small town Canada. There are some real hotbeds of demand for rural land and housing in the "shadows" of large urban areas, and in particular resort areas.

## Table 5.2  Farm Income and Value in Canada

| Variable | 1991 | 1996 | % Change |
| --- | --- | --- | --- |
| Total gross farm receipts ($) | 26,577,357,571 | 32,201,238,975 | 21.2 |
| Average gross farm receipts ($) | 94,905 | 117,115 | 23.4 |
| Total farm capital value ($) | 131,210,056,423 | 156,113,413,831 | 19.0 |

Source: Statistics Canada, Census of Agriculture, *Canada Highlights*, 1997.

## The Canadian Population

The entire collection of Canadian communities, together with the rural and farm population, makes up the population of Canada. As of the 1996 Census, the total population of Canada was 28,846,761. In the years immediately following the Census, Canada's population surpassed 30 million. Although we may be rightly proud of our size, it is important to remember that in the global hierarchy of nations, Canada is a relatively small player. As a point of comparison, consider China at the top of the global population hierarchy, with over 1,133,000,000 people. In fact, seventeen of China's 28 provinces are larger in population size than all of Canada.

For a developed country, Canada is growing relatively quickly. Since 1951, Canada has doubled in population size. During the years 1991-1996 every province and territory increased in population size. A 1997 Statistics Canada report indicates that Canada is a front runner in population growth in the industrialized world. In the period 1991 to 1996, Canada had the highest rate of population growth among the G7 industrialized nations.

Table 5.3 shows provincial populations in 1991 and 1996 and the percentage change over that time interval. It can be seen that, with the exception of Newfoundland, all provinces and territories recorded population growth during the time period. Notable among rates of growth are those for the territories and especially British Columbia.

Do the provinces and territories form a hierarchy? Figure 5.6 uses the data from Table 5.3 in an attempt to create a hierarchy of the provinces. As is obvious from the figure, this is not really a hierarchy at all. The figure is a useful one however, as it provides an interesting viewpoint on the relative

The Future of Communities 89

sizes of the Canadian provinces and territories. Ontario and Quebec dominate the top of the diagram, with Alberta and British Columbia coming in at second place. Clearly there is an east-west split evident here. Dominating the middle of the group are Nova Scotia, New Brunswick, Saskatchewan, and Manitoba all with strikingly similar population sizes. Next comes Newfoundland at about a half a million people, followed by miniscule Prince Edward Island. It is interesting that PEI, with so few people, has provincial status and power, given that there are 23 cities in Canada that are more populous (see Table 5.4). Finally the relatively small population sizes of the two territories are illustrated by their position at the bottom of the diagram. If population size can be equated with *power,* Figure 5.6 gives us a good picture of the power relationships among the provinces.

Table 5.3 Provincial Population Sizes

|  | Population | | % change |
|---|---|---|---|
|  | 1996 | 1991 |  |
| Canada | 28,846,761 | 27,296,859 | 5.7 |
| Newfoundland | 551,792 | 568,474 | -2.9 |
| PEI | 134,557 | 129,765 | 3.7 |
| Nova Scotia | 909,282 | 899,942 | 1.0 |
| New Brunswick | 738,133 | 723,900 | 2.0 |
| Quebec | 7,138,795 | 6,895,963 | 3.5 |
| Ontario | 10,753,573 | 10,084,885 | 6.6 |
| Manitoba | 1,113,898 | 1,091,942 | 2.0 |
| Saskatchewan | 990,237 | 988,928 | 0.1 |
| Alberta | 2,696,826 | 2,545,553 | 5.9 |
| British Columbia | 3,725,500 | 3,282,061 | 13.5 |
| Yukon Territory | 30,766 | 27,797 | 10.7 |
| NWT | 64,402 | 57,649 | 11.7 |

Source: Statistics Canada, *The Daily,* April 15, 1997.

Figure 5.6 is a very useful exercise as it serves to demonstrate that not everything can easily be organized in a hierarchical manner. When it comes time to divide countries into states or provinces, many governments attempt to create units that have approximately equal populations, regardless of their size. This pattern is evident in the United States, for instance, where as populations get less dense across the western half of the country, the states get larger in area. In Canada this is not the case. Rather our provincial and territorial units have been shaped primarily by history.

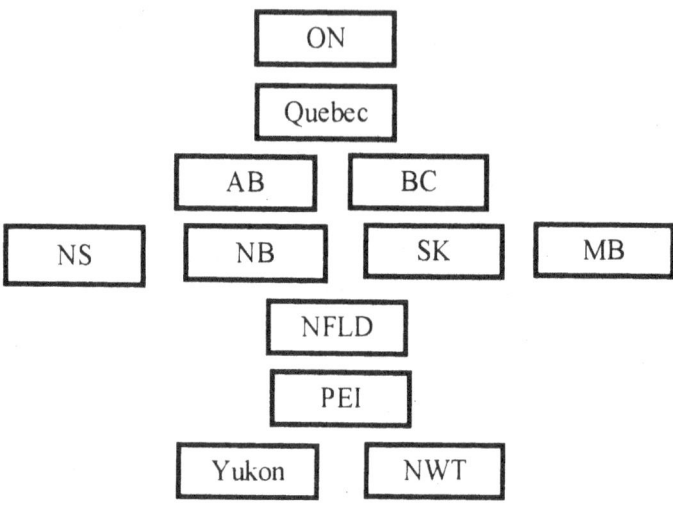

**Figure 5.6 "Hierarchy" of Provincial Populations**

**The Canadian Hierarchy of Communities**

As a modern, industrialized country, Canada should have a highly developed and well-defined national system of communities. The urban system should be comparable to that of other fully developed countries with a highly refined hierarchical structure. There should be a detailed network of a large number of smaller communities, topped by a strong system of large urban centres at the top. Canadians should be proud of their well-developed urban system.

It is possible to subdivide the Canadian urban system into pieces. We could look at the Ontario urban system in isolation, or the British Columbia urban system as separate entities. But such a distinction would be artificial. Canada's urban system should be examined as a single, unified system. On the other hand, the point has been made that Canada cannot really be looked at in isolation from the United States, so we should keep in mind that the Canadian urban system can be considered as just a small part of the larger North American urban system. We will have a look at it in this context, a little later, below.

The Future of Communities 91

As can be see in Table 5.4, Canada has a set of 25 "major" urban-metropolitan areas. These rank in size from Toronto, at the top of the list, with over four million people, to Thunder Bay at the bottom with about 125,000. Of course, there are a large number of other Canadian cities that do not appear on this list of the top 25. Of the 25 cities on the list, nine of them are in Ontario. Of the top twelve, six are in Ontario. This provides a good indication of the degree to which Ontario dominates the Canadian urban system. Quebec, on the other hand, while having Montreal in second place on the list with about 3.3 million people, represents only five of the 25 cities on the list. This suggests that the Ontario urban system is better developed than the Quebec one, even though the provincial populations are different (given in Table 5.3).

### Table 5.4 Canadian Metropolitan Areas by Population and Rank

|  | Rank 1996 | Rank 1991 | Population 1996 |
|---|---|---|---|
| Toronto | 1 | 1 | 4,263,757 |
| Montreal | 2 | 2 | 3,326,510 |
| Vancouver | 3 | 3 | 1,831,665 |
| Ottawa-Hull | 4 | 4 | 1,010,498 |
| Edmonton | 5 | 5 | 862,597 |
| Calgary | 6 | 6 | 821,628 |
| Quebec | 7 | 8 | 671,889 |
| Winnipeg | 8 | 7 | 667,209 |
| Hamilton | 9 | 9 | 624,360 |
| London | 10 | 10 | 398,616 |
| Kitchener | 11 | 12 | 382,940 |
| St. Catharines-Niagara | 12 | 11 | 372,406 |
| Halifax | 13 | 13 | 332,518 |
| Victoria | 14 | 14 | 304,287 |
| Windsor | 15 | 15 | 278,685 |
| Oshawa | 16 | 16 | 268,773 |
| Saskatoon | 17 | 17 | 219,056 |
| Regina | 18 | 18 | 193,652 |
| St. John's | 19 | 19 | 174,051 |
| Sudbury | 20 | 21 | 160,488 |
| Chicoutimi- Jonquière | 21 | 20 | 160,454 |
| Sherbrooke | 22 | 22 | 147,384 |
| Trois-Rivières | 23 | 23 | 139,956 |
| Saint John | 24 | 24 | 125,705 |
| Thunder Bay | 25 | 25 | 125,562 |

Source: Statistics Canada, *The Daily*, April 15, 1997.

92  *Hierarchical Organization in Society*

It should be noted that the population sizes in Table 5.4 are for what are known as *metropolitan areas* and not just *cities*. So, for example, the population size of Toronto of 4,263,757 is not just for the City of Toronto proper, but includes most of the major suburban areas surrounding Toronto. The same idea is true for all 25 cities on the list. They are known as CMA's, that is, Census Metropolitan Areas.

A better picture of the nature of the Canadian urban system comes from looking at it as a hierarchy. Figure 5.7 employs the data from Table 5.4 to create such a treelike hierarchy. Interestingly, the top of the hierarchy is inverted. Toronto and Montreal dominate the top while Vancouver falls distinctly into third place. It is only when we get to the next level that we see the next concise group. Clearly Ottawa-Hull, Edmonton and Calgary form a single group, all of them falling between the 800,000 and one million range of population. Quebec City, Winnipeg, and Hamilton, which could be called "the 600,000's," form the next band of the hierarchy. Finally there are two bands below, one with all of the cities in the 300,000 to 400,000 range, and the other with those cities in the 125,000 and 275,000-population range.

For the retailer, for the planner, for the corporate observer, for the businessperson, or for the casual observer, Figure 5.7 presents an excellent "snapshot" of the Canadian urban hierarchy. It describes the relative size and positioning of all large Canadian communities in a single picture. It conveys much more information, and does it much more clearly, than does a simple list of numbers like that given in Table 5.4.

There are other fascinating properties of Canadian communities. One interesting idea is that population distribution is shifting from east to west in Canada. Statistics Canada reports in April 1997 that in 1951 only fifteen percent of Canada's population lived in Alberta and British Columbia, but that by 1996 that percent had increased to 22. Over the same period of time, the proportion of the Atlantic province's population declined from twelve to eight percent, while Quebec's share dropped from 29 to 25 percent. All told, Ontario represents 37 percent of the national population. Of the major metropolitan areas, the fastest growing, as of the 1996 Census, were Vancouver (+14.3%), Oshawa (+11.9%), Toronto (+9.4%), and Calgary (+9.0%). As a demonstration of just how urbanized Canada has become it is to be noted as well that more than a third of Canada's population (36.2%) lives in four of the most populous metropolitan areas, namely, Toronto, Montreal, Vancouver, and Ottawa-Hull.

The Future of Communities 93

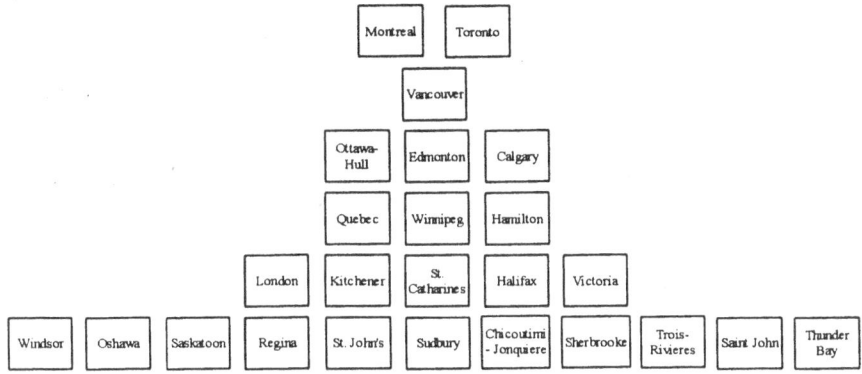

Figure 5.7 The Canadian Urban Hierarchy

The "Americanadian" Hierarchy of Cities

It was suggested earlier that we should keep in mind that the Canadian urban system can be considered as just a small part of the larger North American urban system. Toward that end we can undertake an unusual exercise. We can endeavour, on paper, to integrate the American and Canadian urban systems. The resulting "Americanadian" urban system is probably actually the one that is of the greatest relevance in the era of free trade with the United States. How do our cities stack up against the American ones in the larger American-Canadian hierarchy?

Table 5.5 shows the results. It is a list of the top 75 largest metropolitan areas in the United States, and integrated with it are the nine largest metropolitan areas in Canada (shown in bold). First it can be noted that the *number* of Canadian cities is just about right. Canada is usually considered to be about one-tenth as big as the United States. That means that if the urban system is "balanced," Canada should have about one-tenth as many cities on the list as does the United States. One-tenth of 75 is 7.5 and we have nine cities on the list. We can conclude that the hierarchies are in proportion and that the Canadian proportion of the hierarchy is about as large as it should be.

When it comes to marketing, corporate mergers, or franchising, this listing gives us a good picture of how the two urban hierarchies relate to each other. The larger Canadian metropolitan areas hold strong positions on the list. Toronto is tenth, Montreal is fourteenth, and Vancouver is 26th. The remaining Canadian cities fall further down the list with Ottawa at fiftieth place and the others near the bottom. The useful thing about this listing is that it provides a good indication of how Canadian cities rank with respect to their American neighbours.

### Table 5.5 "Americanadian" Metropolitan Population

| City Name | 1996 Population | City Name | 1996 Population |
|---|---|---|---|
| New York | 19,938,492 | Buffalo | 1,175,240 |
| Los Angeles | 15,495,155 | Hartford | 1,144,574 |
| Chicago | 8,599,774 | Greensboro | 1,141,238 |
| Washington | 7,164,519 | Providence | 1,124,044 |
| San Francisco | 6,605,428 | Nashville | 1,117,178 |
| Philadelphia | 5,973,463 | Rochester | 1,088,037 |
| Boston | 5,563,475 | Memphis | 1,078,151 |
| Detroit | 5,284,171 | Austin | 1,041,330 |
| Dallas | 4,574,561 | Oklahoma | 1,026,657 |
| **Toronto** | 4,263,757 | Raleigh | 1,025,253 |
| Houston | 4,253,428 | Grand Rapids | 1,015,099 |
| Atlanta | 3,541,230 | **Ottawa-Hull** | 1,010,498 |
| Miami | 3,514,403 | Jacksonville | 1,008,633 |
| **Montreal** | 3,326,510 | West Palm Beach | 992,840 |
| Seattle | 3,320,829 | Louisville | 991,765 |
| Cleveland | 2,913,430 | Dayton | 950,661 |
| Minneapolis | 2,765,116 | Richmond | 935,174 |
| Phoenix | 2,746,703 | Greenville | 896,679 |
| San Diego | 2,548,238 | Birmingham | 894,702 |
| St. Louis | 2,548,238 | Albany | 878,527 |
| Pittsburgh | 2,379,411 | Honolulu | 871,766 |
| Denver | 2,277,401 | **Edmonton** | 862,597 |
| Tampa | 2,199,231 | Fresno | 861,753 |
| Portland | 2,078,357 | **Calgary** | 821,628 |
| Cincinnati | 1,920,931 | Tucson | 767,873 |
| **Vancouver** | 1,831,665 | Tulsa | 756,493 |
| Kansas | 1,690,343 | Syracuse | 745,691 |
| Milwaukee | 1,642,658 | El Paso | 684,446 |
| Sacramento | 1,632,133 | Omaha | 681,698 |
| Norfolk | 1,540,252 | **Quebec** | 671,889 |
| Indianapolis | 1,492,297 | Albuquerque | 670,092 |
| San Antonio | 1,490,111 | **Winnipeg** | 667,209 |
| Columbus | 1,447,646 | Knoxville | 649,277 |
| Orlando | 1,417,291 | Scranton | 628,073 |
| Charlotte | 1,321,068 | **Hamilton** | 624,360 |
| New Orleans | 1,312,890 | Bakersfield | 622,729 |
| Salt Lake City | 1,217,842 | Harrisburg | 614,755 |
| Las Vegas | 1,201,073 | | |

Source: Population Estimates Program, Population Division, U.S. Bureau of the Census, Washington and Statistics Canada, *The Daily*, April 15, 1997.

In spite of the interesting perspective afforded by the merged listing of American and Canadian metropolitan areas, it is difficult to talk seriously about the future of Canadian communities without discussing the future of the jewels of the Canadian urban system, namely Toronto and Montreal.

## Toronto - World Class City?

At the pinnacle of the Canadian system of urban places sits the city of Toronto. As can be seen on the list of American-Canadian metropolitan areas, Toronto is the *tenth* largest metropolitan area in the United States and Canada (see Table 5.5). The question is, does Toronto *act* like the tenth largest city in the land?

How do we measure the clout of a city? Size? Fame? Reputation? TV or movie exposure? Sports franchises and successes? International financial power? Industrial and corporate dominance? Specializations in commerce or industry? The answer is that it is probably a lot of one, or a little bit of each. However we measure it, the suspicion is that in the case of Toronto, it does not add up to much. Take away the concrete — the CN Tower and the Skydome — and what have you got left? Just another middle-of-the-road city? Look at where Toronto is on that list of cities (Table 5.5). It is just below Boston, Detroit and Dallas, and just above Houston, Atlanta and Miami. How does it stack up against its neighbours? Apparently, not very well. All of those cities have international reputations in one area of expertise or another. Boston is known as a continental financial centre. Detroit has its global auto industry. Dallas and Houston are world oil centres. Atlanta has Turner Broadcasting, Coca-Cola and worldwide CNN. Miami has an international reputation in tourism and trade. What does Toronto have? What is it well known for? How is it global?

It is clear that Toronto has not lived up to the reputation its size suggests it should have. Sure it dominates the *Canadian* landscape, but in the era of global capitalism and international competition, Toronto seems to be a small "c" city. It should spend less time looking at the minor problems in its own backyard, and more time trying to become the international city that it is supposed to be. Canadians should be able to be proud of it.

Part of the problem is government interference. For example, when the federal government turned down the Canadian bank mergers, this may have hurt Toronto's chance of becoming better known as a centre of international banking. In the new global economy, banks all over the world are merging in order to make themselves stronger, worldwide competitors. And mergers and acquisitions are not regulated elsewhere in the world, like they are in Canada. For instance, within weeks of the announcement that the Canadian banks would not be allowed to merge, it was announced that Spain's largest, and third largest banks would merge to create the Euro zone's largest bank. *The Financial Post* reported that the bank merger, carried out in response to increasing competition and tighter profit margins, would provide estimated annual savings to the merged institution of $1.06 billion dollars. How are "unmerged" Canadian banks supposed to compete with that?

The City of Montreal is another case in point. It too sits high atop the American-Canadian list of metropolitan areas but has yet to distinguish itself as a world class city in any significant way. Look at the list (Table 5.5). Montreal's metropolitan area is in fourteenth place, right up there with Atlanta, Miami, and Seattle. Yet just like Toronto, it is mundane. Montreal probably hit its zenith when it hosted Expo and the Olympics. But that was many years ago, and in the interim it has done little, if anything, to put itself on the world stage. The failed attempt to attract the 2002 Winter Olympics probably only served to illustrate further that Montreal has lost its international sheen.

How can Toronto and Montreal put themselves back in the limelight? How can they earn their place among the cities in the American-Canadian hierarchy of metropolitan areas? Their "place" among North America's big-league cities is illustrated in Figure 5.8 which puts the fifteen largest metropolitan areas in the United States and Canada into hierarchical perspective (data from Table 5.5). It can be seen that New York City dominates, while Los Angeles has a clear hold on second place. Next comes the foursome of Chicago, Washington, San Francisco, and Philadelphia. Finally we see the cities of Toronto and Montreal, together with their American cousins (Boston, Detroit, Dallas, Houston, Atlanta, Miami and Seattle), in the fourth level of the hierarchy. Both Toronto and Montreal should aim to be as well known, as reputable, and as international, as any of the American cities that share the same level as they do. Probably what is needed is greater vision and more inspired leadership — vision to see where these two cities should be on the list of prominence, and leadership to work towards the goal of attaining membership in that elite group of world class cities.

Are Canadian cities ready to face the challenge of the global community? If they are, they will have to think bigger, grander, more aggressively. Corporate and government leaders will have to think on a *continental* scale. The market, the domain of government and business, is no longer in Canada's own backyard. Rather it is in the realm of North America as a whole. The United States, Canada and Mexico are all part of a single, hierarchical, urban-industrial entity, and it is essential, for the future, to view the world from this new perspective.

*The Future of Communities* 97

**Figure 5.8 The Canadian-American Hierarchy of Cities**

A city's reach should exceed its grasp. There is probably no better example of this principle than that demonstrated by the City of Calgary when it managed to win the battle to host the 1988 Winter Olympics. Such a goal should have been far beyond the grasp of Calgary, given its size. But local organizers persisted until they had won the day. They used a motto on the Olympics organizing committee at the time — "The impossible just takes a little longer."

### References

Statistics Canada, 'Census of Agriculture', *Canada Highlights*, 1997.
Statistics Canada, '1996 Census of Agriculture - Characteristics of farm operations', *The Daily*, May 14, 1997.
Statistics Canada, 'Population and Dwelling Counts', *The Daily*, April 15, 1997.
U.S. Bureau of the Census, 'Estimates of the Population of Metropolitan Areas', Population Estimates Program, Population Division, December, 1997.

# 6 Travel, Transport and Continentalization

Transportation is crucial. It is the lifeblood of the economy. In the same way that the human circulatory system is essential in delivering the nutrients and oxygen to the human body that make life possible, the transportation systems of a modern nation deliver the goods and services that enable the economy to function. An excellent demonstration of the importance of transportation occurs whenever a part of Canada suffers from a crippling snowstorm. Factories and businesses grind to a halt — workers, staff and management cannot get to work, parts and supplies cannot be delivered, finished products are stuck in warehouses. The modern economy can come to an almost complete standstill until the roads, rail lines, and airports are cleared.

Other chapters focus on *structures*. Corporations form hierarchic structures. Urban systems are cast as rigid structures. Educational systems evolve into formal structures. This chapter is about *movement*. In particular, it focuses on the movement *within* hierarchic structures. It will look at the movement of goods, services, and people. It will address the issue of how these entities move within hierarchies and how the movements themselves shape and form hierarchies.

Almost every economic transaction is touched by transportation. As a result, transportation plays a critical role in the Canadian economy. As noted in the 1997 Annual Report of the Ministry of Transportation:

> By moving people and goods, and by generating profits and paying salaries, transportation contributes to the economic well-being of Canadians. Apart from its strategic role, the size of the transportation service industry in terms of GDP is significant. This sector is larger than the agriculture, fishing and trapping, logging and forestry industries combined.

Transportation is also a key when it comes to relationships between Canada and the United States. The "buzzword" of the new millennium is often considered to be *globalization*. But from the point of view of Canadians, the more crucial buzzword is *continentalization*. As the economic ties between Canada, Mexico, and the United States strengthen, continental thinking becomes an integral part of the new mindset.

100  *Hierarchical Organization in Society*

Transportation plays an essential role in the continentalization of North America.

## Transportation within Hierarchies

Suppose you live in a small town outside of Kingston, Ontario called Gananoque, and you plan to take a trip to visit a relative who lives in a small town outside of Victoria, British Columbia called Chemainus. Suppose further that you prefer to make as much of the journey as possible by air. How will your trip proceed?

On the first leg of the trip you will make your way by car from Gananoque, to Kingston. You will board a plane in Kingston and fly to Toronto. Next you will probably find it necessary to change planes in Toronto. Following a direct flight from Toronto to Vancouver, you'll change planes again for the flight from Vancouver to Victoria. From Victoria you'll travel again by car to the town where your relatives live, Chemainus.

People make this kind of flight all of the time without ever really giving a second thought to just what is involved. But there is a real pattern to it. Such a trip involves a journey first *upward* in the urban hierarchy, then *across* the urban hierarchy and finally, back *down* the urban hierarchy. The process is illustrated in Figure 6.1. The journey starts at Gananoque, the town, and then proceeds upward in the urban hierarchy by car to the small city Kingston. The next leg proceeds upwards in the hierarchy again, this time by air to the major city Toronto. Next the traveller journeys *across the hierarchy* from the major city Toronto to the major city Vancouver. Finally the trip ends with a journey down the hierarchy from Vancouver to the smaller city Victoria, and then downwards again by car from Victoria to the destination Chemainus.

The journey up, across, and down in the hierarchy of urban places has been illustrated with a simple traveller's itinerary but in reality, almost all travel and transportation in the real world involves a similar pattern of movement. Why does it matter? Being aware of this pattern of movement is significant to anyone involved in shipping, transportation, communications, or travel. But more importantly, it is also of consequence to almost anyone who is involved in the production or manufacturing of goods or products.

Consider as another example, the shipment of grain from the field to the overseas market. The first step of the transportation process is the harvesting of the grain from the field. The gathered grain is transported by truck to a train (either directly, or by going through a grain elevator or other storage). That is the first segment of the journey up the transport hierarchy. Next the grain is loaded onto a train for shipment to a seaport, yet another step upward in the hierarchy. Following transport by rail across country, the grain is then loaded into a ship for transport overseas, which represents the journey across the top of the hierarchy, that is, from major seaport to major seaport. At the other end, the grain will be off-loaded from the ship for transport downward through the urban hierarchy by train or truck, in a series of steps, until it finally makes its way to the consumer's table. The whole journey consists of the grain making its way from the field, to the table, by way of a journey up, across, and down in the transport hierarchy.

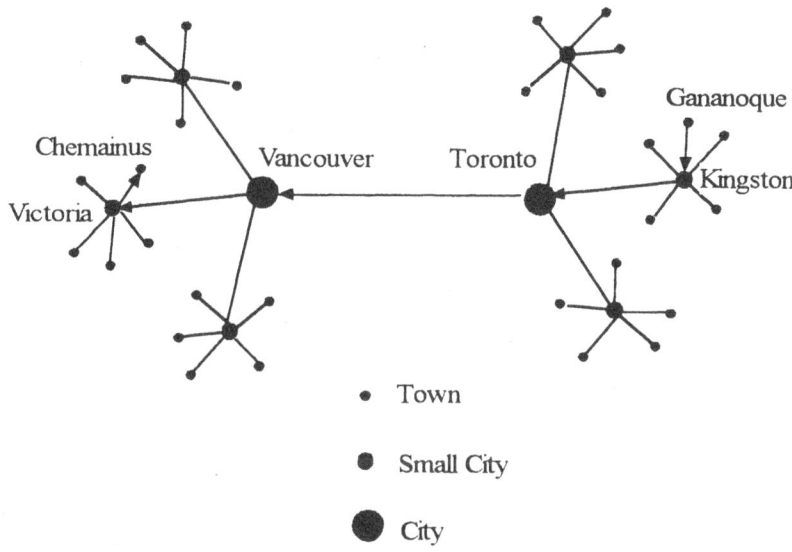

**Figure 6.1 Map of Travel in an Urban Hierarchy**

Both the journey of the traveller and the shipment of the grain share another interesting property. In both cases, as the movement proceeds upward in the hierarchy, the *size* of the "mode" of transport also gets larger. "Mode" refers to the distinction between train, plane, ship, etc. The plane that flies from Toronto to Vancouver will be much larger than the plane that flies either from Kingston to Toronto, or from Vancouver to Victoria. Similarly, the ship that transports the grain across the ocean is a much larger carrier than the train that hauled the grain at the next level below. In turn, the train is a larger carrier than the truck that began the transport process. This change in the size of the *mode* of transport is another common feature of hierarchical movement. Generally, the higher in the transport hierarchy, the larger the mode of transport.

There is a good and interesting reason for the rule just described. As the movement of people or products advances upward in the transport hierarchy, all of the things that are moving will start to converge. For example, when you make your way from Gananoque to Kingston, other people are converging on Kingston for the same flight as well. Similarly, when your flight makes its way to Toronto, other flights are converging on Toronto for the same connecting flight to Vancouver. As we move upward in the transport hierarchy, the amount of movement at each level increases. Larger, longer, or bigger modes of transport are the order of the day. This is illustrated in Figure 6.2 where the thickness of the lines indicates the amount of people or products being transported at each level of the hierarchy. The higher the level, the greater the amount of products or people being transported.

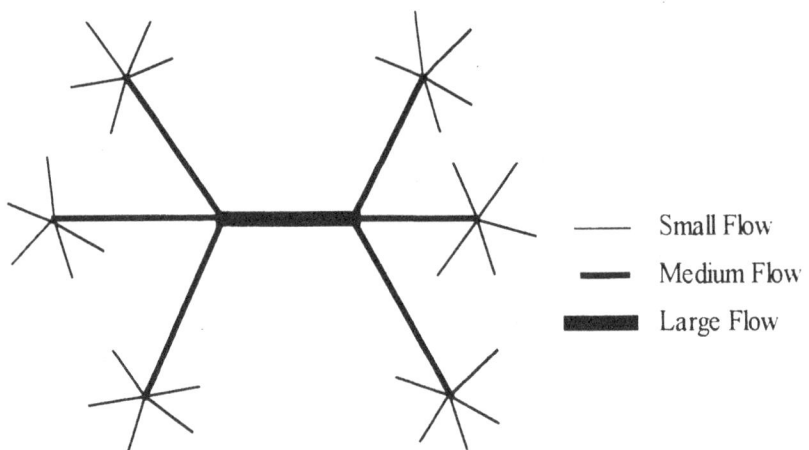

**Figure 6.2 Map of Size of Flows in an Urban Hierarchy**

Hierarchical flow patterns are commonplace in the day-to-day operations of businesses. Consider the notion of "just-in-time" inventory management, for example, which cuts down on the costs associated with maintaining large inventories. In order to truly appreciate "just-in-time" management it is necessary to understand that almost all inventories will move through hierarchical systems of transport. It is important to remember that even inventory that is "in storage" is just as much a part of the "just-in-time" transportation process as is inventory that is "in transit".

*Travel, Transport and Continentalization* 103

Everyone who has travelled by air will have experienced the phenomenon of flying in different sized planes over different routes. Small, local commuter planes fly a small number of passengers over the short haul. "Regional" planes and jets carry a medium number of passengers over medium range flights. Large jets carry huge loads of passengers over long-haul flights. As the plane gets larger, the loading and unloading, the "enplaning" and "deplaning" gets more and more time consuming and difficult to accomplish, but this is offset by the longer duration of the flight. You do not expect them to fully load-up a 747 only to have it carry out a fifteen-minute flight. Neither do you expect to fly from Vancouver to Hawaii on a twin-engine Otter.

The same ideas apply to the shipment of grain. The truck takes the grain over a relatively short distance, from a few to a hundred kilometres. The train hauls the grain one or two thousand kilometres, across part of the country. The ship takes the grain several thousand kilometres across the ocean. Similarly, loading a truck takes a relatively small amount of time, less than an hour, while loading a train takes many hours. On the other hand, loading a large seagoing ship is a very big operation taking several days. You do not expect that a fully loaded seagoing ship will be used to haul grain from Vancouver to Victoria. Nor do you expect the farmer to haul grain by truck from Alberta to Vancouver.

In the case of individual travellers, and in the case of the grain, *economies of scale* work to create hierarchical travel patterns and modes. When we talk about 300 passengers on a 747, or a huge ship full of grain, we are talking about taking advantage of economies of scale. When we talk about the time and expense of loading-up a 747, or a seagoing ship, we are talking about being efficient economically by taking the large cost of loading, and spreading it over a very large distance. In other words, as we have seen time and again, hierarchical patterns emerge when we do things with economic efficiency.

## The National Transportation Hierarchy

Several times now we have discussed hierarchies within hierarchies and it is apparent here that the pattern is repeating itself again. This time it can be seen that the transportation hierarchy seems to exist within the urban hierarchy. Transportation hierarchies do not always coincide with urban ones, but more often than not, they do. The heaviest or largest flows in a national economy tend to occur among the largest places in the urban system. The larger cities at the top of the Canadian urban hierarchy *generate* more flows and also *absorb* more flows. We *expect* a lot of flows of goods and people *directly* between Toronto and Vancouver. We do not expect a lot of direct flows between Gananoque, Ontario and Chemainus, British Columbia.

It is as if the urban system acts as a conduit that guides the flows from place to place. The best analogy is the human circulatory system, which is in itself a hierarchical system. The circulatory system has a structure ranging all the way from the major veins and arteries deep within the body, to the small branching capillaries that connect the veins to the arteries in the extremities. This hierarchical system distributes blood efficiently from the body core to the extremities and back again.

The national transportation hierarchy serves the same kind of function as the human circulatory system. Goods and services are distributed from the "core" areas, usually Ontario, Quebec and British Columbia, to the "periphery" (everywhere else). At the same time, mostly raw materials, natural resources, and agricultural products are collected in the peripheral provinces and delivered to the core areas. For example, automobiles are manufactured in Ontario and distributed to the Prairies, while canola is grown in the Prairies and delivered to Ontario. If the national transport system were a human body, Toronto would be the heart, and the Prairies, Territories, and Maritimes would be the extremities.

We can obtain a glimpse at the structure of the national transport hierarchy by focusing on air transport as an indicator of the whole system. Table 6.1 presents a listing of Canada's busiest airports, measured according to the total annual number of "enplaned" and "deplaned" passengers. As can be seen, Toronto dominates the list with over 22 million passengers. Clearly Toronto is the "hub" of Canada's air transport hierarchy. This listing unfolds quite readily into a hierarchy of Canada's national airport system (Figure 6.3). Toronto dominates the top, while Vancouver, with over 13 million passengers, is evidently the "gateway" to, and from, the west. Next in line come Calgary and Dorval, followed by a large group consisting of Ottawa, Mirabel, Halifax, Winnipeg, and Edmonton. Finally there is a clear break between the top nine airports, and the remaining seventeen others, which handle much smaller numbers of passengers.

Although this hierarchy is presented in the usual fashion, it is interesting to think of the air traffic hierarchy as taking on a different form from most other hierarchies. Specifically, it was indicated above that an air transport system can be thought of as having a "hub." It is illuminating therefore to diagram an air traffic hierarchy in the form of a hub-centred system, as in Figure 6.4. Here the "top" of the hierarchy is equivalent to the central hub, and the other levels of the hierarchy radiate outward to a series of ever-smaller communities that form the "spokes" or "collectors" of the system. Cities in Canada form a sort of "linear" pattern as they stretch across the country, so this diagram does not really seem to apply too well to Canada. But you can imagine it being centred on United States centres of air traffic, such as Chicago or Atlanta. Furthermore you can imagine two major centres of traffic being connected (Figure 6.5) where there would be a very large demand for transportation across the route connecting the two major cities.

### Table 6.1  Canada's Busiest Airports

| City | Enplaning & Deplaning Passengers, 1996 |
|---|---|
| Toronto | 22,669,000 |
| Vancouver | 13,090,000 |
| Dorval | 6,142,000 |
| Calgary | 6,662,000 |
| Ottawa | 2,763,000 |
| Mirabel | 2,392,000 |
| Halifax | 2,462,000 |
| Winnipeg | 2,830,000 |
| Edmonton | 2,897,000 |
| Victoria | 879,000 |
| Quebec | 640,000 |
| St. John's | 626,000 |
| Regina | 640,000 |
| Saskatoon | 633,000 |
| Thunder Bay | 473,000 |
| Kelowna | 539,000 |
| London | 324,000 |
| Prince George | 255,000 |
| Moncton | 222,000 |
| Fredericton | 199,000 |
| Sudbury | 181,000 |
| Saint John | 190,000 |
| Charlottetown | 186,000 |
| Yellowknife | 213,000 |
| Whitehorse | 145,000 |
| Gander | 78,000 |

Source: Statistics Canada, Air Carrier Statements 2, 4 & 6, September, 1997.

106  *Hierarchical Organization in Society*

**Figure 6.3  Canada's Airport Hierarchy**

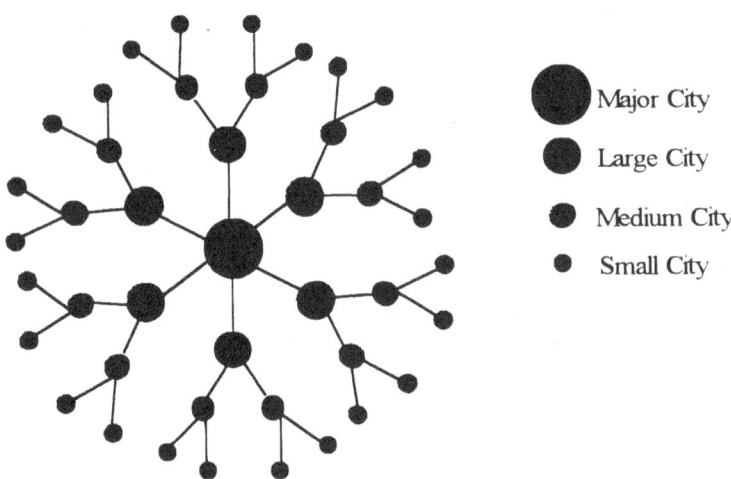

**Figure 6.4  Map of Hub and Spoke Air Traffic Hierarchy**

An article in the 1998 *Globe and Mail* by David C. Johnston discusses the kind of planes that might fly in the future on major routes such as that portrayed in Figure 6.5. The European company, Airbus, has plans to construct double-deck, superjumbo jetliners that would fly nearly 700 passengers at once. Johnson quotes an Airbus spokeswoman as saying:

Travel, Transport and Continentalization 107

The A-3-XX would have 10-across seating (3-4-3) for coach on the main deck, but only nine across (3-3-3) on the upper deck, allowing for slightly wider seats. First class, which would be downstairs, and business class, upstairs, would each be six across. The plane would feature wider aisles than those in 747's, with a wide, almost grand, front staircase and a modest, curving staircase at the tail.

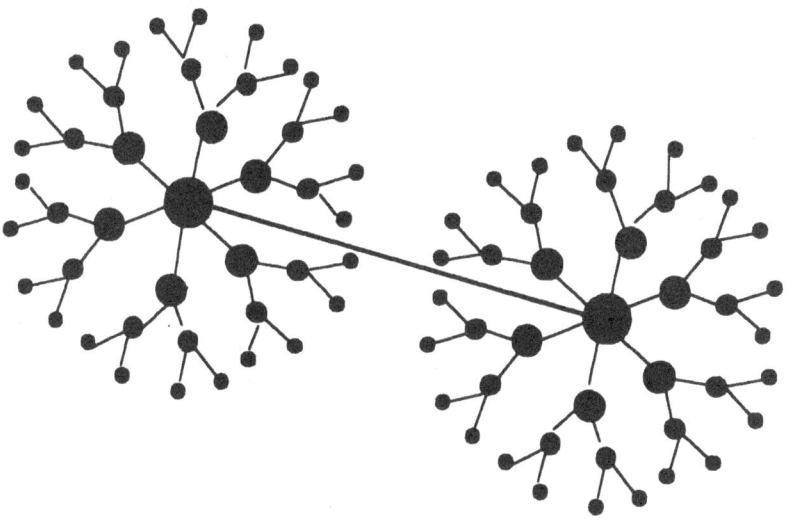

**Figure 6.5 Map of "Double" Hub and Spoke with Connecting Link**

A spokesman for Boeing indicated that planes with 700 to 800 seats make economic sense. The rationale for such large planes is that they would reduce costs. More passengers can be carried, while costs for pilots, fuel, loading and unloading, remain about the same. In addition, "slots" for airline companies at many global airports are currently booked-up, meaning that one company could route more passengers through an existing slot at an airport using bigger planes.

An expert in aircraft design at Stanford University, Ilan Kroo, is quoted as saying:

> Our analyses suggest you can make airplanes reasonably efficient up to 1,000 passengers or so. The problems are much more practical, such as how you get all of those people out in the required time in an emergency and how you build an airplane that is not so tall that it requires unreasonable slides in an emergency situation.

Airbus speaks of using the superjumbos only on "our most popular routes" while British Airways says it would employ them only on "routes between the largest cities." Boeing is quoted as forecasting that over the next ten years, "airlines around the world will be flying 60 per cent more passengers." Superjumbos will definitely fly across the largest "tops" of the world's airline transport hierarchies.

While superjumbos top the airline transportation hierarchy in terms of size, we should not forget that it is possible also to consider *speed* when it comes to identifying those modes of transport that dominate the hierarchies of cities. In this regard, the plane that tops the global list is obviously the Concorde. With speeds of over Mach 2 (about 1300 mph or 2146 km/h) it is undoubtedly a transport mode that is intended only to fly among world class cities. At the moment it flies routes consisting primarily of those between London and New York (British Airways), and Paris and New York (Air France). The cost of a round trip fare between London and New York is about $9000 (U.S.). As of 1996 the fleet of thirteen planes had transported over 3.7 million passengers. The transatlantic flight time is approximately three hours and forty minutes, compared with a time of about seven hours for a Boeing 747. At the moment there are plans for a successor called the Super Concorde which will fly twice as many passengers (200) as the current version. In 1999, in the web magazine *Ride & Drive,* author Thomas Bonsall describes the Concorde experience:

> While the Concorde is fast, the aircraft is also small and a bit cramped — too small, in fact, for a regular galley, which means that Concorde passengers are limited to microwavable meals. Nor is there any in-flight movie — there isn't room, apparently, for the overhead projection equipment. Indeed, it is hard to stand upright in the Concorde if you are over about 5'10" tall, and the aisle is so narrow passing another passenger can be a challenge...It is advanced and retrograde at the same time. Fascinating in its contradictions.

## Ongoing Changes in the National Transportation Hierarchy

As we all know, Canada is a large country geographically, with a very sparse and widely distributed population. As a consequence, transportation is of the ultimate import. The significance of this is highlighted by the fact that Canada is also a very diverse country in terms of its resources and its industries. As is noted in the 1997 Annual Report of the Ministry of Transportation:

Transportation is important for domestic trade. In addition to trade within each province, trade between provinces is vital to regional economies. Each province is unique in its economic makeup, with its own specific industrial structure. Where one may be dominated by natural resources, the other may be dominated by specific manufacturing activities, making transportation a crucial link.

Much of the discussion in this chapter has focused on transport by rail and air, and there is a good reason for that. These are the modes that are the most highly hierarchical. The most important mode of economic transport, however, is by truck and as one might expect, trucks are not constrained to rail lines or ports in the way that trains and ships are. Consequently the structure of truck transport should be expected to be less hierarchical than that for rail or water. Nevertheless, so long as most trucking takes place among major urban centres, and from major centres on "down the line" through the urban hierarchy, it can be argued that transportation by truck is primarily hierarchical as well.

Trucking has long been the most important means of hauling goods in Canada and this trend is continuing into the future. Table 6.2 illustrates the growing dominance of trucking as the most popular mode of transport in Canada. There it can be seen in the third row that in 1981, trucking accounted for 20.8 percent of all goods transported, and by 1997 this had grown to 35.4 percent. Meanwhile, over the same time, the share of rail increased slightly, while that of water declined.

**Table 6.2 The Most Popular Types of Transport**

Distribution of Transportation 1981-1997
(per cent)

|  | 1981 | 1991 | 1997 |
|---|---|---|---|
| Rail | 15.8 | 16.7 | 18.3 |
| Water | 9.4 | 9.7 | 8.7 |
| Truck | 20.8 | 29.8 | 35.4 |
| Air | 16.3 | 13.2 | 14.5 |
| Urban | 17.7 | 10.3 | 6.8 |
| Interurban | 2.4 | 1.1 | 0.6 |
| Other | 17.6 | 19.3 | 15.8 |
| Total | 100.0 | 100.0 | 100.0 |

Source: 1997 Annual Report, Ministry of Transportation.

110  *Hierarchical Organization in Society*

What are the reasons for the growing significance of trucking? Why is it making the most dramatic gains? The 1997 Annual Report of the Ministry of Transportation argues that:

> There are two main reasons for this. First, the structural changes to the overall economy have resulted in a shift in goods production, which in turn means changing freight transportation needs. For example, the current trend is to keep inventories low, and the 'just-in-time' delivery system now in fashion is best suited to trucking. Second, transportation prices have had low increases, prompting shippers to use better quality services, such as door-to-door delivery, for which the truck mode is well equipped.

Given the importance of trucking, it is useful to emphasize that the national network of roads and highways is itself a type of hierarchy. A typical provincial or national roadmap will classify roads into categories by their quality as in the manner shown in Figure 6.6.

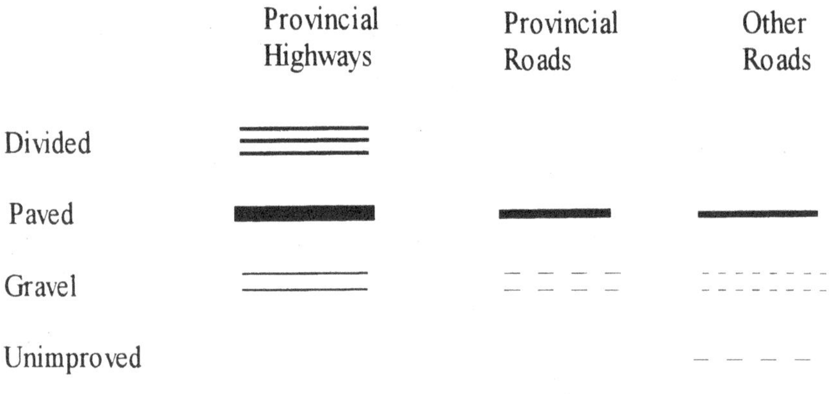

|  | Provincial Highways | Provincial Roads | Other Roads |
|---|---|---|---|
| Divided | ≡ | | |
| Paved | ▬ | ▬ | ▬ |
| Gravel | ═ | - - - - | - - - - - - - |
| Unimproved | | | - - - - |

**Figure 6.6 Typical Road Classification Hierarchy**

This figure is itself a guideline, for drivers, to the *hierarchy* of roads and highways that exists. The higher the quality of the road, and the greater the number of lanes, the higher within the urban hierarchy the road is likely to be. Toronto, at the top of the hierarchy, has the most, and widest, multiple lane highways. Gravelled back roads would be at the other end of the scale. Nationally, the TransCanada Highway should be considered to be the "core" of the highway system, while in the industrial heartland, Highway 401 is usually considered to be "Main Street" Canada.

Finally it is important to emphasize the significance of mixed-mode, or intermodal transport. This refers to transport systems in which two modes or methods are mixed together. The usual form this takes is in the "container on flatcar" that is a common sight at a railway crossing. Similarly, "container on ship" is another often seen method. An article in the January, 1999 *Financial Post* notes that:

> Trains bring in large container boxes filled with everything from liquor to toys from ports such as Vancouver, Montreal, and Halifax. These are lifted by crane off the rail car and placed on trucks for delivery in Canada and the United States.

This form of intermodal traffic is growing explosively in importance and has become an important revenue source for the railways.

### The 49th Parallel - Gateway to the U.S.

"Globalization" is a popular buzzword these days, but in the first instance, Canada should be focused much more on "continentalization." Smart Canadian corporations are pushing the envelope. They are striving to envisage the *North American market*, instead of the Canadian one. The distinction drawn by the 49th parallel is starting to blur. Companies with foresight do not see a boundary anymore. They see a gateway to a market of 300,000,000 people.

Integration with the United States has been a constant theme throughout this book. We have discussed urban, industrial, corporate and other forms of integration with our neighbours to the south. Nowhere is this trend truer than with respect to trade with, and transportation to, the United States. Not only are we trading more than ever with the United States but we are also trading less within Canada. Table 6.3 shows the patterns.

The Free Trade Agreement with the United States is now over ten years old. The results are evident in Table 6.3. The column "Exports to U.S." indicates that in 1988 fifteen percent of all goods moved in Canada went to the United States. By 1996 that figure had increased to 23 percent. That represents a 35 percent increase. Over the same period of time you will see that imports from the United States increased from 13.1 percent to 17.2 percent, a 24 percent increase. By both counts we are trading more than ever before with the United States.

There are two other columns of special interest in Table 6.3. The second column, "Intra-Regional" refers to trade in Canada *within* national regions. The third column, "Inter-Regional," refers to trade *among* national regions. In both of these columns you will see significant decreases, that is, that we are trading *less among ourselves* as a nation and *more* with the

112 *Hierarchical Organization in Society*

United States. What better indicator could there be of our ongoing integration with the United States?

**Table 6.3  Trade Patterns within Canada and with the U.S. and the World**

Percent of Interprovincial and International Trade
Flows of Total Goods
1988-1996

| Year | Intra-Regional | Inter-Regional | Exports to U.S. | Exports to ROW | Imports from U.S. | Import from ROW | Total |
|---|---|---|---|---|---|---|---|
| 1988 | 46.8 | 11.3 | 15.2 | 5.7 | 13.1 | 8.0 | 100 |
| 1989 | 47.3 | 11.2 | 14.5 | 5.7 | 12.9 | 8.3 | 100 |
| 1990 | 47.3 | 10.5 | 15.5 | 5.3 | 12.8 | 8.7 | 100 |
| 1991 | 46.4 | 10.0 | 16.1 | 4.9 | 13.3 | 9.3 | 100 |
| 1992 | 43.8 | 9.5 | 18.0 | 4.6 | 14.5 | 9.6 | 100 |
| 1993 | 41.9 | 8.5 | 20.0 | 4.3 | 15.9 | 9.4 | 100 |
| 1994 | 39.9 | 7.6 | 21.6 | 4.5 | 17.1 | 9.3 | 100 |
| 1995 | 37.7 | 7.4 | 22.5 | 5.5 | 17.3 | 9.6 | 100 |
| 1996 | 37.1 | 7.6 | 23.2 | 5.4 | 17.2 | 9.5 | 100 |

ROW: Rest of World

Source: 1997 Annual Report, Ministry of Transportation.

The same can be said of our trading patterns with the rest of the world. Canada is not only linked strongly to the United States through trade but also with many other regions of the world. Table 6.4 shows Canada's largest trading relationships around the globe.

Table 6.4 shows clearly that Canada and the United States are the world's largest trading partners. Third on the list comes trade between Mexico and the United States. In these two facts is clear evidence of the profound importance of the *continentalization* among the three countries. With the exception of the United States-Japan trade partnership, other global trading relationships pale in comparison to the Canada-United States -Mexico alliance. Another notable pattern in Table 6.4 is that Germany appears on the list five times, far more than any other country.

As such global patterns of trade continue to grow, so too does the international chorus of proponents of *global free trade*. There are those that would have trade barriers all over the world come down as the forces of globalization sweep the world. The United States, for example, is on record as being in favour of international free trade in agriculture, industrial goods, and financial services. Many such ideas evolved out of global trade talks dubbed the Uruguay Round in 1998, and earlier. Future rounds of talks are being scheduled. At the same time, the European Union is in favour of still freer global trade in its proposed "Millennium Round."

**Table 6.4 The World's Top 10 Biggest Trading Partners, 1995**

| Trading Partners | U.S. billion $ |
|---|---|
| U.S. - Canada | 285 |
| U.S. - Japan | 192 |
| U.S. - Mexico | 125 |
| Germany-France | 114 |
| Hong Kong-China | 94 |
| Germany-Italy | 86 |
| Germany-Netherlands | 84 |
| Germany-Britain | 78 |
| U.S. - Germany | 68 |
| Germany - Belgium/Luxembourg | 68 |

Source: *The Globe and Mail*, February, 1998.

The important point is that negotiations are underway for continental and global free trade. The structure of the world is changing, and corporate and other competitors have to be prepared for these new levels of competition. As the amount of trade between the United States and Canada grows, so too will the hierarchical transportation system become ever more integrated.

Good initial evidence of this pattern of unity with the United States is in the linkages that have grown between Air Canada and the United States carriers with which it has been integrating routes. An article in the *Financial Post* by David Olive, suggests that:

> World air travel is falling under the control of just four 'alliances,' each anchored by a major U.S. carrier: Delta Air Lines (the Atlantic Excellence alliance), Northwest Airlines (Wings), United Airlines (Star Alliance, which includes Air Canada) and American Airlines (Oneworld).

North-south, and continental alliances, are becoming the normal approach for Canadian corporations, transportation and otherwise.

114  *Hierarchical Organization in Society*

Significant patterns of international linkage are ongoing in the rail business as well. In fact, only recently CN (Canadian National Railway) acquired the Illinois Central Railway in the United States. This acquisition gives CN a link into the United States market and provides CN's east-west Canadian line with direct access right through to the Gulf of Mexico. The new "Y" shaped transport system, shown in Figure 6.7, gives CN competitive connections into major United States markets.

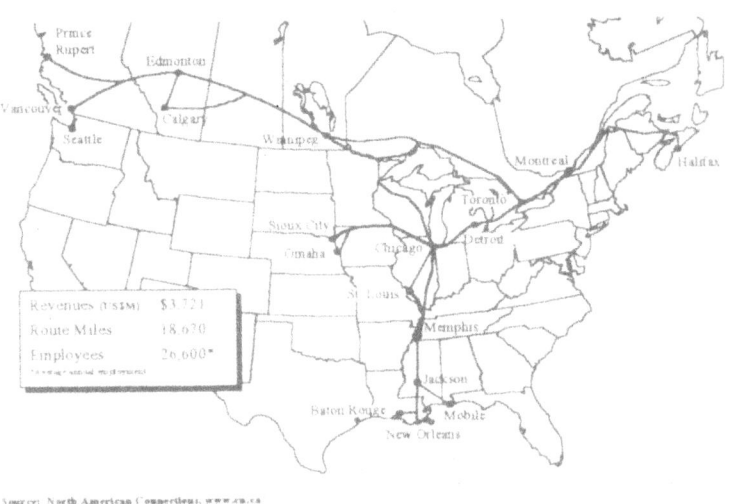

**Figure 6.7 CN Railway Acquires Illinois Central Railway**

A further agreement between CN, Illinois Central, and Kansas City Southern Railway Company gives CN a still greater reach into the United States, including Mexico. A report in the *National Post* indicates that CN "is bucking the longtime east-west trend of North American railways to build up the first continental north-south railway that can tap into the North American Free Trade Agreement."

As the amount of inter-nation trade continues to grow, air and rail transportation systems in Canada are being integrated with those in the United States and Mexico. The form of both the Canadian airline hierarchy and the Canadian rail line hierarchy are undergoing major transformations as they link themselves into continental transportation hierarchies. This is as it should be, as continentalization becomes the new economic reality.

# References

Bertin, O., 'CN bid to buy IC seen as near-perfect match', *Globe and Mail*, February 6, 1998.
Bonsall, T.E., 'The ultimate transportation by air, the Concorde', *Ride and Drive*, January, 1999.
CN-North American Connections, 'Canadian National, Illinois Central and Kansas City Southern Railway form pro-competitive 15-year marketing alliance for linking North American markets with new rail freight services', January, 1999.
Fitzpatrick, P., 'Truckers take on the railways', *Financial Post*, January, 1999.
Johnston, D.C., 'Airlines differ on future of superjumbos', *Globe and Mail*, December 12, 1998.
Little, B., 'The big players in the trading game', *Globe and Mail*, February 9, 1998.
Ministry of Transportation Annual Report, 'Transportation and the Economy', 1997.
Olive, D., 'Fearless forecasts for 1999', *Financial Post*, January 5, 1999.
Statistics Canada, 'Air Industry National Transport System', Transport Canada, Air Carrier Statements 2, 4 and 6, September, 1997.

# 7 Getting Around in the City

Cities are alive. They are not just the rigid pictures you see on maps. They are active 24 hours a day with the flows and movement of people, goods, products and information. People travel to work, to shop, and for social and recreational purposes. Goods and products flow across the city. Pedestrians, trains, buses, trucks, automobiles, and electronic communications are in constant movement. Over a short period of time, the city shapes the flows, but over longer periods of time, the flows shape the city.

Cities are complicated. It is not an easy matter to handle the movements of over 4,000,000 in the metro Toronto area every day, but somehow it gets done. Why do urban transportation systems work so well? How do the flows and movements get accomplished efficiently and effectively? How are so many people able to move from place to place with such relative ease?

The answer is that the only way to handle such complex systems is to organize them hierarchically. In other words, the flows are not just random. There is a pattern — a logic — to the flows that is discernable, and it is crucial to see this pattern if one is to understand the city. The urban transport hierarchy organizes and "channels" the flows. When components of the urban transport system do break down, it is usually symptomatic of a breakdown in the hierarchical structure.

Have you ever noticed those nearly empty buses that run in the suburban areas of Canadian cities? You know the ones. You'll see them at midday or in the evening — typically, large size city buses with only a few passengers on them. There are some that would have us conclude that such occurrences are symptomatic of what is wrong with urban planning and urban transportation. But those nearly empty buses at off-peak hours are normal. They are indicative of a system that has been designed for peak flows. The same buses will be packed full of commuters at the two daily rush hours. Lack of awareness of the hierarchical nature of transit flows within the city is what causes people to criticize what they perceive to be an inefficient system.

David Foot, in his book, *Boom, Bust and Echo,* would have us believe that such problems of urban transportation can be attributed largely to the demographics of the city. For example, Foot suggests that suburban buses are underutilized as a result of the age of the potential suburban riders. The present book maintains that if properly designed hierarchical systems are in place, urban transportation systems — both public and private — are, in general, fast, effective and efficient. The systems that are currently in place have evolved as the city has evolved, and so are, for the most part, appropriate to the systems they serve. The problems and bottlenecks that do exist can be attributed to the failure to appreciate transport systems as hierarchies, and to act accordingly.

**The Journey across Town**

Transportation flows within the city take place in primarily the same manner, as do flows in the national transportation hierarchy. Travellers making a trip tend to move first, *upward* in the hierarchy, then *across* the hierarchy, and finally back *down* the hierarchy. Consider the case of a trip across a city by automobile. Suppose you are leaving a residence in the suburbs and are travelling to visit a friend in another cross-town suburb by car. The journey begins on a residential street as the first stage of the hierarchy. Next you will probably turn on to a suburban "collector" street which represents the second step upward in the hierarchy. It is called a collector street by virtue of the fact that it "collects" the cars from the residential streets. Third, you'll turn onto a major arterial that is still leading you "upward" in the hierarchy. Ultimately, via an interchange, you will enter an expressway that will allow you to zip to the other side of the city. Along the way you may have to change from one expressway to another. At the end of your expressway journey, you will exit via another interchange, only to make your way back "down" the hierarchy of streets at the other end. As you leave the expressway you will drive down an arterial, to a collector street, and finally to a residential street. Without even having been aware of it, you will have journeyed up, across, and down in the hierarchical system of urban streets.

We can visualize the hierarchy of urban streets by using a diagram of the form of Figure 7.1. Interestingly this is roughly the same kind of diagram used to illustrate travel in the national urban system in the previous chapter. This provides convincing evidence of the applicability of hierarchical systems at different levels of the urban system. The journey across town begins, and ends, at the two residences. Each residence can be visualized as being in a neighborhood. In between, the traveller moves up, and then down, through a progressive sequence of roads that reflects the different levels of the transport hierarchy.

In the preceding chapter, the national transportation hierarchy was likened to the human circulatory system, where the transport of goods and people was considered to be analogous to the flow of blood through the human body. Transport was said to be the "lifeblood" of the modern economy. The same can be said of urban transit systems — they bring life to the structure of the city. Interestingly, this is explicitly reflected in the fact that major roads in the city are referred to as "arterials." If we were to carry the analogy further, we could liken residential streets to capillaries (small veins and arteries), and major expressways to the major arteries in the human body. In both cases, the ultimate goal is the same, that is, to achieve "circulation."

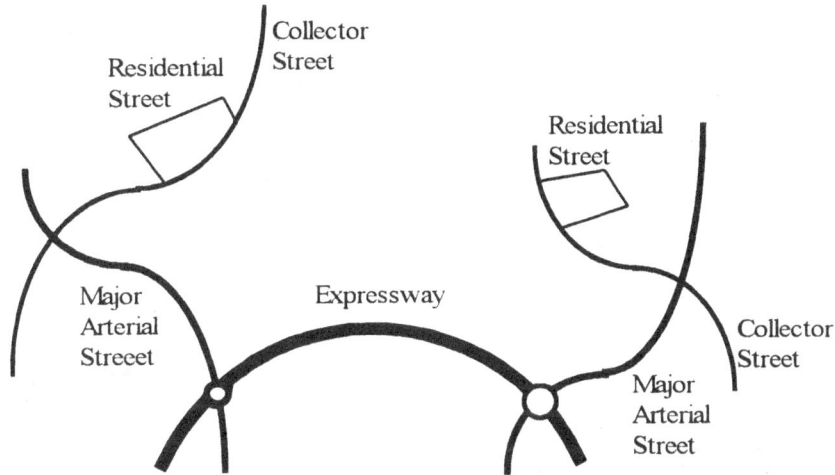

**Figure 7.1 Map of the Journey across Town in the Street Hierarchy**

There are interesting and essential design characteristics of the hierarchy of streets. As you move upward in the hierarchy several things happen. First, the streets get wider. Second, the amount of curbside parking decreases. Third, the speed limit increases with each step upward. Fourth, the amount of lighting increases. Fifth, the quality of the pavement usually gets better. Sixth, the number of stop lights, stop signs, and other signals decreases. Seventh, at some point pedestrians and bicycles are not allowed. Eighth, the roads get "straighter." Ninth, the number of lanes increases. Tenth, the roads get medians and then, later, get "divided." Eleventh, intersections give way to overpasses and underpasses. Finally, the number of "exits" decreases. On the residential street there is a driveway every forty or fifty feet. On the expressway, exits are several kilometres apart.

Interesting also is the design of off-ramps and on-ramps when you are on an expressway. Usually, on-ramps take you downhill to speed you up as you merge with traffic. At the same time, off-ramps normally go uphill in order to slow you down naturally as you exit the expressway. It is interesting that most people are unaware of how the roads are deliberately designed to shape their behaviour.

Why do all of these design changes take place as we move upward in the street hierarchy? Clearly the changes at each step are designed to do two things — move more traffic, and move it more quickly. Can you imagine any better design strategy to move a large number of vehicles through densely populated, congested urban areas? If an urban transport hierarchy is well designed, it can move a huge amount of traffic in a very efficient manner. Unfortunately, what we usually hear about are the problems. For example, when an accident brings a busy expressway to a standstill, that's news. But when the expressway is doing its proper job and effectively moving thousands of cars at a reasonable pace, day after day, not a word gets said.

Cities all across Canada are working on their evolving urban street systems. The classic problem in urban street evolution is that as soon as you make a road wider, faster, or better the amount of traffic on the road will increase, meaning that once again you need to make the road wider, faster, or better (see Figure 7.2). The cycle goes on endlessly. Cities struggle to keep their street systems "up to capacity" but of course there are always budget limitations with which to deal. As a consequence, urban transportation systems evolve as best as they can, given the constraints of budgets. Usually the major transportation problems arise, not as the result of some inadequacy of road design, but rather in response to inadequate budgets. Bottlenecks usually can be "solved" if sufficient money is available.

## The Public Transit Hierarchy in the City

The same ideas about travel that apply to the urban street system apply also to urban public transit systems. The principal difference is that usually urban transit systems focus on a single "hub" which is normally located in the downtown area. This reflects the fact that the downtown is the most popular destination for transit riders. Typically public transit is organized hierarchically, around the central hub. "Collector" routes of buses that run through neighbourhoods or industrial areas often have suburban transit centres as their first destination. In many cities these suburban transit centres will then have direct routes, or express routes, that connect to the downtown transit centre (see Figure 7.3). In larger cities having rapid transit or subway systems, the bus routes will also link-up with those systems. In either case there is a definitive hierarchical pattern. Transit riders make their way "upwards" through a series of hierarchical steps until they reach some downtown destination. As is typical of a hierarchical system, at each upward step, the system should be designed to move more people and do it faster. It should get larger, faster, and have fewer stops, as will be the case in the step from a bus to a light rapid transit (LRT) or subway system.

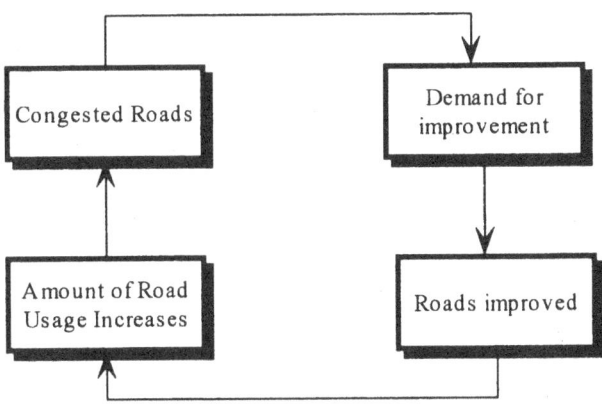

**Figure 7.2 The Endless Cycle of Road Improvement**

The major difference between the hierarchy of roads and the mass transit hierarchy is that the latter focuses on the downtown. Consequently if a mass transit rider wishes to take our earlier journey from a suburban residence to another suburban residence this usually requires a journey through a downtown terminal or at least through a more complicated route on a rail or other transit system. These extra constraints on the mass transit user reflect the simple fact that, unlike the individual automobile, mass transit is designed to serve the "masses." As a result the system is not as flexible as that of the automobile. It is important to point out that in the case of transport by bus, the buses do travel in the hierarchy of urban streets, and so enjoy the design features of the system that were described in the section above.

As was the case with the urban traffic hierarchy, the effectiveness of the public transit system is largely at the mercy of civic budgets. There is a fine balance between limiting spending, on the one hand, and providing excellent service, on the other. Most communities strive to provide the best possible service, subject to the budget limitations that are imposed.

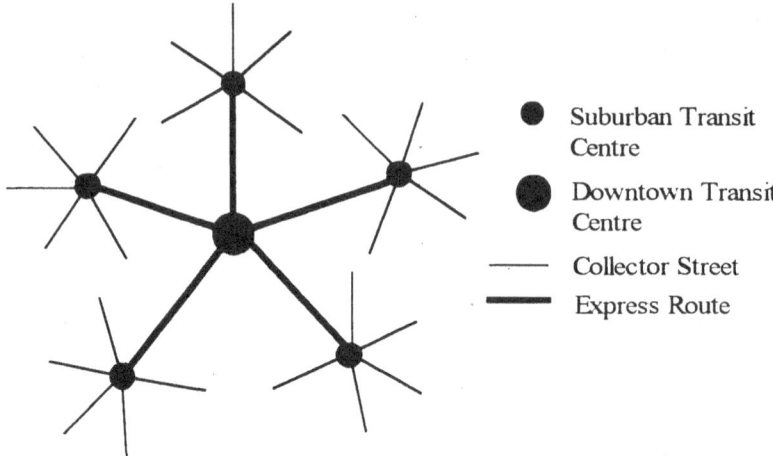

Figure 7.3  Map of Mass Transit Flows in a City

**The Timing of Urban Flows**

An essential criterion of urban transport systems is that they be designed to be able to handle the "peak" flows that occur in the system. In the city, these peak flows typically are associated with the morning and evening rush hours. It is interesting to break down the flows that occur in the city according to the time of day that they occur. In this way we can see how the flows "surge" through the urban transit systems at different times of the day. The hierarchies must be designed to accommodate not just trips to work, but all trips that are taking place within the city.

Figure 7.4 presents a series of four graphs showing the amount of travel in the average city according to different purposes. These are drawn from an article in the book *The Geography of Urban Transportation*. The first graph (a) shows the percent of *work* trips at various times during the day. As expected, work trips represent the largest flows that we see. There is a morning peak at about 8:00 a.m., followed by a late-day peak at about 5:00 p.m. There is a very low "trough" during mid-day. Graph (b) shows *shopping* trips during the day. This graph is virtually the opposite of the work-trip line, with low levels in the early morning and late afternoon, peak times at mid-day, and a small surge in the evening. Graph (c) indicates trips for *social or recreational* purposes and, as we might expect, there is a smaller mid-day peak followed by a huge surge in the evening hours, between 6:00 and 11:00 p.m. Finally graph (d) shows the averaged *total* trip pattern resulting from the sum of the others. It can be seen that there is an early morning peak, followed by a general pattern of increase throughout the entire afternoon that finally "crests" at about 5:00 p.m.

Although traffic moves all day, the urban travel hierarchies are stressed to their limits twice a day, and it is by their capacities and effectiveness at those times of day that traffic managers and planners will judge the performances of the systems. The phenomenon of a "wave" of people "washing" in to the downtown area in the morning, only to "wash" out again at the end of the workday, is sometimes called "the urban wave." It is this wave that tests the mettle of urban transportation systems, planners, and managers.

## Urban Transportation and the Automobile

Evolution. Most people associate the idea of evolution with Charles Darwin and the evolution of species. But it is possible to look at the idea more broadly. It is the point-of-view of this book that urban systems also evolve, through "natural selection," such that in most cases the systems we see around us at present are the ones that have evolved into their optimum form, given their circumstances. A case in point is the urban transportation system. The point of view presented here is that modern urban transport systems represent the current stage of a process of evolution that has produced the best possible solution to the transportation problems faced by the modern city.

There are all kinds and manner of automobile and expressway "critics" out there who argue that we should all but abandon modern transport systems, apparently, so that we can all ride bicycles to work. Such a perspective ignores almost totally the form of the contemporary city, and the needs of its residents. *There are good reasons why so many people drive a car.* To ignore these reasons is to ignore the realities of the modern world. At the same time there are those who mock the provision of public transit to suburban areas, taking the point of view that this is an inefficient waste of resources.

In the modern North American city there are two co-existing methods of transportation, the automobile and public transit. The two systems have evolved over time through the last century. In the first half of the century, public transit was more popular. Since World War II the automobile has taken over the top spot. Nevertheless the two systems still co-exist, each serving its own particular role in the urban transport system.

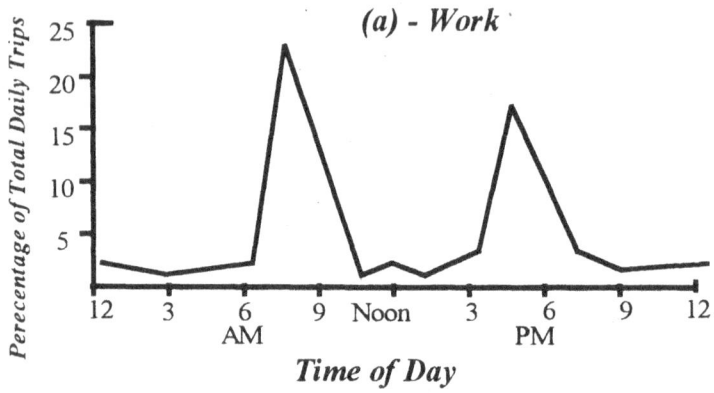

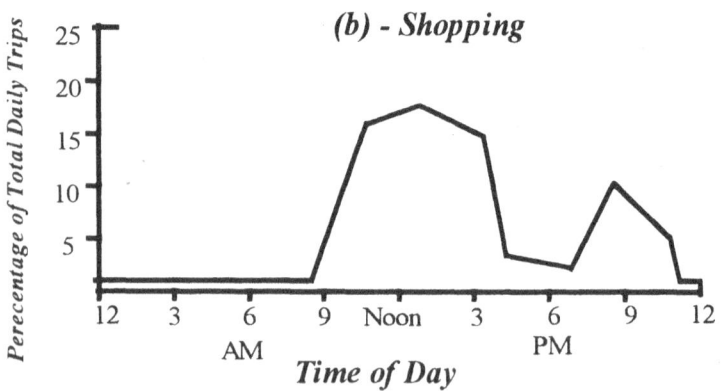

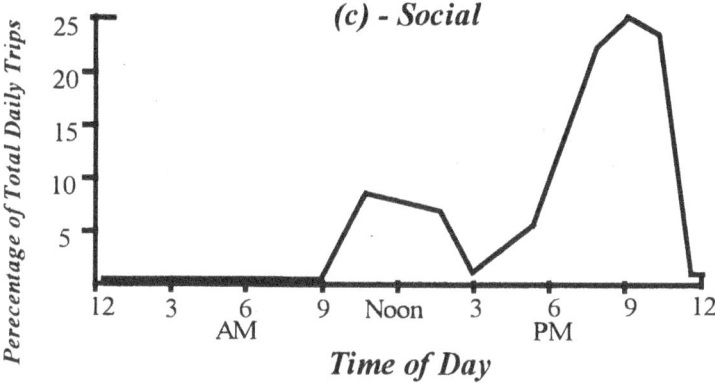

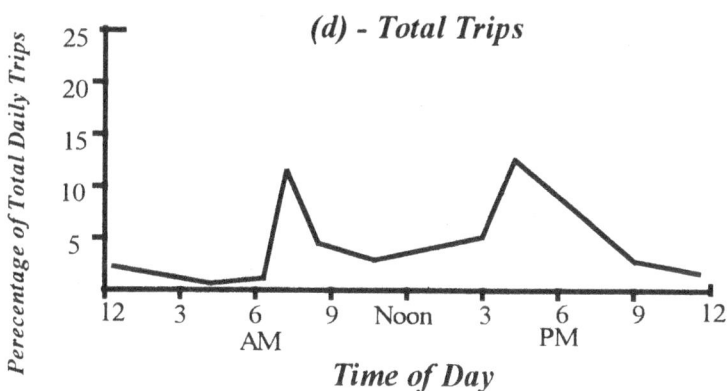

Source: Reprinted with permission from *The Geography of Urban Transportation*, 1995.

**Figure 7.4 The Timing of Flows in the City**

Public transit was invented when cities were smaller and the automobile was less popular. As a result, buses, subways, and streetcars are designed to serve primarily older areas of the city that are close to the downtown. This was their original purpose, and this is what they are still best at doing. They serve areas of the city that have high population densities in what is typically referred to as the inner-city. An illustration of the typical pattern of *public transit* usage is presented in Figure 7.5(a) that shows daily volumes of users of public transit in the City of Edmonton. The map shows the flows of users, where the thicker the black lines, the greater the flow. The most obvious characteristic of the pattern is that it focuses on the downtown area. The heaviest concentration of users surrounds the inner-city, and there are only a few "branches" reaching into the suburbs (the actual city centre is left blank on the map, as it would turn solid black if mapped).

The evolution of public transit pre-dates the evolution of suburban sprawl and consequently, public transit was never intended to solve the problems of urban sprawl. The suburbs evolved later, and as they did, they evolved their own solutions to their own transport problems. City transport systems adapted themselves to the automobile through the use of hierarchies of road systems as described earlier. This pattern is evident in Figure 7.5(b) that shows daily volumes of *automobile users* in Edmonton. This map is strikingly different from the map of public transit users (Figure 7.5(a)). In particular there is a much stronger emphasis on large volumes of hierarchical flows in suburban areas.

Between them, the two systems get the job done. The older public transit portion of the transport system serves primarily people who live in the areas closer to the downtown, while the road-based portion serves the suburbs. Each system provides appropriate transport for the majority of users in each of the areas served. But, of course, there are exceptions. Some residents of the suburbs need or prefer to use public transit while some residents of inner areas of cities need or prefer to use the automobile. As a result it is necessary to have some overlap in the systems. This is where the critics come in. They bemoan the fact that it is not only necessary, but also logical to extend some public transit lines into the suburbs. Not everyone in the suburbs can avail themselves of the use of an automobile. Not everyone has a driver's license. As a result there is some demand for buses or other public transit in the suburbs. City planners and managers are aware of this demand and do their best to solve it by running buses in suburban areas.

How do you design public transit for the suburbs? Clearly the answer is that you build the system to handle the peak loads that occur. There would be little point in using smaller than usual buses, for example, if they won't handle the rush hours. The public transit system, just like the system of roads, has to be designed to handle flows when they are at a maximum. This means that during off-peak times of the day the public transit system will appear to be inefficient. Half-full buses will make the system look as if it is wasteful at mid-morning or mid-afternoon. But it has to be designed for 8:00 a.m. and 5:00 p.m. It is at those times that the system is doing what it is designed to do.

Getting Around in the City   127

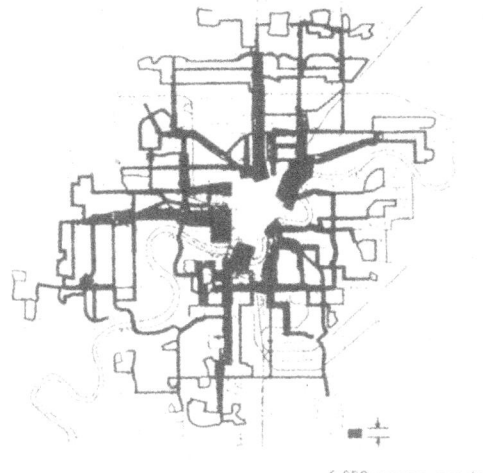

(a) Public Transit Users

(b) Automobile Users

Source: Reprinted with permission from the *Canadian Transit Handbook*, 1980.

**Figure 7.5 Daily Transit and Automobile Flows in Edmonton**

David Foot exemplifies the illogical nature of the argument against "almost empty" buses or subways in this passage from the book *Boom, Bust and Echo*:

> It makes no sense to build expensive subway systems or even to run conventional buses in most suburban areas because, no matter how good the service, not enough people will use it. This fact can be seen by anyone who drives down a suburban Toronto freeway unofficially called the Spadina Expressway, which connects a northern suburb to the city. The expressway has a subway line running above ground down its centre median. *Except for brief periods during the weekday rush hours*, these subway cars are almost empty.

Exactly. So are the roads.

By analogy, do you ever hear anyone say that the expressways are excessively built because they are "almost empty" at 10:30 in the morning or 10:30 at night? Should we criticize the expressways because they are not being used to full capacity during the entire day? Of course not. Everyone understands that expressways are designed for the peak, rush hour flows. Saying we should not run conventional buses in the suburbs is tantamount to saying that an expressway is a waste of money because "not enough people use it." The subway line above the Spadina is full during the rush hours, just as it was designed to be.

One of Foot's solutions to the "problem" of suburban public transit is as follows:

> since conventional large buses don't work in suburbs because the population densities are insufficient to support them, why not use more cost-efficient smaller buses? Since many people won't walk several blocks to a major street to find a bus stop, why not let the little buses circulate into the side streets to get them?

We need to ask how popular this approach to the provision of public transit to the suburbs will be at rush hour, when the "little buses" leave commuters stranded at curbside. The transit system is designed for the weekday rush hours. Sure, inner-city bus routes are more heavily used and therefore more profitable, but so are inner city streets used more. These patterns of use reflect the fact that cities are circular, and the most accessible place in them is in the middle. Of course there are higher densities in the inner-city, and of course transport systems there get more heavily used, but that does not mean we should abandon the suburbs when it comes to providing public transit.

Two separate systems of urban transit have evolved over this century. The current state of affairs represents a situation where the two systems coexist, each serving a different set of users, but working to maximum efficiency, given the constraints imposed by the geography of the city. The present situation represents the best of both worlds. Hierarchical road systems serve automobile users in an efficient manner, while public transit systems do the same for non-drivers.

In spite of the efficiencies described above, there are still those who will do their utmost to get drivers out of their cars. These people extol the virtues of mass transit and argue that we could improve the quality of life in cities by encouraging much greater use of mass transit.

This book says people "vote with their feet." If you want to judge what people prefer, look at what they do. Public transport accounts for only about ten percent of all passenger trips in North America. That tells us something. It says that the private automobile is overwhelmingly the choice of about ninety-percent of urban residents. There are obvious reasons for this. The car is private and personal. Unlike public transit, you do not have to wait for it. It goes directly where you want it to go. It is fast and flexible. And it is perfectly suited to the typical lifestyle of most people who run a half-dozen errands a day. Obviously there is a strong personal preference for the private automobile, and it smacks of arrogance to tell people they should not use their automobile, or make them feel guilty for doing so.

## Planning for the Future of Urban Transport

Transportation systems are so important to cities that it is impossible to understand, or study, the history of cities without giving due diligence to their transportation systems. The modern city evolved hand-in-hand with a series of transportation innovations and advancements that determined the course of urban evolution.

The first city was the pedestrian city, small and compact, where people walked to work, shopping and leisure activities. This city was small and compact, with high population densities, and it was devoid of any internal transport system. Typical of this time would be the shop owner who lived directly above his store. The first uses of transport in the city involved the horse-car, or horse drawn car. The horse-car hauled goods and people, and gave the city its first chance to start to expand. Next came the steam engine. Loud and noisy, it was incompatible with the horse-car system and so was of limited impact in the city. But still it enabled the city to continue to grow outward. In between times, railways had come into limited use in some cities. Although they were really intended for travel *between* cities, in some cases they were used to set up the first "commuter" lines. These lines, affordable only to the very wealthy, enabled the city to expand beyond its original boundaries for the first time.

The next technological invention was the one that revolutionized the modern North American city — the electric streetcar. This stunning new technology was immediately successful. There were over 200 streetcar systems installed in North America in just a three-year period, ending in 1892. This was *mass-transit* for the first time — public transit for the *masses* had never existed before. The streetcar set the stage for the beginning of the widespread expansion of the city. Cities grew outward and densities started to decrease. The form of the city was being altered by the new technology.

Ultimately, and some time later, came the invention of the internal combustion engine, bringing with it, automobiles, trucks, and buses. Now the city was truly ready to undergo a revolution in form. The invention of the automobile literally created the suburbs. Unlike the electric streetcar, this immensely popular mode of transport was *private*. Not only that, but it was affordable and offered a number of other advantages that only a private vehicle could. The city started to expand far beyond its original borders as the automobile extended the ability of people to acquire the single family, detached home in the suburbs. The final innovation to affect the modern city was the invention of the "expressway" which served only to exacerbate the patterns already being etched into the surface of the city by the automobile.

It was said earlier, that the flows shape the city, and the city shapes the flows. It can be seen now quite clearly what this means. In the history described above, there is an evolution of transportation technology that both shapes and responds to the form of the city. When transport innovations came along, they were constrained by the existing form of the city. The automobile, for example, was initially limited to travelling in the existing "gridded" street pattern that existed. The city shaped the flows. But with the invention of the limited access freeway, rapid cross-town travel became a reality. The flows started to shape the city. This cycle of form and function can be illustrated in a simple diagram. Figure 7.6 shows how the act of improving an existing road, for example, can set off a chain of events that results in an endless cycle of further improvement to the road, followed by greater usage of the road. In other words, when a road is improved, this will lead to additional traffic using the road. This, in turn, will cause more "development" to occur along the road, for example, more businesses may be built. The new businesses cause still more traffic to use the road, which in turn causes a need to improve the road again. And so on.

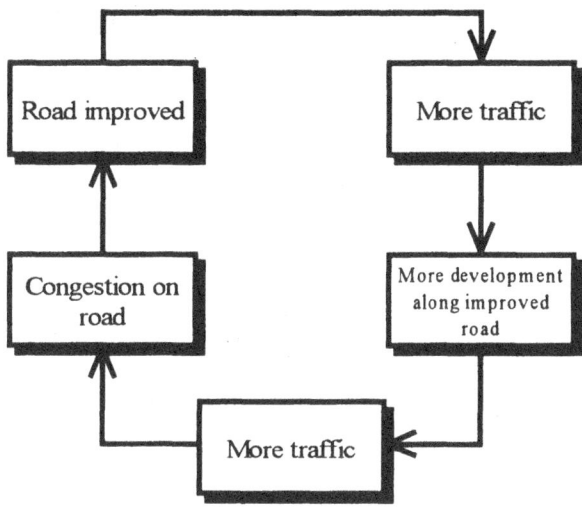

**Figure 7.6 The Endless Cycle of Traffic and Development**

As Figure 7.6 shows, the flows affect the city, and the city affects the flows. In the first case, new development occurs as a result of traffic, and in the second case, new traffic occurs as a result of development.

## Urban Evolution

The point was made earlier in this chapter that urban systems evolve to their optimum configuration, in the same way that species do. This form of evolution can be seen in the development of urban transportation systems. Most people would tend to look at Figure 7.6 as an indicator of the *problems* of modern transport systems, that is, that there seems to be no end to the cycle of change and improvement. We prefer instead, to see Figure 7.6 as an illustration of *the natural evolution of urban systems*. It illustrates the way in which cities and their transport systems *should* evolve. It indicates that as problems arise, solutions are found for them that correct any temporary imbalance in the system. This is how evolution proceeds in the natural world. Members of species *adapt to changes in the environment* and by so doing increase their competitive advantage. As a city grows and evolves, solutions are found to transportation problems. Any of these solutions will be temporary, because as the city continues to grow and evolve, it will continue to require new solutions to new problems. At any given point in time, the existing structure of the city represents a temporary balance between the opposing forces of budget constraints, and the need for change and improvement.

The more recent history of the modern city is a history of the impact of the automobile. The private car is without a doubt the greatest innovation to impact the form of the city in this century. Henry Ford's use of mass production had many implications far beyond the factory floor. Since World War II we have seen urban sprawl, together with the development of suburban centres and their surrounding communities. These sprawling suburbs surround older, more compact, inner cities. As John Hartman of the Transportation Association of Canada notes, these trends were spurred on by a number of factors, namely:

- A shift of population from rural to urban areas
- A booming economy with healthy tax bases
- Affordable housing and automobiles
- Inexpensive gasoline, and
- Plentiful road space.

The excesses of the period between the 1950's and the present are upon us now. There are problems with urban transport that have arisen from the halcyon days of the past. But these problems are really nothing new or surprising. They are just another part of the natural evolution of urban transport systems. Unfortunately many urban managers and planners see the focus of the problem as too much dependence on the automobile. As true as this may be, it flies in the face of reality that for the foreseeable future we are stuck with the automobile as *the overwhelmingly preferred mode of travel for the majority of residents of cities.* And that is not going to change.

Across Canada, practitioners of the practice of planning urban transport are almost unanimous in their vision of the future of cities and their transportation systems. There is usually a consensus on a number of issues, most of which focus on reducing the use of the automobile. The Transportation Association of Canada produces a typical list of Decision-Making Principles for the future:

1. Urban Structure and Land Use
   *Plan for increased densities and more mixed land use.*
2. Walking
   *Promote walking as the preferred mode for person trips.*
3. Cycling
   *Increase opportunities for cycling as an optional mode of travel.*
4. Transit

*Provide higher quality transit service to increase its attractiveness relative to the private auto.*

5. Automobile
   *Create an environment in which automobiles can play a more balanced role.*
6. Parking
   *Plan parking supply and price to be in balance with walking, cycling, transit and auto priorities.*
7. Goods Movement
   *Improve the efficiency of the urban goods distribution system.*
8. Inter-Modal Integration
   *Promote inter-modal and inter-line connections.*
9. New Technology
   *Promote new technologies that improve urban mobility and help protect the environment.*
10. System Optimization
    *Optimize the use of existing transportation systems to move people and goods.*
11. Special User Needs
    *Design and operate transportation systems, which can be used by the physically challenged.*
12. Environment
    *Ensure that urban transportation decisions protect and enhance the environment.*
13. Funding/Financing
    *Create better ways to pay for future urban transportation systems.*

Clearly the focus of such a list is often on discouraging the use of the automobile in favour of walking, biking, and transit. While many items make a lot of sense, many of the ones focusing exclusively on the decreased use of the automobile (particularly numbers 1 to 6) are unrealistic.

In spite of the fact that there is a social consensus that items such as 1 to 6 are laudable goals that are "environmentally friendly," the reality is that ninety-percent of the population *prefers* to use the automobile. Given this huge constraint, it is inconceivable to suppose that any *major* change can be wrought in urban transport systems by convincing or encouraging people to change their behaviour or preferences in regard to the automobile.

In addition to the impenetrable wall of personal preference that will be encountered in trying to discourage the use of the automobile, there is a far more practical reason why it won't work, especially in Canada. It was indicated earlier that transport systems have to be designed and built to handle maximum or peak flows. Usually we think of these flows, as we did above, as occurring at certain times of *day*. But in Canada we also have to allow for time of year. In spite of the fact that we might successfully encourage people to use mass transit or bicycles at certain ideal times of year, in Canada we have to deal with the harsh realities of the climate. As a result, *an urban transport system should be designed to handle the peak flows that will occur in ninety percent of the country when it is -20 degrees Celsius, there is a northwest wind at 30 kilometres, and there is a foot of snow on the ground.* We need to ask, "to what extent are people likely to use mass transit, let alone a bicycle, under *these conditions*?"

To be fair, critics of the automobile do have some valid points. Here is a list of some of the problems with the automobile as suggested by the Transportation Association of Canada:

- wasted fuel and inefficient operation of motor vehicles
- wasted time for drivers and passengers
- increased operating and maintenance costs for motor vehicles
- higher roadway maintenance costs
- less effective public transit services
- air and noise pollution
- increased accidents
- increased costs to the health care system from air pollution, driver stress and accidents
- the spread of "urban blight", when homeowners move to cleaner, quieter, safer neighbourhoods
- less competitive cities, as industries seek sites with better access and tax based are eroded
- a lower quality of urban life.

There are some legitimate criticisms here. But several of these so-called problems are typical of the vague accusations that are often levelled at the automobile. For instance, the last one, "lower quality of urban life" is particularly galling. How many people would agree that their everyday use of the automobile lowers their quality of life? Imagine trying to take your kids to a hockey practice, for example, using mass transit instead of a car. Is there anyone who would seriously argue that they would prefer mass transit? Certainly there are lots of people who cannot afford an automobile, single mothers for example, who have a lower quality of life for that very reason.

From the evolutionary point of view, a list like that above represents a set of problems to be solved, as opposed to a list of reasons to knock the automobile as a mode of transport. It is just as easy to create a similar list of the problems involved in mass transit:

- Pollution spewing buses
- Noise pollution
- Long waiting times at subway and bus stops
- Crowded, dirty facilities
- Lack of privacy
- Feeling of lack of safety
- Lack of security at night
- Long walks to stops
- Walking and waiting in cold or inclement weather
- Time lost to circuitous routes taken
- Inconvenient scheduling
- Longer commuting time
- Lack of ability to run errands
- Lack of ability to chauffeur children around.

And so on. The list could go on and on. But rarely do we see such a list. Rather there is a mentality in the transit planning community that a list, such as the thirteen Decision-Making Principles given above, is the accepted route to follow. In fact, the Transportation Association of Canada indicates that its New Vision for Urban Transport, represented by the list of thirteen principles above, has been endorsed by a number of Canadian municipal and regional governments.

Urban and transportation planning has to recognize the realities of the love affair with the automobile. In an earlier section, a list of the advantages of the automobile was recited. It is virtually impossible to imagine another mode of transport that has so many positive features for the user. Until that other mode is invented, people will continue to use automobiles as they have in the past. Planners have to recognize that fact. As well, they need to recognize the realities of the Canadian climate. Creating visions of commuters, happily pedaling to work, clouds the real issue of handling those peak flows that will occur on those bitterly cold, blustery winter days that occur across most of the country.

In attempting to deal with the realities of automobile use, there are many new initiatives on the horizon. This is in keeping with the evolutionary point of view that says technologies will evolve to meet demands. Some of the solutions to automobile congestion problems that are being promoted include the following:

136  *Hierarchical Organization in Society*

- Develop a better *hierarchy* of roads and expressways
- Decentralization of jobs to suburban areas, especially through zoning
- Encourage use of mixed modes, e.g., park and ride
- Flattened traffic peaks
- Ride sharing
- Flexible working hours
- More and better parking structures
- Substitution of telecommunications for commuting
- Computerized, real time, traffic management
- Build new "toll roads," e.g., Highway 407 in Toronto, with automatic toll technology
- Privatize road building and maintenance
- Build new "toll lanes" where new toll lanes are constructed in the medians of existing highways.

The last technology on the list, the use of toll lanes, has been implemented in California. Peter Samuel, in the *Financial Post*, indicates just how the system works:

> The San Diego Association of Governments, which runs carpool lanes in the San Diego area, began allowing single-occupant cars into its I-15 carpool lanes by charging a toll which can vary as frequently as every six minutes, by amounts of 25 or 50 cents, depending on the traffic. SANDAG's toll express operation is the first variable toll to change dynamically, in line with increasing or easing congestion. Because legislation requires SANDAG to maintain free flow conditions for the car poolers, SANDAG increases the toll to discourage overuse whenever the facility threatens to become overloaded. When it has empty space, it lowers the toll. Motorists pay between 50 cents and $4 for a 13-km trip, depending on the congestion. The variable toll idea works well. Message signs announcing toll rates keep the lane reasonably utilized while keeping numbers down to allow free flow. To the astonishment of many officials, the variable toll is uncontroversial. Motorists love it. Polls show strong support. Although a few naysayers dubbed them 'Lexus lanes' — and higher-income people do use the lanes more — those lower on the ladder also value them, since they are more likely to be penalized for being late for work.

The San Diego approach provides an excellent example of the response of technology to a problem in urban transportation. There exist truly innovative solutions to automobile transit problems that are indicators of where the future will lead us.

# References

Barber, G. (1995), 'Aggregate Characteristics of Urban Travel', in Hanson, S. (ed.), *The Geography of Urban Transportation*, The Guilford Press: New York, pp. 81-99.
Foot, D.K. (1996), *Boom Bust & Echo*, Macfarlane Walter & Ross: Toronto.
Hanson, S. (1995), *The Geography of Urban Transportation*, The Guilford Press: New York, p. 85.
Samuel, P., 'Toll lanes a fast track to easing traffic woes', *Financial Post*, January 23, 1999.
Soberman, R.M. and Hazard, H. (1980), *Canadian Transit Handbook*, University of Toronto/York University Joint Program in Transportation, Toronto.
Transportation Association of Canada Briefing, 'Creating a common vision - the urban mobility challenge', May, 1992.
Transportation Association of Canada Briefing, 'A new vision for urban transportation', March, 1993.
Transportation Association of Canada Briefing, 'Achieving livable cities', November, 1998.

# 8 Retail in the City and the Countryside

Shoppers buy inexpensive goods more frequently, and are not willing to travel far to get them. Shoppers are likely to want to purchase a loaf of bread, a dozen eggs, or a carton of milk quite often, and they do not want to drive a great distance to get them. In fact they are usually willing to pay a little extra to get such perishable items at a convenient location.

Shoppers buy expensive goods infrequently, and are willing to travel farther to get them. Shoppers are unlikely to want to purchase big-ticket items like expensive jewellery, automobiles, or furniture very often. They are probably also more willing to drive a greater distance to shop for such items, and are more likely to be concerned about finding appropriate selection or pricing.

The same ideas that apply to *goods,* apply to *services* as well. For example, when it comes to going to church, attending to a minor medical emergency, or renting a movie, people want the service to be reasonably close-by. People carry out such activities quite often. But when it comes to something like having surgery, visiting a lawyer, or seeing an orthodontist, people are usually quite willing to travel a greater distance. And such activities normally happen less frequently.

Is it possible to predict where consumers will shop, or what kinds of things they will buy? It is obvious from the descriptions above that consumers do alter their patterns of travel according to the type of good or service they are interested in acquiring. We can say a lot about *where* consumers will shop. We know they usually shop at the nearest facility that provides whatever it is that they are looking for. We know also that they are willing to travel farther for some things, more than others. We can also say a lot about the *kinds* of things they want to acquire. We know that everyday, common items are expected to be found close to home, while big-ticket, or specialty items and services can be found almost anywhere.

These ideas are important to retailers. These ideas say that if you are in the business of providing everyday items like movie rentals, perishable goods, or emergency medical services, you'd better be located close to your customer base. At the same time they say that if you are providing rare, specialized, expensive or infrequently purchased items — such as furs, an art gallery, or financial advice — you can get away with locating at a greater distance from your customers. There may be substantial cost savings for some businesses (e.g., furniture or automobile sales) in following the latter approach.

A retailer's ability to satisfy customer demands depends on his or her location within the retail hierarchy. We will see below that there are hierarchies of retail businesses, and that the type of goods or services offered depends upon the level in the hierarchy.

It is not necessary to carry out market surveys to figure out what it is that people want to be able to buy close to home. You need only look at the contents of the nearest convenience store to answer this question. The convenience stores have learned the hard way, through trial and error, what it is that people want to buy in a neighbourhood store. We all know the mix — milk, bread, eggs, basic foodstuffs (with little selection from which to choose), newspapers, movies, soda pop and other children's food products, and so on. Basically the selection consists of things that people run out of, that they are willing to replace immediately at a higher than usual price, together with high markup items that people will buy on a whim such as chocolate bars, chips, or soda pop. For example, if a household runs out of fresh produce or fresh meat, that usually implies a trip to the grocery store. But when a household suddenly runs out of milk, cigarettes, or bread, it usually means a trip to the convenience store. And, in addition to the item that is really needed, people will usually indulge themselves in some other nonessential product, such as a treat or junk-food for themselves or the kids.

What are people willing to travel farther for? Just look at the evidence. What kinds of businesses are *not* located in your neighbourhood? What are the businesses that *make you drive* to get their goods and services? Automobile dealers are an obvious answer, but there are many other such business or service types, for example community colleges or universities, farmers' markets, medical specialists, major sports franchises, and so on. These are the businesses and services that understand you are willing to travel the extra distance in order to take advantage of them. They have more freedom to locate wherever they want or, alternatively, to offer their goods or services at fewer locations, often just one. Importantly, there are extra costs for the consumer. Greater travel means greater expense and more time spent.

However we look at it, the retail system contains provocative and meaningful properties for retailers and consumers alike. The retail hierarchy has implications not only for the competitive success of retailers, but also for the budget-wise consumer. It is important to note that the retail hierarchy exists both within urban areas, and in rural areas. As we shall see, the implications of it for consumer travel and expense are far greater in rural, than in urban areas.

## Shopping and Travel

Imagine the flow of consumers to and from places of shopping during the day. Consider either urban shoppers or those in the countryside. Suppose further that you could observe the flows from the air. You're looking down at shopping consumers as if they are ants on an anthill. What will the flows look like? Is there any pattern to them?

A picture, they say, is worth a thousand words. Lest the reader not yet be convinced of the presence of *patterns* in the daily lives of people, let's begin this chapter with a look at a picture that is over 60 years old, taken from *Market Centers and Retail Location* by B.J.L. Barry and J.B. Parr. Figure 8.1 shows the shopping patterns of farmers for various types of retail goods and services in a rural area of the state of Iowa in 1934. Farmers were asked the simple question "Where do you obtain your.....?" From the farmers' responses, a series of maps were constructed, one for each different type of retail good or service that the farmers were asked about. *The spoke-like lines drawn on each map connect each farmer with the town or village where he obtained his.....?* For example, in Figure 8.1(a) the lines show to which towns farmers travelled to go to church.

What you see in this series of maps is a fascinating progression. In each succeeding map, the pattern of lines gets longer and longer. For example, farmers go to a nearby town to go to church (a). To get groceries, they travel further (b). To see a doctor they travel further still (c). And so on.

It is an interesting picture. The distances keep getting longer until finally we see map (g) representing the sources from which farmers get their daily newspapers. Here you can see the newspapers come from much farther away. In fact, they come from the major cities in the area, namely Omaha, Nebraska on the left, and to the right (off the map) Des Moines, Iowa.

What the maps show quite clearly is that in a *retail* context, consumers are willing to travel different distances to obtain different types of goods and services. The result is that you can literally see different *hierarchical* patterns of flow over the different maps.

142 *Hierarchical Organization in Society*

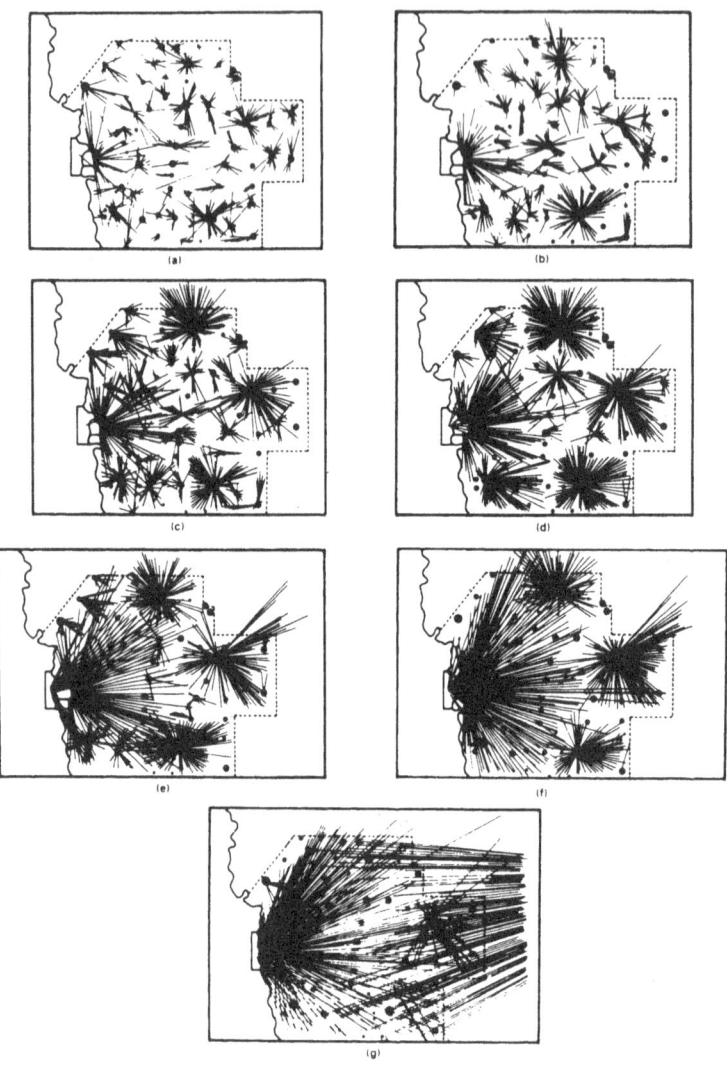

(a) Where farmers went to church (b) grocery stores' market areas (c) Patronage of physicians (d) Where farmers went for legal advice (e) Centers visited to purchase women's coats and dresses (f) Hospital service areas (g) Which center's daily newspapers were read by farmers.

Source: Reprinted with permission from *Market Centers and Retail Location*, 1988.

## Figure 8.1 1934 Map of Where Farmers Got Their Goods and Services

What do these patterns have to do with the everyday retail environment? The answer is "everything." Modern consumers travelling in modern vehicles exhibit the same kinds of travel patterns in their daily shopping trips. If we wish to understand the pattern of retail shopping in the city, it is important to understand consumers and the shopping trips that they make.

**Retail Hierarchies in the City**

The hierarchy of retail centres in an average city is illustrated in Figure 8.2, which is repeated from the introduction. The essential ingredients of this hierarchy are that as we move from top to bottom, there are more shopping opportunities at each level. The average Canadian city usually has one major, downtown shopping area, several major malls, dozens of minor shopping centres, and hundreds of convenience stores or neighbourhood convenience centres. The question now is how does this pattern of retail shopping come into existence? How does the shopping behaviour of thousands of individual consumers cause a retail hierarchy to emerge?

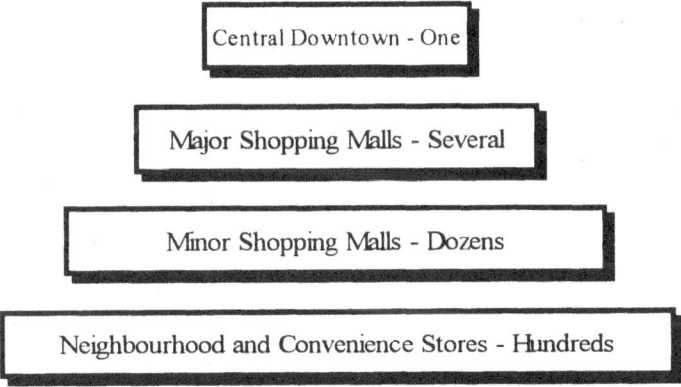

**Figure 8.2 Urban Shopping Hierarchy**

Consider the shopping patterns of a stay-at-home housewife or househusband during a typical span of a few days. Let's suppose on Day 1, our consumer needs milk and bread and so travels to a neighbourhood convenience store. Oftentimes, such a store is located in a neighbourhood "convenience centre" that might also provide gasoline, propane, and so on.

This is the closest shopping opportunity to the home. Normally the local convenience store is able to charge higher prices in exchange for the "convenience" that it provides. This convenience not only includes its closer location but also that it has extended hours of operation.

On Day 2 our consumer needs to make a trip for fast food and a visit to a florist. Along the way he or she visits the bank. This might involve driving to a minor shopping mall that is not too far from the home. The minor mall is referred to as a B- or C-class mall and offers other essential services such as a small drug store, a dry-cleaner, movie rental store, etc.

On Day 3 the consumer desires to go shopping for groceries and children's clothing. Typically this might suggest travel to a major shopping mall, and visiting two of the big "anchor" stores in the mall. In all likelihood the consumer will find it necessary to travel further on Day 3 than on the previous two days. There are fewer major malls, and they tend to be farther apart.

On Day 4 our shopper decides to travel to the downtown-shopping district to shop for adult clothing, in particular, evening or formal wear. This trip covers a still larger distance in order to access some of the "specialty" shops in the downtown.

What this consumer has defined in these daily travels is the hierarchy of retail shopping in the city. Figure 8.3 portrays the hierarchy in visual form. On the first day the *suburban* consumer travels to a neighbourhood center, on the second, a minor shopping mall, on the third, a major shopping mall, and on the fourth, the downtown shopping area. On each day the consumer travels a greater distance than on the day before. On each day, the goods or services that the consumer acquires, also become more specialized or higher in value.

All consumers tend to have the same kinds of shopping habits as our example shopper and, as a result, their collective behaviour creates the type of hierarchy illustrated in Figures 8.2 and 8.3. These travel patterns have taken place in the same basic way as those of the farmers, discussed above. Travel patterns implied by Figure 8.3 are the same as those of the farmers described in Figure 8.1; that is, different goods and services are acquired at different distances. In turn, the travel over those various distances defines a hierarchy of retail shopping.

There would be quite strong links between the map of the retail urban hierarchy (Figure 8.3) and the hierarchy of the urban transportation system described in Chapter 7. In particular, Chapter 7 discussed a hierarchy of roads in the city as consisting of those in Figure 8.4.

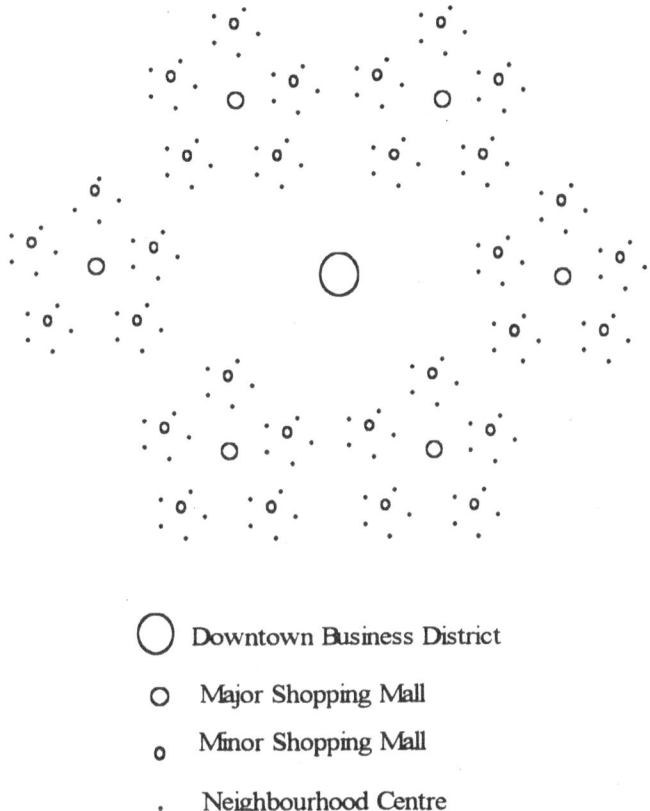

○ Downtown Business District
o Major Shopping Mall
₀ Minor Shopping Mall
. Neighbourhood Centre

**Figure 8.3 Map of the Retail Hierarchy in the City**

The retail hierarchy in Figure 8.3 would tend to correspond quite closely with the hierarchy of roads in Figure 8.4. We could expect to find neighbourhood convenience centres on collector streets, minor malls on major arterials, and major malls on expressways. Although the system of streets is designed primarily to serve rush hour commuters, commercial developers take advantage of the street system by locating shopping facilities at the most *accessible* points within the system, whenever possible. Thus shoppers also benefit from the existence of the urban transport hierarchy.

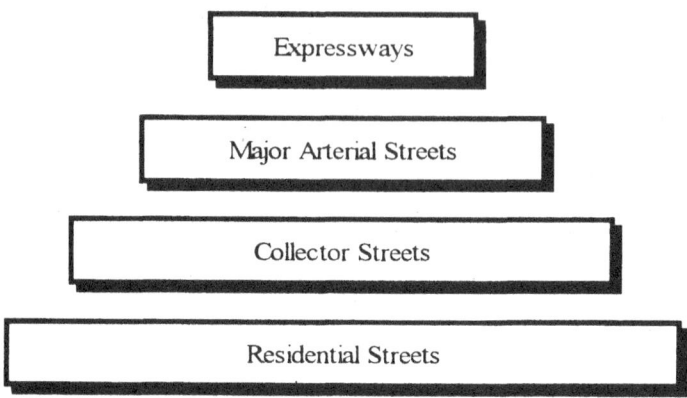

**Figure 8.4 The Hierarchy of Roads in the City**

In any retail market, storeowners strive for an edge — any edge that will give them a foot-up on their competitors. *Location* can sometimes provide such an edge. It is clear in the example above that consumers *expect* certain goods and services to be available at certain convenient distances. If an entrepreneur can satisfy that demand, he or she can be successful. Finding a business opportunity in a mall or plaza location requires the identification of a marketing "niche" that has yet to be filled in that location. It is necessary only to look at other successful entrepreneurs, in other locations, in order to identify market niches that have been profitable elsewhere.

What is interesting about consumer behaviour in the hierarchy of shopping is that at each stage, not only does the consumer travel farther, but also he or she invests more time and money in travelling. The time and travel costs expended to shop for evening or formal wear downtown are far greater than those that are involved in going to the convenience store.

Why is there not a shop that sells evening or formal wear in the neighbourhood mall? Because there are usually not enough customers in a single neighbourhood, or even two or three, to support such a business. It is the type of enterprise that typically requires a market size of the entire city to be successful. The downtown retail area attracts customers from all over the city.

Recognizing that there is a city-wide market for some goods is another way for a potential entrepreneur to identify market niches that have not been filled. In other words, it is necessary to ask what kinds of new businesses could survive if they were the only one, or one of a few, in the city. This is how really specialized stores come into existence. A good example is a store that sells only costumes for special occasions such as

Halloween. Only one or a few such specialized businesses usually can survive in a city. The number will depend upon the size of the city.

**Retail Hierarchies in the Countryside**

The same basic processes that cause retail hierarchies to emerge in the city, will also cause them to develop in rural areas. The main difference is that the pattern of shopping exhibited in the city, will repeat itself in rural areas in a pattern of shopping in *towns, villages, and hamlets* as illustrated in Figure 8.5. Significantly, the retail shopping patterns that exist in rural areas are also slowly causing the decline of smaller communities in those areas.

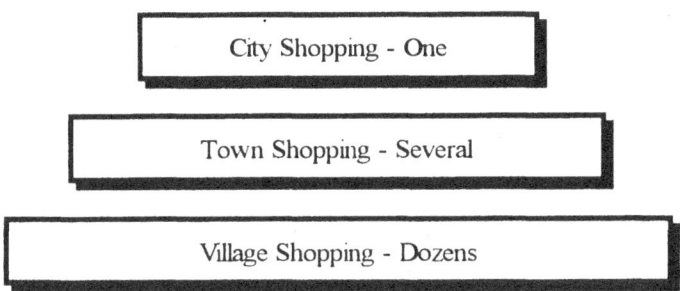

**Figure 8.5 Shopping Hierarchy in a Rural Area**

Consider the rural resident of a small village. What will be the shopping facilities available to such a resident? Just like his counterpart in the city who lives near a neighbourhood convenience store, the resident of a small village will probably find only local "convenience" goods available in his community. There may be a single business that duplicates the services of the neighbourhood store in the city — bread, milk, eggs, candy, soda pop, junk food, movies, newspapers, etc. And just like its counterpart in the city, the village convenience store is able to charge higher prices for the goods it sells. The reason is simply that there is little or no other competition in the village.

If the resident of the village wishes to shop for more specialized goods that are not available at the local convenience store, he or she will likely have to travel to obtain them. In the city this required a trip to the minor shopping mall. In a rural area, this usually means a trip "upward" in the hierarchy, to the next largest community, a town. It is expected that the town will have its own convenience store plus some additional, more specialized goods and services. In the city example, these were fast-food, a florist, and a bank. In a rural area these might be a restaurant, a lumber/hardware store, and a bank. Whatever the particulars of the case, the point is that the rural resident has to drive farther for these more specialized items, just like his urban counterpart. Only, for the rural resident, it is a much longer drive.

Taking the argument to the next level, we can now consider residents of both the village and the town who both wish to obtain still more specialized goods. As in the urban example, consider groceries and children's clothing. In order for the rural residents of towns and villages to obtain good value for the dollar on groceries and children's clothing they are very likely to want to shop in the city. Like their urban counterparts they will journey to major urban shopping malls and/or the downtown area to acquire the goods and services they require. Once again, rural residents have to travel much farther than urban residents to obtain more specialized goods and services. Normally they will compensate for this by making fewer trips but purchasing more, on a given trip. Shopping lists of urban goods are deferred for an all at once shopping trip.

The pattern of the rural shopping hierarchy is illustrated in Figure 8.6. There is a one-to-one correspondence between the hierarchy of communities (Chapter 5) and the hierarchy of shopping. Rural residents, when they wish to consume more specialized goods than are available locally, find it necessary to travel "upward" in the urban hierarchy. This is the same pattern we saw when we looked at travel for educational purposes in the hierarchy of communities in Chapter 4.

**Impacts of the Rural Retail Hierarchy**

What are the consequences of this pattern of shopping by rural residents? There are two, and they are both of importance. First of all, we need to consider the retail history of the towns and villages. Years ago, most of the goods that are now acquired in the city, used to be bought in the local towns and villages. Local merchants were able to compete effectively with the cities when it came to selling goods such as groceries or clothing. Nowadays, of course, any small rural retailers that there are, are forced to compete with "super-stores" and "big box" stores in the city. These have driven many small town businesses out of existence, and that in turn, has hurt the economies of smaller communities. When local residents shop outside the local community, their money does not stay in the local economy.

There is a paradox in this. The paradox is that the more we work to improve highways in rural areas, the more we do to hurt small towns. Every time that the highway to the city gets improved, it makes it that much easier for rural residents to take their business to the city. There is a direct link between improvements to rural transportation routes and the decline of small towns, all across Canada.

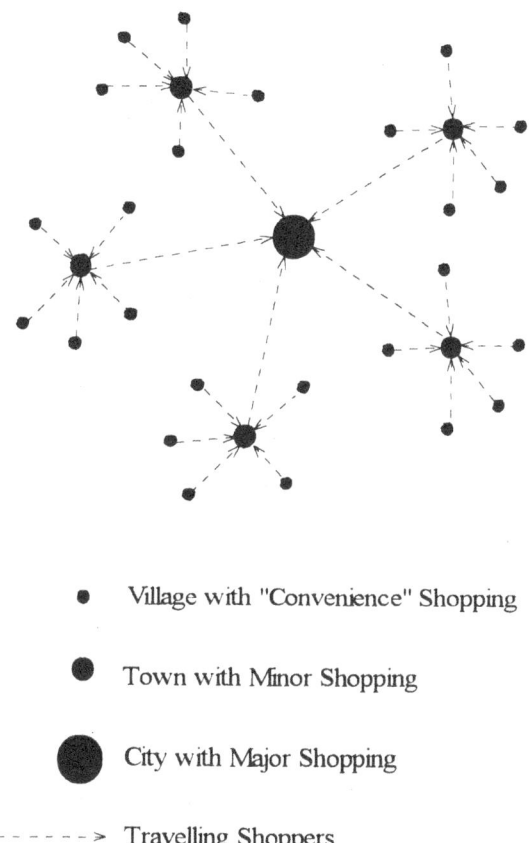

- Village with "Convenience" Shopping
- Town with Minor Shopping
- City with Major Shopping
- - - - - > Travelling Shoppers

**Figure 8.6 Map of Rural Shopping Hierarchy**

A second consequence of the fact that rural residents shop mainly in cities is found in the extra transportation costs born by them. Urban residents can make a trip for more specialized goods or services with relative ease. A trip downtown (in the urban transport hierarchy — see

Chapter 7) is fairly easy for the city resident. The rural dweller, on the other hand, pays a premium cost, in time and gasoline, for those shopping trips to the city.

What are the implications for retailers of the rural hierarchy of retail shopping? We have already indicated what the impact is on smaller, local retail outlets. Many of them have to learn to survive by being "super" convenience stores, with a maximum amount of convenience type goods and services. It is perhaps not enough to offer just the basic necessities. Rather, local merchants have to be more creative in offering a more diverse or eclectic line of merchandise. Many of them have learned by experience that there is strength in diversity.

Those larger retail outlets that currently serve an existing market segment in a local town or village, would do well to compete with larger urban chains by providing *services* that are unavailable in the big city. A small town grocery store, for example, might increase its success by offering things that usually are not found in the city such as individual customer attention, home delivery, or custom meat cutting.

For the retailer in the city, it would be sensible to cater to the rural shopper by "bundling," that is, by providing a bundle of goods and services all under one roof. Many retailers are, of course, already doing this by providing, for example, one-hour photo finishing, a pharmacy, and an automotive centre all in a single establishment. Such retail operations will be especially attractive to out of town shoppers.

The bottom line is that for the rural resident the existence of the retail hierarchy has an important effect on determining the shopping and other patterns of rural life. If consumers want to acquire more than is available in the local community, whether it is retail goods or medical services, they need to make their way to higher levels in the hierarchy of communities. This is a daily way of life for rural residents — they constantly travel through, and deal with, the extra travel and extra problems that are part and parcel of the rural hierarchy.

**Rural Communities in Decline**

The point was made in Chapter 5 that farms in rural areas are getting larger but fewer in numbers. As a consequence it was argued that as the size of the rural population base declines, that local, small town businesses will suffer. The end result was said to be the "erosion" of the bottom levels of the community of hierarchies. We can see the same pressures and forces at work in the retail hierarchy as well.

Retail businesses in the countryside are suffering a triple blow. Not only is there the problem of declining population size as a result of changes in the farming industry, but there is also the additional and growing problem of competition with retailers in larger urban centres. As we have seen here, the geographic make-up of the retail system in rural areas encourages people to shop in communities larger than their own. It was true in 1934 (see Figure 8.1) and is still true today. At the same time, economic forces compel retailers to locate in larger communities where they know the chances of success are better.

What does the future hold? We have seen several forces at work against small rural communities, namely:

- Fewer, larger farms and therefore declining rural farm population
- Retail shopping by rural residents in larger communities and therefore declining customer base for small town businesses
- New and improved transportation systems, leading to more shopping in large communities by rural residents.

The combination of these factors is leading to the erosion of the smaller communities at the base of the hierarchy of communities. It is important to make note of the fact that these changes are affecting primarily *small* and isolated rural communities. Moderately sized communities are withstanding these forces of erosion and in most cases are holding their own, or growing, as a result of their still viable place in the hierarchy of communities (see Chapter 5).

## Retail Strategies

One of the most difficult decisions a business owner has to make is with respect to location. Imagine that you yourself are going to open a new business, the one of which you have always dreamed. One of your first and biggest problems will be to decide the question of *where* the business should be located. A good location can mean large numbers of customers, huge sales potential, and the success of the venture. A poor location can lead to poor customer flows, disappointing sales, and the failure of the enterprise. Moreover, the choice of a store location is a weighty decision that has long term consequences. A business can always match a competitor's prices, promotional campaigns, or services. However, if a competitor has a better *location* it will be difficult to compete with that.

We have seen here that, just like people who live in cities, businesses have a tendency to cluster together location-wise. Why is this so? What are the benefits of businesses locating close to one another? If you were opening a new business wouldn't you prefer to be *far away* from your competition? What are the advantages and disadvantages of particular location strategies?

With the exception of the single neighbourhood convenience store, we have seen that businesses and services in the retail hierarchy have a strong tendency to locate near to one another in malls. What is the popularity of malls? According to *Location Strategies for Retail and Service Firms* by A. Ghosh and S. McLafferty there are several reasons why businesses prefer mall locations. Clustered shopping opportunities encourage *multipurpose* shopping trips, that is, trips where the consumer carries out several purchases or errands in a single trip. An example might be a trip to the drugstore that is combined with a visit to a bank, a florist, and a video store. When consumers wish to be efficient in their daily travels they tend to undertake multiple-purpose-shopping trips. If a large number of consumers are carrying out multipurpose shopping trips that will increase the volume of shoppers in the mall.

Greater numbers of shoppers means more business for everyone. If neighbouring stores in a mall are related to each other they all tend to help each other. For example, a paint store, a wallpaper store, and a drapery shop would draw similar customers and would benefit each other by being located close together.

Large department stores in malls, known as "anchor" stores, tend to draw large numbers of consumers and therefore draw more customers to the mall in general. Small specialty stores benefit from the presence of large department stores as a result of multipurpose shopping trips. Consumers who are patronizing the large anchor store will tend to patronize the smaller stores located nearby.

Surprisingly, stores that sell similar or competing products often tend to locate near to one another. For example, you might expect shoe stores to stay away from each other when they choose locations. Instead they always seem to locate in clusters in malls. The reason for this is that they wish to take advantage of the fact that large numbers of customers will be drawn to the *cluster* of shoe stores because it is convenient for them to comparison shop. This is a good example of "co-opetition," that is, a system where there is cooperation among competitors.

Malls, as we have already indicated, increase accessibility. They tend to be located on major arterials or expressways, they usually have a lot of parking, and they tend to be in highly visible locations. Malls attract a lot of customers that individual stores might not. They normally provide a pleasant, indoor, controlled environment, which is attractive to consumers. Sometimes they may go beyond the conventional bounds of customer satisfaction. A recent news report indicated that a major, international airport had experimented with the use of various "pumped-in" pleasing odours in passenger areas. After trying a number of possibilities, including fresh baked bread, they decided ultimately to use the smell of fresh cut grass as the odour of choice. Here is definitely a marketing strategy that malls can be expected to use shortly, if they are not already.

In the hierarchy of malls, including the downtown shopping area, most stores appear to take advantage of the benefits that clustering provides. Moreover, the features of mall locations seem to offset the extra expenses — usually higher rents — that such locations demand.

**Shopping Malls as Hierarchies**

Interestingly we can characterize the very layout of malls and shopping centres as being hierarchical in themselves. Think of the "transportation" systems of the typical shopping mall. We can characterize the parking lots of malls as being similar to residential streets, where individual shoppers leave their individual cars. The flows of pedestrians are "collected" at the mall entrances. In turn the "side streets" or arterials of the mall typically flow into the major "expressway" that runs lengthwise through the main part of the mall. Consumers moving from one part of the mall to another, say from anchor store to anchor store, flow along this expressway that runs the length of the mall. The layout of a typical urban mall illustrates the patterns (Figure 8.7). This is the Yorkdale Mall in Toronto, second in size in Canada only to West Edmonton Mall.

A critical element of all mall designs is to have at least two anchor stores, and preferably more than two. These are always strategically placed at opposite ends of malls to encourage pedestrian traffic and to get it to stream past the smaller specialty stores in the mall. This pattern is illustrated in Figure 8.7, which shows anchor stores at all four corners of a square shaped plan. There is a reason why you always seem to have to walk from one end of the mall to the other. The designers planned it that way.

Interestingly the same hierarchical patterns that can be attributed to the layout of the mall as a whole can also be applied to individual stores. If one considers the layout of a large department store, the hierarchical design patterns are apparent. Congested areas where shelves, racks of goods and customer counters are located, are not intended to improve the flow of traffic. If anything they are designed to impede the flow of people and stimulate "browsing." Just like the mall, however, the store can be described as having secondary aisles as well as major, or primary aisles, each intended to handle appropriate amounts of traffic. A constant element of the layout is also to place displays of merchandise in or near major aisles to slow flows and encourage browsing. Another deliberate part of the browsing design is to create primary and secondary aisles that are circuitous, that do not run directly through the store.

Malls themselves also have interesting design patterns, many of which are apparent in Figure 8.7. One aspect of the pattern is to create primary aisles that do not allow the shopper to see down the entire length of the mall, but rather to see only segments of it at a time. This gives a mall a less cavernous appearance and also makes it seem smaller than it really is. Another design strategy is to avoid the use of windows in order to keep the consumer focused on the shopping experience. Similarly you will not find clocks in a mall. The architects do not want shoppers to be conscious of time and therefore hurrying along. Generally the goal is to keep the customer "immersed" in the mall environment, making the shopping experience more focused, and having fewer intrusions from the outside world.

Many other features of malls are designed simply to create a positive atmosphere that is conducive to shopping. Indirect lighting, soft colours, soft music, pleasant textures in building materials, pools and fountains, greenery, mirrors and glass, brass and wooden accents, artwork, and so on, are all designed to keep the shopper in a positive frame of mind.

Shopping malls are facing stiff new competition these days however. Stand-alone "mega-stores" seem to be presenting a new challenge to the malls. A report by K. Barnett from *CNN Financial Network* indicates that:

> There are fewer department stores to 'anchor' malls, and women are now working more and shopping less. In addition, a creeping sameness to malls across the country is also blamed for a mall malaise sweeping older, smaller shopping centers from Denver to Des Plaines. In their heyday, America's malls were hailed as the 'new Main Street' — a place to shop and socialize. Today, the average shopper spends 20 percent less time per mall visit than she used to, which translates to spending less money. Some developers are fighting back by offering entertainment, food, and even virtual reality. Analysts say the survivors will be mostly super-premium malls, which might even thrive by taking over weaker competitors.

In Canada, the big-box stores are certainly presenting a head-on challenge to the big malls. In fact, the latest trend is towards the development of "super-malls" consisting of *clusters of big-box stores*. Time will tell how the balance tips, but one thing that Canadian indoor malls have in their favour is in their ability to let shoppers get out of the winter weather. This may turn out to be a crucial variable in the future of

Canadian malls as the large market of aging, baby-boom consumers continues its present dominance of the retail market.

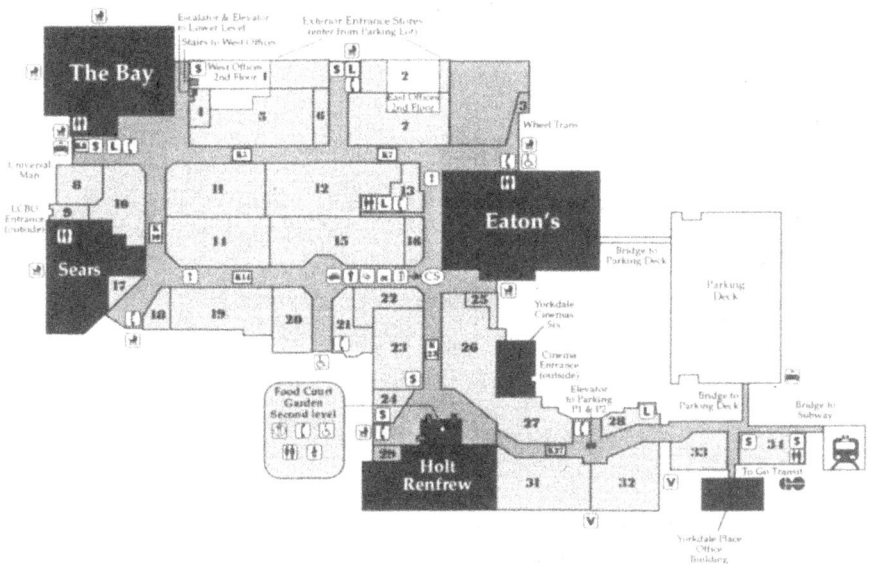

**Figure 8.7 Typical Shopping Mall**

## References

Barrett, K., 'Shopping malls in decline', CNN Financial Network, January 29, 1999.
Berry, B.J.L. and Parr, John B. (1988), *Market Centers and Retail Location: Theory and Applications*, Prentice-Hall, Inc.: New Jersey. p. 12.
Ghosh, A. and McLafferty, S.L., (1987), *Location Strategies for Retail and Service Firms*, D.C. Heath and Company: Toronto.

# 9 Leaving Home

Migration has a significant effect on the quality of peoples' lives. Children grow up, receive an education and move off to new places to seek out employment opportunities. For young adult movers, this can be one of the most exciting times of life. A migration of this sort means challenges and opportunities in what is usually an exciting new environment to investigate and explore. For the parents and family of the young movers, this can present one of the most stressful times of life. Children who have been constant companions of their parents for twenty or so years are gone away suddenly. The nest is empty. The loneliness of the newly quieted house may offset the happiness for the success of the children. Grandchildren may move away with their young parents.

Migration has a direct and emotional impact on almost every person at some time during his or her lifetime. Families and friendships are torn apart by geography, as migrants pursue new opportunities in distant places. Migrations are among the most profound events in people's lives and they usually happen, literally, overnight. Very few people are untouched by the personal turmoil of migration.

Most people that do migrate, move to jobs and, as a consequence, most migrations take place within the context of hierarchies. Whether we look at migrations from community to community, or from country to country, a hierarchical pattern can usually be discerned. Typically these movements are "upward" within a hierarchy, as individuals strive to improve their lot in life. Such migrations are usually for the economic benefit of the individual or the individual family unit. As emotionally difficult as they might be, it is important to appreciate that migrations are usually a part of the "natural" progression of people through hierarchies of economic advancement. In other words, if people wish to "get ahead in life" this often implies the necessity of moving upward through economic and urban hierarchies.

There are real dollar costs associated with long distance migration. Most of the usual kinds of costs involve those for moving, and then those for staying in touch, such as:

- Telephone or other communication costs
- Costs of shipping parcels, mail, etc.
- Costs of occasional return trips.

Most people would probably agree however that these kinds of real dollar costs are relatively incidental as compared to the *emotional costs* of migration. How does one put a dollar value on the joy of being able to hug a grandchild, or not being home for Mom's birthday, or Christmas? The emotional costs of migration are enormous, but are so deeply felt as to be almost impossible to quantify. The emotional costs of moving are born equally by those who are moving away as well as by those who are left behind. Family and friends are separated from one another in the interests of jobs and economic advancement.

Migration, and the splitting apart of family relationships, is as old as the ages. In the recent human history of the planet there has been an endless succession of migrations all over the world. One of the biggest known migrations of all time was the movement of people from Europe to the Americas from the 1500's to the 1900's. Literally millions of people pulled up stakes and moved across the Atlantic Ocean in search of a better economic life. Seldom, however, do we remember the millions of family and friends that were left behind over the years. Imagine all of the personal letters that have flowed across the ocean over the years, and all of the emotion that has been spent, on the human consequences of this historic pattern of migration.

An even more compelling story comes from the history of the Slave trade between Africa and the Americas from the 1400's to the 1800's. Estimates put the number of slaves moved across the Atlantic at up to fourteen million people, where approximately one-quarter died en route. These horrendous numbers illustrate the magnitude and misery of the slave trade, but they also represent the millions of people who were forcefully removed from family and friends, never to be in touch with them again. It is one of the most wrenching stories in the history of humanity.

Canada is a country made up of migrants. In spite of the fact that most people are proud to say that they are Canadians, in every family there is somewhere in the past a history of migration from another part of the world. Even Native peoples have roots in the migration thousands of years ago of their ancestors. At one point in the past, North America was uninhabited, and everyone who now resides here brings with them a legacy of migration.

Although international migration to Canada continues to be important, what currently comes to life as an equally significant focus of interest is the migration of people *within* Canada and North America. As continentalization becomes ever more a key concept in the economic evolution of North America, the migration of people comes to play an ever more important role in Canada and in the continental economy. This book has discussed several times the significance of Canadian integration with the United States and nowhere is this more apparent than with respect to migration to and from the United States.

There are some big issues. Is there a brain drain to the United States? Are we spending millions of dollars to educate young Canadians, only to see them move away to the United States? Is our educational system suffering from a loss of trained professionals? Are there too many migrants being allowed into Canada? Do "foreigners" take jobs away from Canadians? These, and many other important issues, are addressed below.

**Canadians on the Move**

If there is a national hierarchy of migration, it takes place among the *urban* system of communities. As was indicated in Chapter 5, the *provinces* do not lend themselves very well to treatment as a hierarchical system. They represent instead an eclectic collection of boundaries and different population sizes that is more an accident of history than any logical geographical system. Nevertheless, Statistics Canada collects much of its information at the level of the provinces. Accordingly, if we wish to investigate population migration trends in Canada it is useful to look briefly at the provinces. The focus on a hierarchy of flows among communities is reserved for the section that follows this one.

Canadians are a mobile population. According to a Statistics Canada report, 43 percent of Canadians moved between 1991 and 1996. Of those, 23 percent moved within their municipality while the remainder moved either to another municipality or another province. Table 9.1 shows the patterns of migration for each of the provinces and territories for 1991 to 1996. The columns "In-migrants" and "Out-migrants" show the number of people moving into and out of each province over the five-year period. For example, Newfoundland gained 16,225 people, while it lost 39,465. The difference between the "In" and "Out" migration is called the "Net migration" and it is in that that we are most interested. This shows whether a province was "attractive" and gained population, or was "repulsive" and lost population. As an example, consider Newfoundland again which had a net loss of -23,240 migrants. This means that Newfoundland lost over 20,000 people to other provinces.

The column of net migration in Table 9.1 shows that the most attractive province to migrants over the period 1991 to 1996 was British

160 *Hierarchical Organization in Society*

Columbia, with a gain of nearly 150,000 people. This suggests a definite western trend. No other province was a big "winner" of population during the period. The table shows that the largest losers of population were Ontario, followed by Quebec, Newfoundland, Saskatchewan and Manitoba. One of the clearest long-term trends in the net flow of population (not shown in the table) has been for Quebec, which has shown a net loss of people every year since 1976, when the Parti Quebecois was first elected.

**Table 9.1 Net Interprovincial Migration of Population, 1991-1996**

| Province | In-migrants | Out-migrants | Net Migration |
|---|---|---|---|
| Newfoundland | 16,225 | 39,465 | -23,240 |
| Prince Edward Island | 8,945 | 7,485 | 1,460 |
| Nova Scotia | 47,455 | 53,905 | -6,450 |
| New Brunswick | 34,060 | 36,025 | -1,965 |
| Quebec | 68,895 | 106,345 | -37,450 |
| Ontario | 194,030 | 241,040 | -47,010 |
| Manitoba | 43,215 | 62,595 | -19,380 |
| Saskatchewan | 47,520 | 67,295 | -19,775 |
| Alberta | 162,645 | 159,055 | 3,590 |
| British Columbia | 252,625 | 102,680 | 149,945 |
| Yukon | 5,955 | 5,285 | 670 |
| Northwest Territories | 8,715 | 9,100 | -395 |

Source: Statistics Canada, *The Daily*, April, 14, 1998.

The pattern of flows from province to province is an interesting one. As Statistics Canada indicates:

> The census showed that 89,500 people moved from Ontario to British Columbia between 1991 and 1996, the largest flow between any two regions. The second largest was the flow of 83,800 people from Alberta to British Columbia, while the third largest was the movement of 66,100 people from Quebec to Ontario. In turn, about 44,800 people from Ontario took up residence in Quebec.

There are many other trends of interest in patterns of province to province migration. Not surprisingly, young people are the most mobile in the country. Men and women between 25 and 29 years of age are the most mobile group in the country. These are the peak years when young people move in search of employment opportunities. In the age range 15 to 24, women are more likely to move than men. This, says Statistics Canada, reflects in part the fact that women in this age range tend to have male partners in the 25 to 29 age group.

Notably, the number of anglophones (English-speaking people) moving out of Quebec continued to be strong. Statistics Canada reports that of the 37,450 people that moved out of the province, almost two-thirds were anglophones. This compares dramatically with the provincial proportion of anglophones, which is just nine percent.

Education is another factor that has a strong link to migration. Statistics Canada reports that "University graduates with a bachelor's degree or higher were far more mobile than the overall population." With respect to migration within hierarchies, this suggests that those with a university degree are seeking *more specialized* job opportunities, and therefore are more likely to have to move, or move farther. As will be argued again below, people move for jobs.

**The Hierarchy of Migration**

In order to be able to answer questions like those posed in the introduction it is first useful to examine migration in greater detail in order to see what kinds of patterns emerge. It is the contention of this book that patterns of migration within Canada, to the United States, and to and from the rest of the world, are best understood as taking place within national and international hierarchies.

The idea that migration takes place in a hierarchical form is certainly not new. In fact, when we look at the history of the study of migration one of the earliest ideas put forward was that human migration follows the pattern of the hierarchy of communities. As far back as 1885 a British scientist, E.G. Ravenstein was studying recorded registers of migrants within England when it came to his attention that there was a certain regularity or pattern to the flows. Ravenstein described one of his observations roughly as follows: Movement takes place from rural areas to urban areas, and is made in stages.

The gist of Ravenstein's argument is that cities grow by attracting migrants from surrounding rural areas. As those migrants move out of rural areas they are replaced by migrants from still more remote areas. Thus

162  *Hierarchical Organization in Society*

there is a pattern of migration that takes place in "stages" upwards in the hierarchy of communities. Migrants from hamlets will move to villages, migrants from villages will move to towns, and migrants from towns will, in turn, move to cities. Thus the migration of people follows the hierarchy of communities and, as people advance forward economically, they also advance upwards in the hierarchy of cities. The pattern is illustrated in Figure 9.1.

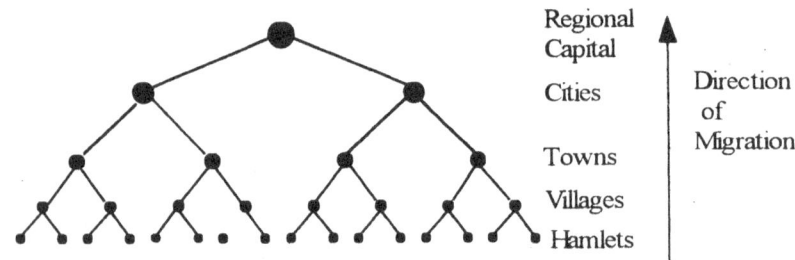

Figure 9.1  The Hierarchy of Community Migration

Why does migration follow the hierarchy of communities? One idea is that as an individual moves upward in the hierarchy of communities they will gain more information about jobs and opportunities at the next higher level. This makes common sense. If a person lives closer to a larger community, they will tend to get more information from it, for example, in the form of newspapers, visits with friends, etc.

There is another good reason to believe that migrants tend to move from smaller to larger communities. This line of thought says simply that, the bigger the community, the more likely there are to be jobs there. J. Vanderkamp, quoted in *Intermetropolitan Migration in Canada*, puts this argument in the form of an example. Vanderkamp suggests that the size of the destination community could play a role:

> for example, consider the choice faced by a potential migrant in London (Ontario) between Windsor and Toronto, which are roughly equi-distant destinations. Would not the size of the Toronto labour market make that a more attractive destination than Windsor, all other things equal?

Looking at Figure 9.1, the argument would be that as we move upwards in the hierarchy of communities, there are more jobs available at every successive level. Thus most migrants would keep moving upwards to larger communities.

It is possible to imagine this hierarchical migration sequence happening in the real world. Consider the situation of an entrepreneur who starts a small business in a small community. If the business is growing, it may be only natural for it, and its employees, to continue to move to larger and larger communities as it expands. Similarly, one can imagine an employee of a company being given promotions, where each promotion involves moving to a larger community than the one before. Ultimately, the employee would hope to be promoted to company headquarters, which as we saw in Chapter 5, is very likely to be located in one of the largest cities in the hierarchy. As a further example, consider the young person who moves from the small town to the big city to obtain a college or university education. As the saying goes, once the young person has experienced the "bright lights" of the big city, it is difficult to get them to go back to a small town lifestyle.

Chapters 5 and 8 make the point that smaller communities at the bottoms of hierarchies are in decline, and that the bottoms of the hierarchies are dissipating. Here again in this chapter we see forces at work that will serve to erode the base of the hierarchy of communities. At the same time that the rural farm base is disappearing, and rural stores are losing their customers, so too are migrants tending to move away from smaller communities and toward larger ones. Jobs are the big attraction. Typically, young residents of smaller communities need to look to larger communities to find employment. Smaller communities suffer as a result. There is no one to blame for this. As we have seen, it is simply the nature of urban systems to evolve in this manner.

## Migration among Canadian Cities

In spite of the arguments made above about migration within the hierarchies of communities, the actual flows of migrants among the system of Canadian cities do not support entirely the idea that migration usually takes place in the direction of larger communities. Statistics Canada (February, 1999) published facts and figures on the migration of people among Canada's major cities. While some of these numbers support the idea that people move upward through the hierarchy of communities, others do not.

Table 9.2 illustrates the patterns of *migration* among Canadian cities. The column on the left contains those cities (called Census Metropolitan Areas) that gained migrants over the year 1996 to 1997 while the column on the right lists those cities that lost migrants. It can be seen that more cities gained migrants than lost them, indicating that most cities at the top levels of the hierarchy of communities got larger as the result of migration.

**Table 9.2 Net Migration for Canadian Cities, 1996-1997**

| Cities that gained population | | Cities that lost population | |
|---|---|---|---|
| Toronto | 76,601 | Winnipeg | -4,101 |
| Vancouver | 45,638 | Sudbury | -1,462 |
| Calgary | 21,232 | Regina | -1,330 |
| Montreal | 6,537 | St. John's | -1,030 |
| Edmonton | 6,124 | Thunder Bay | -879 |
| Hamilton | 5,893 | Chicoutimi-Jonquiere | -683 |
| Kitchener | 4,884 | Saint John | -669 |
| Ottawa-Hull (Ontario part) | 4,525 | Trois-Rivieres | -240 |
| Windsor | 3,513 | Ottawa Hull (Quebec part) | -87 |
| Oshawa | 3,027 | Quebec | -7 |
| St. Catharines-Niagara | 2,682 | | |
| Halifax | 2,001 | | |
| London | 1,523 | | |
| Victoria | 906 | | |
| Sherbrooke | 731 | | |
| Saskatoon | 344 | | |

Source: Statistics Canada, *The Daily*, February 17, 1999.

The patterns show that Toronto, Vancouver and Calgary were the biggest "winners" of migrants, while only Winnipeg had a substantial loss of population due to out-migration. Clearly the conclusion to be drawn is that although not all cities are acting as magnets to migrants, most are. It may be that the negative aspects of cities — crime, pollution, and congestion — are causing some urban places in Canada to have a loss of population due to out-migration. This leads one to suspect that it may be the mid-sized communities, or those small ones near to urban areas, that are leading the way in attracting migrants. This argument is consistent with the ideas advanced in Chapter 5. It is important to clarify that, in spite of the *migration* numbers, almost all of those cities did grow in population size, as a result of births and foreign immigration. Table 9.3 shows the percentage rates of growth of major Canadian cities between 1991 and 1996.

With the exceptions of Chicoutimi and Saint John (which both recorded minor declines) it can be seen that all other Canadian cities are experiencing growth.

What is even more startling is the growth being experienced by smaller municipalities. Table 9.4 shows the rates of growth and population size for Canada's fastest growing communities (municipalities with over 5000 people).

Notable on the list in Table 9.4 are resort communities such as Whistler, Canmore, and Wasaga Beach. Interestingly the largest of these fast growing communities is Kanata, Ontario, home to many of Canada's high tech industries.

**Continental and International Migration among Cities**

It was said earlier that it is the contention of this book that patterns of migration are best understood as taking place within national and international economic hierarchies. We should expand the scope of our look at Canadian cities then, and consider instead patterns of migration among cities at a grander scale. The process is the same as that described above, that is, that migration should proceed upward in the hierarchy of cities. Figure 9.2 provides a picture of the expected pattern of migration among cities at the national, continental, and international scales.

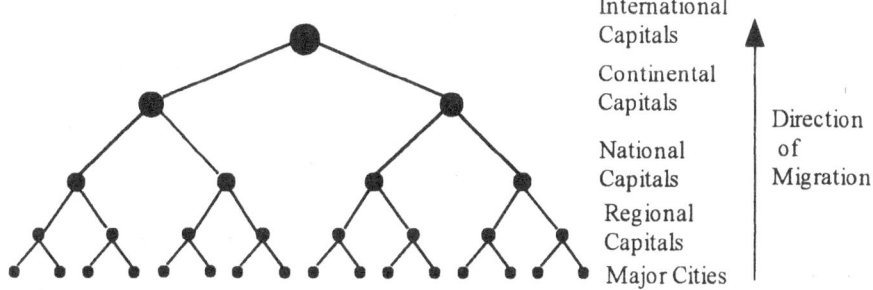

**Figure 9.2 The Global Hierarchy of City Migration**

166  *Hierarchical Organization in Society*

## Table 9.3 Percentage Rates of Growth of Major Canadian Cities

| City | % Population Change |
|---|---|
| Vancouver | 14.3 |
| Oshawa | 11.9 |
| Toronto | 9.4 |
| Calgary | 9.0 |
| Kitchener | 7.4 |
| Ottawa-Hull | 7.3 |
| Windsor | 6.3 |
| Victoria | 5.7 |
| Sherbrooke | 4.7 |
| London | 4.5 |
| Quebec | 4.1 |
| Hamilton | 4.1 |
| Saskatoon | 3.8 |
| Montreal | 3.7 |
| Halifax | 3.7 |
| Trois-Rivieres | 2.7 |
| Edmonton | 2.6 |
| St. Catharines-Niagara | 2.2 |
| Sudbury | 1.8 |
| St. John's | 1.3 |
| Winnipeg | 1.0 |
| Regina | 1.0 |
| Thunder Bay | 0.5 |
| Saint John | -0.1 |
| Chicoutimi-Jonquiere | -0.3 |

Source: Statistics Canada, *The Daily*, April 15, 1997.

## Table 9.4 Fastest Rates of Growth for Canadian Municipalities

| Municipality with population over 5,000 | 1996 Population | 1991 Population | % Change |
|---|---|---|---|
| Whistler | 7,172 | 4,459 | 60.8 |
| Saint-Colomban | 5,569 | 3,638 | 53.1 |
| University Endowment Area, B.C. | 6,833 | 4,534 | 50.7 |
| Courtenay | 17,335 | 11,698 | 48.2 |
| Canmore | 8,354 | 5,681 | 47.1 |
| Saint-Emile | 9,889 | 6,916 | 43.0 |
| Cochrane | 7,424 | 5,267 | 41.0 |
| Sainte-Catherine | 13,724 | 9,805 | 40.0 |
| Masson-Angers | 7,989 | 5,753 | 38.9 |
| La Plaine | 14,413 | 10,576 | 36.3 |
| Wasaga Beach | 8,698 | 6,457 | 34.7 |
| Notre-Dame-de-l'Ile-Perrot | 7,059 | 5,261 | 34.2 |
| Lavaltrie | 5,821 | 4,365 | 33.4 |
| Saint-Lin | 9,336 | 7,029 | 32.8 |
| Ladysmith | 6,456 | 4,875 | 32.4 |
| Qualicum Beach | 6,728 | 5,137 | 31.0 |
| Blainville | 29,603 | 22,679 | 30.5 |
| Val-des-Monts | 7,231 | 5,551 | 30.3 |
| Central Okanagan | 22,901 | 17,770 | 28.9 |
| Parksville | 9,472 | 7,381 | 28.3 |
| Kanata | 47,909 | 37,344 | 28.3 |
| Airdrie | 15,946 | 12,456 | 28.0 |
| Varennes | 18,842 | 14,758 | 27.7 |
| Nanaimo | 19,930 | 15,619 | 27.6 |
| Saint-Jean-Chrysostome | 16,161 | 12,717 | 27.1 |

Source: Statistics Canada, *The Daily*, April 15, 1997.

168  *Hierarchical Organization in Society*

It can be seen that Figure 9.2 is the same as Figure 9.1 except that the *size* of the system is changed. Now we are looking at migration upwards through a system of very large cities, all the way up to cities whose reach is at the international scale.

It is difficult to create an actual hierarchy of international cities, because their population size does not necessarily measure their economic "clout." For example, although Sao Paulo (Brazil), Bombay (India), and Shanghai (China) are among the world's biggest cities in population size, they do not carry the same economic impact as do the "smaller" cities of New York, London, or Paris. Which city is at the "top" of the global hierarchy? New York? Tokyo? The answer depends on how we measure it. The point, however, is that once we strip away political and trade barriers, international patterns of trade and migration should start to appear like those illustrated in Figure 9.2. The patterns should be truly global, and upwards flows of people should take place irrespective of borderlines.

How does Canada fit into the international scheme of cities? Clearly Toronto and Montreal should fall into the class of major cities in the world. In order to demonstrate the validity of this point, Figure 9.3 presents them in juxtaposition with their major American cousins. Once again it can be seen that Toronto and Montreal hold a very strong place within the hierarchy of Canadian and American cities and, judged by their size, should be considered to be "major cities" at the global scale.

**Figure 9.3  The Hierarchy of Major American and Canadian Cities**

Given their level in the international hierarchy of cities, both Toronto and Montreal should be considered to be well positioned within the international hierarchy of migration. As major cities they should be "destinations" for some of those moving upward in the system of cities, and at the same time they are "jumping off points" for those who are moving to higher levels in the hierarchy of communities.

We have seen, as well, that there is expected to be a correspondence between the hierarchy of communities and the hierarchy of corporations. Bigger companies will tend to have locations or head offices in larger cities. For example, Toronto houses most of the corporate headquarters in Canada while New York houses most of the corporate headquarters in the United States. Migrants who aspire to move upwards in the economic or corporate worlds will, almost of necessity, move upwards in the urban world as well.

It could be said that Toronto and Montreal used to be "end-points" in a corporate world that was confined largely within Canada. Usually Canada was considered to be little more than the home of American "branch plants," and thus the corporate hierarchy in Canada ended at Bay Street. However with the advent of the Free Trade Agreement (FTA) and the North American Free Trade Agreement (NAFTA), the corporate perspective in Canada now extends well beyond the $49^{th}$ parallel.

As corporations make their way across the border, so too will individuals. We can expect to see a pattern, more and more, of Canadians heading south, not just for vacations, but to advance their lives and their careers. "Snowbirds" will be joined by "sunbirds." Newly defined in this book, sunbirds are considered to be those young, ambitious, entrepreneurial Canadians who "fly" to the United States to reside permanently.

## The Brain Drain - Canada as a Competitor in the International Jobs Hierarchy

Corporate integration with the United States is leading ultimately to demographic integration as well. As the impediments to trans-border migration fall, more and more Canadian sunbirds will take advantage of the new economic and career opportunities that become available to them in the United States. This means wonderful new possibilities for individual Canadians, but it also means a formidable task for Canada, as the best, the brightest, and the most entrepreneurial seek out new challenges in the "land of opportunity."

Lest the reader believe that Canada is still economically a "hewer of wood, and drawer of water," we should make it clear that the economy is changing. In particular, there is a growing emphasis on high technology and all that goes with it. The *Globe and Mail's Technology.com* reports, that in a speech to a group of IT (information technology) executives in 1998, Finance Minister Paul Martin indicated that, "The growth and output of

Canada's high-technology industry is now proceeding at a rate twice the size of the economy as a whole", pointing out that there has been a fundamental shift in the nature of our economy. For example, in 1980, he said, 60 percent of Canada's exports were represented by basic commodities. Today, that number is less than 35 percent. "What that tells you is that the perception of the Canadian economy [being dependent on its natural resources] is very much backed by myth and does not conform to the reality that we are the world leaders in the new economy."

A common point of view in Canada is that there is a "brain drain" from Canada to the United States. News reports and companies alike deplore the loss of educated, young Canadians to the United States. Typically the emphasis is especially on graduates in programs of science, technology, engineering and computing. The point is made that Canada is already suffering shortages in these crucial areas, even if there were no ongoing losses to the United States. Brain drain alarmists raise the warning call, demanding that governments do something to stem the tide.

There are several reasons cited for the brain drain. Usually the United States is considered to have the upper hand in a number of ways, namely:

- Higher salaries
- Better facilities and laboratories
- Employer reputation
- Lower tax rates
- Higher job creation
- Higher starting salaries
- Stronger dollar
- Better weather.

In the media, stories abound of individuals being enticed away by higher salaries in the United States. Here's just one anecdotal example from a 1998 article in *The Globe's Technology.com*:

> As director of the school of computer science at McGill University in Montreal, Prof. Therien has to compete with U.S. industry every bit as much as Canadian businesses do when it comes to hiring IT faculty.
>
> "I have four positions open in my department now," says Prof. Therien.
>
> Wonder why? Prof. Therien had a recent strong candidate in mind, a post-doctoral student from McGill whom he could short-list for an appointment with a starting salary of $52,000, "or maybe I can go to $57,000 or $58,000 if you twist my arm."

Leaving Home 171

You'd have had to twist Prof. Therien's arm to the point of intervention by Amnesty International before he could match U.S. conditions. Thank you very much, responded the alumnus, but he now had a position at a major IT manufacturer in Portland, Ore., at a salary of over $100,000 U.S. with bonuses layered on top of that.

A recent survey by the Canadian Advanced Technology Association (CATA) indicates that 77 percent of graduates in IT are willing to move south and that twenty percent believe their salaries will be lower if they stay in Canada.

What are we to do? How is Canada supposed to respond to this dilemma? The usual response is to suggest several courses of action, including:

- Lower taxes
- Increase university spending and enrollments
- Invest more in research facilities and laboratories
- Undertake joint initiatives between the university and private IT sectors.

Given the Free Trade Agreement (FTA) between Canada and the United States there has been a relaxation on the traditional restrictions placed on migration between the countries. This is as it should be. If there is going to be an economic union, then citizens on either side of the border should be freer to pursue their career or entrepreneurial goals wherever they choose. If any one thing is clear, it is that the solution to the brain drain problem is certainly not to be found in placing restrictions on the freedom of individuals to migrate. Canada is a country where one is free to pursue one's ambitions. If a migration is part and parcel of that pursuit, then that is taken as accepted. People are free to pursue their dreams within Canada wherever that may take them. No one would argue, for example, that "Yes, you are free to pursue your dream." but, "Only insofar as it doesn't require you to move to Calgary." In fact, the freedom to move within Canada is guaranteed in the Canadian Charter of Rights and Freedoms.

What are we to do then? What is the solution to the problem of the shortage of skilled workers in Canada? The answer is to be found in looking at Canada within the international economic hierarchy, and choosing a course of action that is consistent with Canada's place in the hierarchy. It was noted in the introduction that the point of view put forth by brain drain alarmists, ignores the fact that Canada is part of the international community of science and engineering.

The flip side to the "Brain Drain" is referred to as the "Brain Gain." The idea is that Canada is also an *importer* of skilled workers and that such immigrants help to offset the losses of Canadian trained, skilled workers to the United States. The question is whether the flows into Canada are adequate to offset the flows out of Canada. Given the international hierarchical position of Canada, there should be more flows of skilled workers into than out of the country. According to a study by Ivan Fellegi, Canada's chief statistician and head of Statistics Canada, the numbers bear out this point of view. Fellegi is quoted in the *Globe's Technology.com* article by Edward Greenspon entitled, *Why some of our brightest are heading south*:

> In a presentation to university administrators last fall entitled Brain Drain or Brain Gain, he recounted that between 1990 and 1994 Canada lost an average of 834 engineers, computer specialists and natural scientists to the United States and gained 201 for a net loss of 633 people — a reasonably stable figure during the past decade.
>
> At the same time, though, the worldwide inflow of knowledge workers into Canada far outstripped the emigrants — by a ratio of about 4 to 1 between 1986 and 1996, he said.
>
> Dr. Fellegi concluded that it is a myth that Canada is losing its best and brightest to the United States.

Fellegi's conclusions are consistent with Canada's place in the international hierarchy of migration. Yes, Canada *should* suffer a net loss of skilled workers to the United States. The United States represents a market for skilled employees that is ten times bigger than that of Canada, so of course it will be able to attract more skilled professionals than it sends out. The reader will remember an example used above in the context of city-to-city migration (Chapter 9). It asked the reader to consider the choice faced by a potential migrant leaving London (Ontario), and choosing between Windsor and Toronto, which are equi-distant from London. It was said that the larger Toronto labour market would make it a more attractive destination for the migrant, simply because of its larger size. The same principle applies here. Movement for jobs tends to be "upward" in the hierarchy of cities and countries, and the Free Trade Agreement has made Canada and the United States unified parts of a single system of migration.

At the same time Canada, as one of the more attractive destinations in the world, should also expect to attract more than its fair share of skilled workers from other places in the world. In the international hierarchy of "attractive" countries Canada would be somewhere near the top. Perhaps it is not so powerful a "magnet" to migrants as the United States, but certainly it has considerable drawing power. This should mean that skilled professionals from all over the world are drawn to Canada as a desirable place to live and work.

A recent study by Statistics Canada entitled, "Brain Drain or Brain Gain? What do the Data Say?" comes to the conclusion that Canada is a net importer of educated and talented people from around the world. In answer to the question, "Is there a brain drain to the U.S.?" the study answers:

> Yes, but this drain is offset by a brain gain from all over the world, especially in the high-tech sector, where the gain is many times greater than the drain. Given the severe shortage of workers in the high-tech sector, this gain is making an important contribution in meeting the high demand.

According to Don DeVoretz, a C. D. Howe Institute expert on immigration, we should consider ourselves involved in a "trade in brains" rather than a brain drain. According to his calculations (quoted in the Greenspon article cited above), Canada is a "net importer" of brains from the rest of the world. While we educate students for the U.S. market, other countries educate students for us.

> In the 15 years up to 1994, the rest of the world spent $14.1-billion on the postsecondary education of Canadians whereas Canada spent $9.1-billion educating people who left for greener pastures, primarily the United States.

To be fair, it should be pointed out that in spite of the discussion of the brain drain, the majority of students educated in Canada do stay in Canada. This says that in spite of the list of factors cited above, that make the United States attractive, there are still many Canadian educated students who prefer to stay at home to work. Not surprisingly, students usually cite quality of life factors, especially crime and Medicare, as important considerations. What surveys do not show or measure however is probably the most important factor — the emotional cost of moving across the border and giving up being "a Canadian." It is hard to put a finger on precisely what that is, but people understand what it means.

## Migration from Canada to the Rest of the World

International boundaries are purely arbitrary. What we are seeing emerge presently is the true global hierarchy of international relations based on economic relationships. This is the new economic reality within which corporations must learn to exist. As was indicated earlier, there are ongoing international negotiations led by the United States in which there is a serious push towards true international free trade. Canada will have to learn to compete internationally and will also have to learn to compete at home without the benefits of trade barriers and protectionism. With the international fall of socialism and communism, the capitalist form of free enterprise is sweeping the globe. Even the last bastions of communism, such as China, are beginning to participate in the international capitalist economy. There are even predictions that new, giant global corporations will soon come to have more international power and control than countries. This is a world in which unfettered hierarchies of trade and migration span the globe.

As corporations move to make their operations global, so too will population migration become a more global phenomenon. It will become ever more the norm for employees of companies to be expected to work and live abroad. There are literally thousands of examples of Canadian corporations currently working overseas, and tens of thousands of Canadian employees working with them. It should be expected that the trend will be for more of these relocations. It should also be expected that more of them will become permanent ones. At the moment, most employees head overseas with the expectation that the transfer is a temporary one. But as the trade barriers continue to fall, and as increased numbers of people get used to the idea of living abroad, we should expect more Canadians to elect to make these relocations long term.

We spoke above about the historical large-scale migration of people from Europe to the Americas. That scale of migration was appropriate to the time and era in which it occurred. Steamships and railroads dominated the transportation scene. At the present "turn of the century", the international migration trend is continuing, but now the scale is a global one and international corporations are dictating the pattern of migration. Intercontinental air travel, and global communications, have shrunk the size of the world. People and places are "closer" together than they ever have been before. This is the "new geography" of the hierarchical age and there is no turning back from the course that it has set.

If someone needs evidence of globalization, they need look no farther than the clothes on their back or the food in their cupboards. More than ever, the things we consume come from around the globe. People's tastes have internationalized. No longer are people satisfied with just locally produced products. An excellent demonstration of this is obvious in any large grocery store. Only a few years ago those stores were stocked primarily with food and products that were produced locally or nationally. Nowadays, however, those shelves are stocked with exotic and specialized goods from all over the world. People are becoming more international in their preferences, and their tastes have become truly global.

We should not only expect to see international migration taking place at the behest of corporations. We should also see more and more that individual entrepreneurs will take advantage of unprecedented opportunities in global markets. We should anticipate freer international flows of business ideas, information and people. We should expect to see more migrants who are willing to take on the financial risks, and opportunities, offered by the global marketplace.

As population growth slows in the developed countries of the world, the less developed regions become the source of new markets of growth for businesses and entrepreneurs. There are huge "markets" in the world, in China in particular, that global Canadian corporations are anxious to tap into. As they do, they will find it ever more necessary to have their employees live and work in those foreign lands.

## Migration from the Rest of the World to Canada

Canadians come from hearty stock. As was said above, all Canadians have ancestors that at one time or another had the temerity to pull up stakes and move half way around the world to try and better themselves. Migration takes courage, boldness and confidence. There are always risks associated with migration and for all the success stories we see, there are countless others who fail in the attempt to migrate to a better life and end up back where they started, or worse off then before. But most Canadian families have paid the emotional price and have made a success of themselves through migrating.

Most of the large number of migrants to Canada came in the past, when "the gates were open." In fact, prior to World War I there were no migration restrictions in place anywhere in the world. People were free to move where they wanted to, primarily because large-scale international transportation had not yet come into existence. Since that time, of course, migration restrictions have been put into place in many countries.

It is interesting that when we talk about the migration of Canadians to other countries, that we never have to talk about restrictions on that immigration. By and large Canadians are free to move to whatever countries they so desire. But consider the reverse situation, that is, are people from the rest of the world who wish to move into Canada, free to do so? The answer is no. What is the difference?

Basically we can sort all of the countries in the world into two groups, those that are highly attractive to migrants and those that are not. For the most part, it is the developed nations of the world that fall into the attractive class. They are known around the world as having healthy economies and are regarded as good places, not only to live, but to get ahead in life. Places, if you will, where people can live out "the American dream" and make a life for themselves through hard work and ambition. Then there are the less developed countries of the world. Many of these can be regarded as good places to live if you are already well off financially. In fact, it is often possible to live in luxury on what would be a modest income, in other parts of the world. But for most people these less developed countries are places from which they desire to escape. These unattractive countries do not require restrictions on immigration. There is no demand for what they have to offer.

Canada is one of the attractive destinations. Canadians should feel both lucky and privileged to reside in one of the most desirable destinations in the world. There is an international demand for what Canada has to offer and as a consequence, like most developed nations, Canada finds it necessary to put in place restrictions on immigration. These restrictions vary from year to year but are usually in the neighbourhood of about 200,000 immigrants per year. That may seem like a lot but if you compare it to Canada's population size of about thirty million it turns out to be less than one percent of the total.

How many immigrants should we allow in? What are the ideal numbers? On the one hand it should be realized that the worldwide demand to enter Canada is enormous. One can only imagine what would happen if we opened the doors wide open and let in as many people as wanted to come. We could expect that the country, and its social, economic, medical and educational institutions would literally be swamped with new arrivals. So we do need to have controls, if only to pace the arrival of immigrants to the rate at which the country can absorb them. But how much is enough?

Like many of the developed countries in the world, Canada has a "population problem" of its own. The problem is not an overabundance of people but rather an inadequate supply of them. There is a delicate balance between growth too fast, from opening the doors wide, and growth not fast enough, from Canadian birth rates that are not high enough. Canada's *natural* rate of growth, the one that results from the surplus of births over deaths, is slowing. Yet in any country it is desirable to have a population that is "growing," that is not just replacing itself, but getting at least somewhat larger in size as time goes by. Such growth goes hand-in-hand with the growth of jobs as the economy expands. It is important. If the economy is healthy, and is growing and expanding, it will require an ever larger workforce for success.

As of 1996, according to Statistics Canada, the number of births in Canada had declined for six years consecutively. Between 1990 and 1995 natural growth rates for Canada's population dropped from 7.7 to 5.7 per 1000 population. This trend of slowing growth is showing no signs of reversing itself and it is unlikely that fertility rates will return to levels observed previously. Meanwhile, as Canada's population continues to age, death rates rise. The combination of the falling birth rate, together with the increasing number of deaths, leads to an ever-smaller rate of natural growth of Canada's population. By 2020, Statistics Canada estimates that Canada will have a natural growth rate close to zero.

Given the population scenario described above, it is clear that Canada will have to rely increasingly on immigration as a source of population renewal and growth. This trend is evident already. As of 1996, 47 percent of the total growth of Canadian population growth was attributable to natural growth, while 53 percent was due to immigration. Thus the Government of Canada strives to maintain that precious balance between maintaining a small but steady rate of population growth, while at the same time trying not to overload social or economic systems with "too many" migrants.

Do migrants "steal" jobs from Canadians? The evidence suggests they do not. When the government admits immigrants to Canada it makes an attempt to match their skills and qualifications to the needs of the country. The process is not perfect, of course, but strives to achieve the best-fit possible. What do the actual numbers look like? Figure 9.4 presents the number of immigrants to Canada by province during 1996.

It can be seen that of the total 225,508 migrants represented in the table, 119,345 settled in Ontario. Thus Ontario, as the economic heartland of the country, takes in about half of all international immigrants. With respect to immigration to the other provinces, British Columbia is second, Quebec is third, and Alberta is fourth. Clearly Quebec does not take in its "fair share" of migrants, given its population size. The numbers of immigrants going to other provinces are relatively small compared to the population sizes of those provinces (see Table 5.3).

Statistics Canada reports that Toronto is the number one destination for immigrants to Canada. Between 1991 and 1996:

> The Toronto census metropolitan area was the preferred destination of Canada's most recent immigrants. About 441,000, or 42% of all new arrivals to Canada, settled in Toronto, nearly three times its share of the total Canadian population (15%). This was the largest influx into any census metropolitan area. In comparison, 18% of recent immigrants to Canada settled in Vancouver, and 13% in Montreal.

178  *Hierarchical Organization in Society*

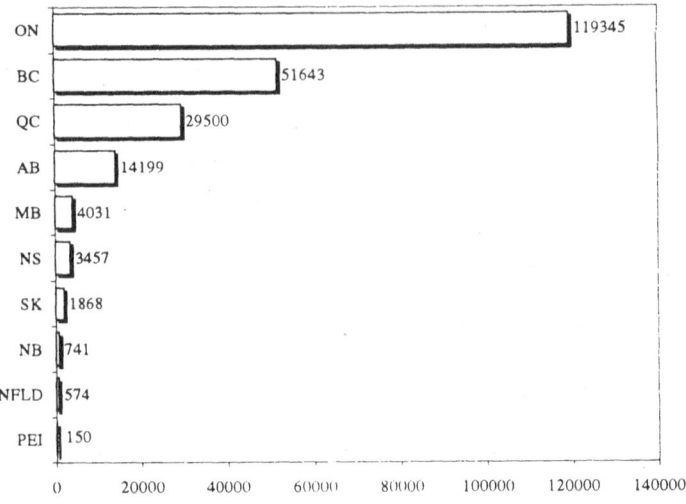

**Figure 9.4  Immigration to Canadian Provinces**

Source: *The Top 10 of Everything 1999*, 1998.

Perhaps a more important question is "What is the perception of immigrants as takers of jobs?" A study carried out in 1997 indicates that 44 percent of Canadians believe that too many immigrants are accepted, while 44 percent believe that levels are "about right." At the same time, 51 percent of Canadians surveyed believe that immigration causes unemployment. Clearly there is a gap between the perception of immigrants as "stealers of jobs" and the actual reality of the situation. Most studies show that immigrants add positively to the growth of the economy. In recent years there has been put in place an "investor immigrant" program whereby immigrants who plan to make an investment in Canada are admitted to the country. A recent study from Statistics Canada shows that:

> Between 1992 and 1995, a total of 9,093 individuals immigrated into Canada as investors from all over the world. Not only are some of them likely the best managers of businesses in the world, they have also brought a minimum of $2.3 billion investment dollars into Canada.

The flow of migrants to Canada from other parts of the world is but one small part of the total international flow of immigrants. Huge flows take place all over the world as people everywhere seek out better opportunities in places other than where they live. It is difficult, if not impossible, to characterize the international flow of migrants from less developed to more developed countries as a hierarchy, because flows everywhere are restricted by governments. If we were to allow the unrestricted international flow of migrants a definitive hierarchy of flows would emerge which would reflect the *population sizes* of the "sending" countries together with the *economic size* of the "receiving" countries.

What is truly ironic is that the developed countries of the world are promoting unrestricted free trade, but want it only in *goods and products*, not in people. In effect, the argument they make is to ask the less developed countries to open their doors to our manufactured goods and agricultural products. But at the same time they do not intend to offer to open their "migration doors" to those same countries' peoples. It could be argued that free trade is free trade, and that truly free trade allows the unrestricted movement of people as well as goods. Would the developed countries be so anxious to gain access to global markets, if these were the conditions under which they had to do so?

## References

Ash, R. (1998), *The Top 10 of Everything 1999*, Reader's Digest Association Canada, Ltd.
Globetechnology.com, 'Success for Canada depends on plugging the brain drain', February 21, 1998.
Globetechnology.com, 'Why some of our brightest are heading south', February 28, 1998.
Globetechnology.com, 'Lower taxes will only slow brain drain, Martin says', September 21, 1998.
Statistics Canada, '1996 census: immigration and citizenship', November 4, 1997.
Statistics Canada, '1996 census: education, mobility and migration', *The Daily*, April 14, 1998.
Statistics Canada, 'Population Estimates', *The Daily*, September 26, 1996.
Statistics Canada, 'Brain drain or brain gain? What do the data say?', October 1, 1998.
Statistics Canada, 'Migration 1996-1997', *The Daily*, February 17, 1999.
Statistics Canada, 'Census of Canada - Population and Dwelling Counts', *The Daily,* April 15, 1997.
U.S. Department of Commerce, 'Geographical mobility: March 1996 to March 1997 (update)', *Current Population Reports*, July, 1998.
VanderKamp, J. in Shaw, R.P., (1985), *Intermetropolitan Migration in Canada*, NC Press Limited: Toronto, p. 49.

# 10 How Our Communities Shape the Quality of Our Lives

There is no underestimating the great significance that the size of communities has on the nature and quality of peoples' lives. In fact, several chapters have made the point that there is a strong connection between the hierarchy of communities and other important kinds of hierarchies. Chapter 4 linked the educational hierarchy to the hierarchy of communities and demonstrated the significance of the link in regard to the availability of, and access to, higher levels of education. Chapter 8 talked about the retail system and showed how it is strongly linked together with the hierarchy of communities. This drew attention to the important implications for consumers of living in different sized communities.

There are a number of other interesting facets of the communities in which we live. There are subtle ways in which the hierarchy of communities shapes and molds our lives. Everyday events and occurrences, taken for granted by most people, are often intertwined with, and determined by, the size of the community in which we live. This chapter takes a look at a few of the other ways in which the hierarchy of communities influences our daily lives.

## Sports Hierarchies

John Elway. Wayne Gretzky. Michael Jordan. Mark McGwire. What do these four names have in common? The reality is that they are probably the most well known athletes in each of their respective sports. Sports of all kinds take on the form of hierarchies and Elway, Gretzky, Jordan, and McGwire all sit atop the four leagues that top those hierarchies. Below those "big leagues" there exists a whole array of lower levels of sports leagues, many of them acting as "feeder" systems for the professional sports leagues at the top.

The level of sport that is available locally to fans or spectators usually depends upon the level of their town or city in the hierarchy of communities. If we regard convenient access to spectator sports as something that enhances the quality of peoples' lives, then this provides

182  *Hierarchical Organization in Society*

another instance of where the size of the community in which one lives, plays a role in determining one's quality of life.

Consider Canadian hockey as an example that can be considered to be a hierarchy in itself (see Figure 10.1). It can be seen in Figure 10.1 that the hockey hierarchy has properties consistent with the others we have looked at. Once again in this inverted "tree" there are but a few teams at the top, but literally thousands at the bottom.

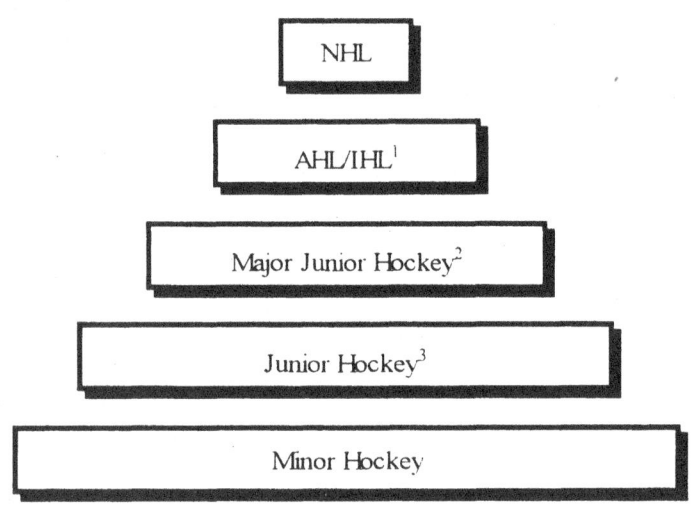

Notes:
[1] American Hockey League (AHL)/International Hockey League (IHL)
[2] Major Junior Hockey or the Canadian Hockey League (CHL) consisting of: Western Hockey League (WHL), Ontario Hockey League (OHL), and Quebec Major Junior Hockey League (QMJHL)
[3] Junior A, Junior B, Junior C, etc.

**Figure 10.1  The Hockey Hierarchy within Canada**

This hockey hierarchy represents the feeder system from the minor ranks all the way to the NHL. But what is interesting about it from the hierarchical point of view is that there is a general correspondence between this hierarchy and the hierarchy of communities. In other words, NHL franchises tend to be in the largest cities (e.g., Calgary), AHL franchises in medium sized cities (e.g., Halifax), Major Junior Hockey franchises in smaller cities (e.g., Kamloops), and Minor Hockey teams in communities of all sizes. So there exists a one-to-one correspondence between the hockey hierarchy and the hierarchy of communities.

There are several levels in hockey and each has unique characteristics. Interestingly there are many parallels between the hockey hierarchy and the educational hierarchy discussed in Chapter 4.

The bottom level of the hockey hierarchy is defined by Minor Hockey. Here players range from about four or five years of age right up to those at the end of high school. The amount and distance of travel to games and practices generally increase as players get older, though even at young ages quite a bit of travel is involved. This results from the fact that, in the era of "indoor" hockey, rinks are few and far between. Leagues within cities imply travel within the city, while rural areas usually have "town leagues" that require travel among the hamlets, villages, and towns. At this level of play, positioning in the hierarchy of small communities is usually unimportant. Geographical closeness and the existence of a rink are usually all that are required for membership in a league.

There is a rather strange feature of minor hockey that most people accept without a second thought. This is the fact that young children are expected to play the game on the same sized rinks that adults use. In a perfect world, there would be perhaps three different sizes of rinks and kids would advance from one to another as they got older. We can only imagine the existence of a hierarchy of, say, small, medium, and regular sized hockey rinks in each community. Wouldn't it be nice if every neighbourhood in the city had its own mini-plex of small, kid sized, indoor ice surfaces? But because of the great expense of building and maintaining arenas, we have a system where "one size fits all." The exception is in those cases where half-ice or cross-ice play is sometimes employed. Back in the good old days, when outdoor rinks were more common, there was probably more of a match between the size of the child and the size of the ice. The discrepancy is most obvious when one watches really young children play a game of hockey on a full size sheet of ice. The pace of the game is incredibly slow as little tykes gradually make their way from one end of the long ice to the other.

We can also compare hockey to other sports wherein it is possible to organize team or league play at the *neighbourhood* level. Usually ball diamonds and soccer pitches, being inexpensive compared to rinks, are found in plentiful supply in neighbourhood parks in a city. As a result, travel for players and parents is less of an issue and local leagues can be organized for very young children. This is in sharp contrast to minor hockey, where neighbourhood-level leagues are almost unheard of.

Even from the beginnings of minor hockey, players are judged and sorted into different levels of skill. Some communities sort their players into groups or "tiers" that continue to play locally for the most part, while others create elite teams of players often known as travelling teams. The idea is that in order to find other teams with comparable, highly skilled players, it is necessary to travel. The travelling team consists of the best players, who then play the best players from other communities. The point is that even at the level of minor hockey, highly competitive teams search out competition at a higher level in the hierarchy of communities.

The final levels of hockey within minor hockey occur towards the end of high school. Many players lose interest and drop out along the way, others turn to "recreational" or other such informal forms of hockey, while the chosen few advance to higher levels of play. For those that do advance, more long distance travel becomes required. In other words, as the calibre of play advances, the number of highly skilled players declines. *There are fewer but better teams.* As a result, the level of play moves to a higher level in the community of hierarchies. *Inter-city league play* replaces league play within the city and local area, as the "best of the best" rise to a higher level of play.

In Canada, as players advance beyond minor hockey they move to the next level of the hockey hierarchy — Junior Hockey. Here again the players are sorted by skill level into Junior A, Junior B, Junior C, and so on. The very best players advance to Major Junior Hockey — or the Canadian Hockey League (CHL) — consisting of the Western Hockey League (WHL), the Ontario Hockey League (OHL), and the Quebec Major Junior Hockey League (QMJHL). All of these levels of hockey take players to higher levels within the hierarchy of communities. Generally the higher the level of the team, the bigger the community in which it will play. You might expect to find Junior A in small cities, Junior B in large towns, Junior C in medium sized towns, and so on. In all cases however the leagues are organized at the inter-town or inter-city level. The amount of travel required intensifies.

A clear example of how the level of play matches the level in the hierarchy of communities comes from the CHL or Major Junior Hockey. At this level of play, teams exist only in larger communities, in most cases, "medium" sized cities. Travel becomes very extensive. The WHL, for example, consists of teams all the way from Manitoba to British Columbia and the States of Washington and Oregon. There is even talk of having inter-league play among the WHL, OHL, and QMJHL. In Major Junior Hockey, players are recruited from all over Canada, the United States, and Europe.

Those players that advance beyond the CHL move to various levels of professional hockey. A selected few move directly to the National Hockey League (NHL) but most move to the other two major developmental leagues, namely the American Hockey League (AHL) and the International Hockey League (IHL). Many of the teams in the "A" and the "I" are affiliated with teams in the NHL and serve as places for "player development." Once again there is another advancement upward in the hierarchy of communities. Teams in the AHL and IHL tend to be found in larger cities than those with CHL teams.

In addition to the AHL and IHL there are several other professional hockey leagues in existence, each of them finding a place in some set of communities that is unserved by either the AHL, the IHL or the NHL. Some of these leagues include the East Coast League, The West Coast League, The United League, the Western Pro League, and the Central League.

At the top level of the hockey hierarchy comes the NHL Here again the sizes of the cities that are able to support franchises increases again and the travelling distance increases greatly. Only major cities, those at the "top" of the hierarchy of communities, are capable of keeping and maintaining teams. The "best of the best" play in the largest cities in Canada and the United States. The feeder system that starts in the local neighbourhood rink results in teams playing in major cities with players from all over the globe.

As a general rule, it can be suggested that the relationship between level of league play and community size looks somewhat like that below.

| | |
|---|---|
| NHL | Major Cities |
| AHL/IHL | Medium to Smaller Cities |
| CHL | Smaller Cities |
| Junior Hockey | Large Towns |

There are, of course, many exceptions to this general rule, but basically it can be taken as a guide to the level of hockey team that any community should have. It should be noted too that major cities will sometimes be able to support all of these levels of hockey simultaneously. That means that larger communities not only have a higher calibre of play, but usually also have a greater diversity of it as well.

Hockey is just one spectator sport but it serves well to illustrate the point being made. It is quite clear that the calibre and diversity of spectator sports is usually associated with the size of the community in which those sports are housed. People who enjoy spectator sports are clearly advantaged by the size of their community. The bigger the community, the better the level of play to be seen, and the more variety available. For those people who live "farther down" in the hierarchy of communities, the choice is to enjoy a lower calibre of sport, or to travel the extra distance required upward in the hierarchy.

186  *Hierarchical Organization in Society*

The same match up between calibre of play and community size exists for all other sports as well. Pro football and pro basketball have feeder systems that are based more strongly on college and university leagues in the United States. Pro baseball has a feeder system in the United States that is more akin to that for hockey in Canada. In all cases, however, as the calibre of play advances, so does the size of the communities in which it takes place.

When it comes to comparing sports hierarchies with city hierarchies, it was noted that there is a match-up in Canada between the size of cities and their ability to support sports teams. Figure 10.2, repeated here for convenience, shows the hierarchy of Canada's largest cities. The point to be made is that the six largest cities on the top of the hierarchy — Montreal, Toronto, Vancouver, Ottawa-Hull, Edmonton and Calgary — are the cities where NHL hockey has proven itself to be viable. At the same time, the next three cities in the hierarchy of Canadian cities — Quebec, Winnipeg and Hamilton — have all shown themselves to be unable to acquire or maintain NHL franchises. Both the Quebec and Winnipeg teams moved to the United States. The Quebec Nordiques became the Colorado Avalanche and the Winnipeg Jets became the Phoenix Coyotes. Meanwhile, the City of Hamilton not only built an arena, but tried in vain to acquire an NHL franchise. It is thought that competition with NHL markets in nearby Buffalo and Toronto has been one stumbling block to Hamilton's success.

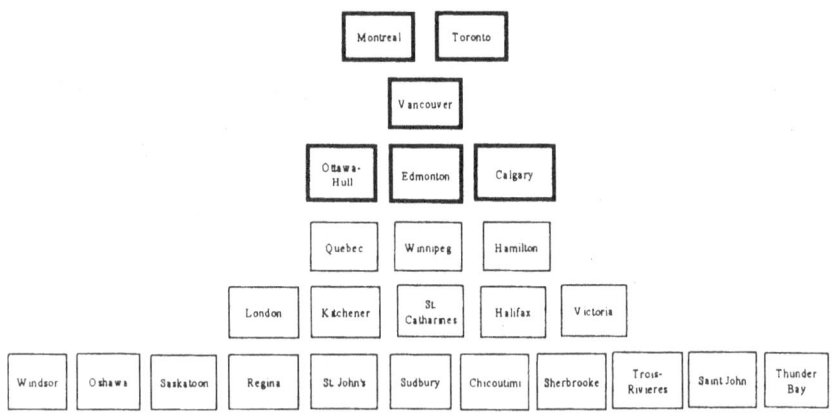

**Figure 10.2 The Canadian Urban Hierarchy and the NHL**

If we apply the same kind of reasoning to the combined hierarchy of Canadian and American cities we come to the inescapable conclusion that the city of Toronto (and Montreal) should have long ago acquired an NFL football franchise. Figure 10.3 shows the combined hierarchy of Canadian and American cities. Quite clearly the figure shows that Toronto and Montreal are in the "big leagues" in terms of their size, and should have sports and other facilities that are comparable to the other American cities in the diagram. Every American team in Figure 10.3 has, has had, or will have again, an NFL franchise. Toronto and Montreal are quite definitely out of step with their American counterparts and the citizens of those two cities are deprived of a source of entertainment that they should justifiably expect to have.

Figure 10.3 The Canadian-American Hierarchy of Cities and the NFL

While Montreal, and especially Toronto, continue to wait in their efforts to acquire an NFL franchise, the price keeps escalating further and further out of reach. News reports out of Toronto indicate that not only would Toronto need to build a new football-only stadium to NFL specifications (the Skydome isn't up to snuff) but it will also have to come up with a franchise fee that is fast closing-in on $1 billion U.S. dollars. Clearly Toronto should have pushed harder for a NFL franchise many years ago. Never mind the fact that even the Skydome went bankrupt. Given the huge franchise fee, Toronto may have lost forever its chance to join the exclusive club of cities shown in Figure 10.3. On the other hand, if those cities are capable of funding and supporting NFL teams, so too should Toronto and Montreal. Or are they members of the club in *size* only? The Super Bowl in Toronto. Will we ever see it?

## Information and News from the Media

News and information used to travel over the world at quite slow speeds. Studies have shown that when Abraham Lincoln was assassinated in the United States, it took several days for other parts of the country to hear the news. Nowadays, of course, information about such an event would be transmitted to the entire globe literally within seconds. It is important to people that "news" be timely and up-to-date.

The fact that news must be timely is illustrated by the fact that in the study of commodities, newspapers are considered to be a "perishable" item. Just like yesterday's bread, over-ripe bananas, or expired milk, an old newspaper is, as they say, "yesterday's news." The "shelf-life" of the typical daily newspaper is a single day. When the day is over, the paper "expires" and literally becomes worthless. It is not the newsprint you pay for, it is the news content of the paper that has value. And interestingly, people are willing to pay in order to receive that information.

Consider the huge amount of information available to people on a day-to-day basis. Satellite and cable TV, newspapers, Internet, and radio bombard the average citizen with an overabundance of news at almost every minute of the day. An interesting question to ask is whether all of this information is distributed evenly. Do all citizens get their "equal share" of news and information? Does everyone get the news in a timely manner? Are citizens of different sized communities served equally well by information sources?

The truth of the matter is that there is a great variation in the amount and timeliness of information availability across the hierarchy of communities. Not only are smaller communities disadvantaged by their position within the hierarchy, but they are also less likely to be "heard" when they make news of their own.

The most obvious case where there is a substantial difference in the amount of information received by different sized communities is with respect to newspapers. Newspapers tend to be as big and as frequent as they can be, given the size of their markets. In other words, the publisher of a paper, who is in business to make money, will strive to make the paper as large as possible, and to distribute it as often as possible, to the point of whatever the local market will bear. Imagine if you yourself set up a new newspaper in a small town with the intention of making a living at it. You would try to extract the maximum amount of profit from that paper by publishing as much, and as often, as possible. Your goal would be to maximize your profit by selling as much ad space as you could.

A small *village* will typically have a weekly paper that is fairly small in size. Sometimes such a small paper will serve several small communities. The published news is local. A *town* may be large enough to support a daily paper, but again it would tend to be on the small size. It might not publish on Sunday. The news emphasis is local and "regional." A *moderately sized city* will have a larger, daily paper that will publish every day but Sunday. More and more such papers are able to include colour graphics. The news in such a paper will be a mixture of local, national, regional, and international. A *full size city* will have more than one daily paper and, as a result of competition, those papers may publish every day of the week. They will feature local, national, and international news, and the local coverage will be limited to more important local stories and events. In a *really big city* the news goes a step further. Not only are there multiple newspapers, but the larger ones will publish several new editions per day. There is more news and it is more up-to-date. The coverage is at all levels but again small, local issues are not given much emphasis. Finally there are the *"national"* newspapers, distributed from coast to coast, but only in larger cities. News coverage is regional, national, and international, but local news (from the place where the paper originates) is all but ignored.

Clearly there is a correspondence between community size and the amount of information conveyed by newspapers. The size of the paper, the frequency of the paper, the freshness of the paper, and the quality of the paper all correspond with community size (see Table 10.1). This is not to say that people in small towns, for example, do not also read the daily paper from a nearby large city. But it does mean that the general amounts of information available increase with increasing city size. Stories, news, and information that get printed in the thicker, large-city daily for instance, may never see the light of day in a mid-sized city daily. The fact of the matter is that people who live in larger communities will, on the average, tend to be better informed.

Variations in the availability of information can be crucial to some people. Consider two people dealing in the stock market, one in Toronto and the other in Kamloops, BC. Which of the two market players has better access to more, and more up-to-date, information? There may be stories about national and world events in the Toronto newspapers that would never make the pages of the smaller papers read in Kamloops.

At the same time that less news gets reported in smaller communities, news *from* smaller communities also gets less national attention. Figure 10.4 illustrates the idea. This "map" of Canadian cities represents their relative positions according to the news flows that get reported from them. The study was done by looking at the "bylines" on news stories reported in papers all over the country. The closer a city is to the "centre" of the map, the more it dominates national news coverage. In other words, if a city's news stories get a lot of national coverage, it will be closer to the centre of the map. Meanwhile, if a city's news stories get very little national attention it will be closer to the edge of the map. It can be seen that all of the cities that dominate the centre of the map — Toronto, Ottawa, Vancouver, Montreal, Edmonton, and Calgary — are all of the largest Canadian cities. Similarly, the cities that are relegated to the periphery of the map tend to be the smaller ones. The large cities not only generate a lot of news, but it also gets reported more than the news emanating from smaller cities. Like the "noisy" neighbours down the street, the big cities draw a lot of attention to themselves.

**Table 10.1 Newspapers by Community Size**

| Community Size | Frequency | Size (number of sections) | News Emphasis |
| --- | --- | --- | --- |
| Big City | multiple editions daily | 5-10 | National, International |
| City | daily - 7 days | 3-5 | Regional, National |
| Town | daily - 6 days | 2-3 | Local, Regional |
| Village | weekly | 1 | Local |

The availability of television corresponds very much with community size. There are still many rural and small town areas of Canada that are served by only one or two TV stations (CBC and or CTV). Although this discrepancy is easily offset these days by the availability of satellite TV, the fact of the matter is that not everyone living in a small community or rural area can afford it. Many people still rely on just one or two TV stations to bring them news and information. Similarly, while cable TV continues to advance into smaller and smaller markets, there are still many communities in which it is unavailable. While many city people would claim they suffer from "information overload" there are still many areas of Canada that are relatively isolated in terms of information availability from television.

*How Our Communities Shape the Quality of Our Lives* 191

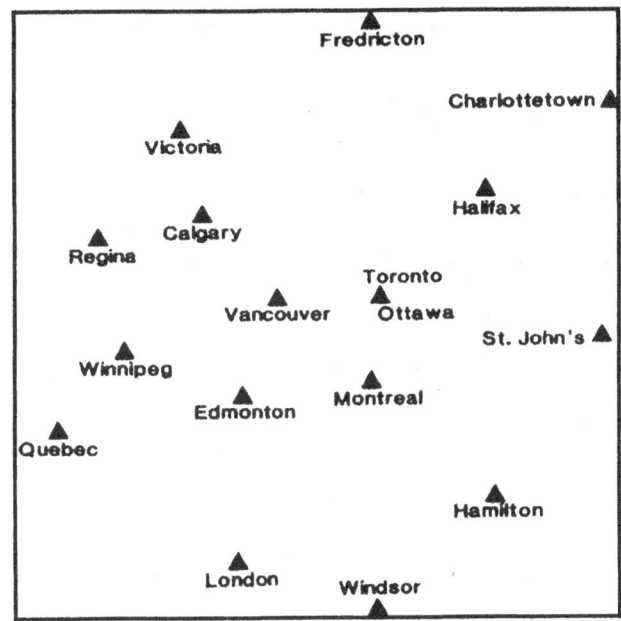

Source: Reprinted from *The Geographer At Work*, 1985.

**Figure 10.4 "Map" of Canadian Cities According to News Flows**

Radio is another story. Unlike cable or satellite TV, radio is still a method of communication that is literally "broadcast," from a point to an area, in the same way it was when it was first invented. Just like newspapers, the number and power of radio stations in an area is limited by the amount of advertising revenue that can be generated. Sparsely populated rural areas just do not generate the advertising dollars that big cities do. As a result there is a very strong correspondence between community size and the number of radio stations almost everywhere in Canada. Highly populated areas like southern Ontario will be awash in radio stations, while the more sparsely settled areas like the Atlantic Provinces, Prairies and the Rocky Mountains will be underserved by radio. Given the great extent to which people rely on radio as a source of up-to-date information and entertainment, this represents one of the more serious consequences of living "too far down" in the hierarchy of communities.

There is also the Internet to consider. Access to it depends on access to either telephone lines or cable. At the present time, high-speed access to internet service is most readily available through cable and so those internet users in communities large enough to have cable, have a distinct advantage over those who rely on phone lines. Nevertheless, the Internet is available to anyone, anywhere, with a phone line, although costs may vary in some areas. High-speed access to the internet by phone is currently limited to large cities so here again there is an advantage to living higher in the hierarchy of communities.

Finally, one other simple difference between life in the big city and life in a smaller community is just in the simple amount of daily, *personal information* that people receive. As big city residents go about their daily business they simply have more contacts, with more people, on a day-to-day basis. This would be especially true of people who work in industries where personal contact and information is particularly important. The obvious example is in a business like the stock market where information plays a crucial role. A good analogy is to think of molecules bouncing about in a container. In a crowded container, with more molecules, there will be more collisions that will occur simply as a result of chance. The same kind of thing happens with people living in a crowded city — more contacts are made and more information gets passed around. Where do you wish your stockbroker lived? Would you rather she be in Toronto, or would you rather that she lived in Come-by-Chance, Newfoundland?

## Social and Cultural Facilities and "Critical Mass"

Another reason for citizens of smaller communities to be concerned about their quality of life is that they are often said to suffer from social and cultural "deprivation." If someone wants to attend the theatre, go to a movie, visit an art gallery, go to a museum, patronize a posh restaurant, go to a rock concert, hear a symphony orchestra, or see a Broadway musical, the implication is that they have to be in a large city in order to do so.

It is obvious that large-scale social and cultural facilities and events exist primarily in large cities, but what is less obvious is that they cannot occur "in part." In other words, it is impossible to have a "scaled down" version of these events and activities for smaller communities, like we can for other things. For example, a small town might have a small grocery store or a scaled down library, but that does not mean it will have a "small" symphony orchestra, part of a Broadway musical, a small-scale posh restaurant, or a miniature movie theatre. For many social and cultural facilities to exist, a "critical mass" of people is required.

Unfortunately, critical mass is usually achieved only in larger cities that sit among the top echelons of the hierarchy of communities. Even medium to mid-sized communities often do not have the population base to support some of these more sophisticated facilities and events. In fact many people will be judgmental of a community that does not have an adequate share of such high-class facilities. It is the "mark" of a city to achieve success at calling itself a city, by having its own symphony orchestra, for example. And even residents of large cities will "look down their noses" at communities that are not properly endowed with worldly social and cultural facilities. Such things are often taken to be the badge of a truly civilized city.

Once again the implication for residents of communities lower in the hierarchy is that travel is required to take advantage of more sophisticated facilities and events. Such travel becomes a way of life for people who live anywhere but in the very largest cities. It is commonplace to travel down the highway to take in an event such as those described above. The extra time and expense are usually not even considered, but are chalked up to part of the cost of not living in the largest cities. And, of course as we have seen, the trends indicate that many people *prefer* the smaller-town or smaller-city life to the big-city life. The extra cost of an occasional trip into the city is considered to be well worth the advantage to be had from living in the safer, cleaner environment of the smaller community.

**Goods and Services on the Move**

In spite of the negative aspects of smaller town life outlined in the sections above, there are some cases in which the goods and services available in larger cities actually do become "mobile" in order to make themselves available in smaller communities. When the demand for a particular good or service in a town is not large enough for that good or service to exist in that town, an option is to offer that good or service just *some of the time* in that town.

A good example of this process in action is in the case of a lawyer who visits a small town one-day a week. On that one day the lawyer can provide all of the legal services the town needs. There are not enough clients to keep the lawyer in business five days a week, but there is enough demand to require her services one-day a week. Many other such services are commonly offered in smaller communities, for instance, dental services, optometrists, travelling salespeople, insurance sales, mutual funds, financial services, and so on. Basically anything can be offered in this way that does not have a need for a large inventory.

The retailer or service provider in this situation can literally "make the rounds" of a series of small towns on every day of the week. Thus legal services could be offered in town A on Monday, in village B on Tuesday, and so on. The creative, itinerant businessperson can create an entire clientele, simply by travelling to where the demand is on different days of the week.

An interesting variant on this pattern is the well known idea of the farmers' market or the flea market, where buyers and sellers have a common agreement to come together and meet, once a week at a pre-determined location. Often there is not enough demand to warrant opening the market five days a week, nor is there a desire on the part of the vendors to set-up in a retail market for five days a week. It is only by mutual agreement that the supply and the demand come together at the right time, at the right place. The consequence is that a smaller community hosts an event it could not otherwise support.

**Travelling Entertainment**

A more interesting variation of the idea above comes to life even in the bigger cities. The best example of what we mean comes from the circus. In most cities there is not enough demand to warrant running a circus in a single place, all year-round. The people that run the circus know this and so, in response, they take the circus on the road. Circuses travel constantly to new communities every few days. From an economic point of view, what the circus is doing is taking the "supply" of entertainment to where the "demand" exists. Instead of the customer coming to "the store," the store, in effect, travels to the customer. The travelling around of a circus is just the same as the lawyer travelling to the small town. In the case of the circus there is enough demand to keep it in town, one or two days a year.

Exactly the same process happens with other travelling shows and entertainment. A well-known instance is in the case of the travelling "Broadway" style of show or musical. On Broadway, in New York, there is enough demand for such shows that they can stay in place, on Broadway, the year round. In fact, many of the more popular shows stay on Broadway literally for years at a time. But when such shows go on the road, to smaller cities, it is necessary for them to travel around in order to find adequate audience numbers. They may play for a week or two in a larger Canadian city, but only for a night or two in a smaller market city.

Other entertainment that follows this pattern of bringing big-city attractions to smaller market cities includes things like amusement rides, ice shows, children's shows, plays, rock and other musical concerts, "professional" wrestling, truck races, rodeos, and so on. In all cases the promoters are taking the "supply" on the road to find the "demand." From the communities' points-of-view it is usually in their interest to build facilities of sufficient size (e.g., halls, arenas) to host these "travelling shows." This is one way in which the residents of communities that are lower down in the hierarchy of communities are able to avail themselves of big-city attractions without having to undertake extra travel. In this case, it is the entertainment that does the travelling.

**Fads and Innovations**

Another subtle area where the hierarchy of communities has an influence on the quality of people's daily lives is when it comes to fads, innovations, or inventions. Believe it or not, most new fads that "come down the pipeline" arrive by way of the largest cities. In Canada, the expectation is that the latest trend in music or fashion will originate in Toronto and then spread downward through the hierarchy of communities. This being the case, the newest innovations will follow the paths outlined in Figure 10.5 from the top to the bottom. The implication is that a fad or innovation will spread across the country, among large cities, before it spreads to closer communities. For example, a fad that originates in Toronto should spread to Vancouver, before it finds its way to more nearby communities such as Kingston or Windsor. An example of the kind of trend that will "flow" down the hierarchy might be in something subtle such as a new style of clothing or fashion. The new clothing style first adopted in the "clubs" in Toronto will eventually appear on the streets in St. John's, Brandon and Cranbrook. The big cities are usually the first adopters, and by the time the fad spreads to the bottom layers of the Canadian urban hierarchy it is probably already becoming passé at the top in Toronto. An interesting question is where fads come from before their arrival in Toronto. Most new innovations probably come from the top cities in the American hierarchy of cities, especially New York and Los Angeles, and probably the same pattern of datedness applies there as well, that is, by the time an innovation reaches the bottom end of the hierarchy it has already become obsolete at the top.

In addition to fashion trends and fads, other more significant innovations and inventions are also considered to spread downwards in the hierarchy of communities. The latest medical techniques, recent innovations in construction or manufacturing, and so on, have all been shown to be adopted first in larger communities and then to spread to smaller ones later on. This can have important implications for residents of smaller communities. For example, in the case of medical care, it is more likely that your doctor or surgeon is "up-to-date" on the latest medical technology or breakthroughs if he or she lives in a larger city. The same

196  *Hierarchical Organization in Society*

probably goes for your stockbroker or financial planner. We have already seen that more information flows around in larger cities and those "in the know" tend to be located in such cities.

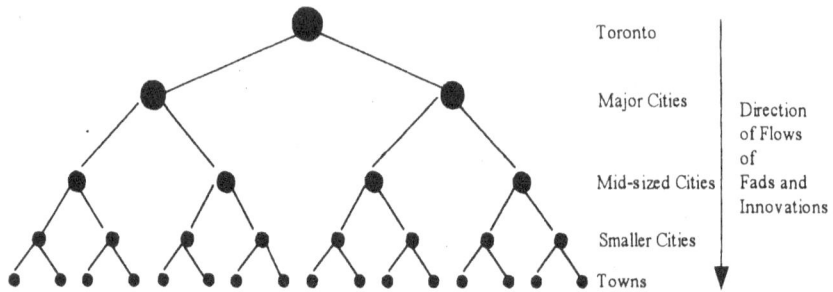

Figure 10.5  Flows of Fads and Innovations in the Hierarchy of Communities

**References**

Gould, P. (1985), *The Geographer at Work*, Routledge & Kegan Paul: London.

# 11 Canadian Medical Care - Equal Treatment for All?

Most Canadians would agree that Canada has one of the best health care systems in the world. Universal Medicare is truly a wonderful program that provides equal, high quality health care for all Canadians regardless of national origin, social status, age, race, gender or ability to pay. Any Canadian, from anywhere in the country can walk into any health care facility, anywhere else in the country, and receive top quality medical care at no charge whatsoever. Canada's health care system "sets the bar" for other nations anywhere in the world that wish to establish universal health care. The system is timely as well. Although there are occasionally some local problems with waiting lists or delays for procedures, for the most part the system is also very fast and efficient at providing Canadians with a level of health care unsurpassed anywhere in the world. Canadians are proud of their health care system, and rightfully so.

If there is any one thing that represents a weakness of the health care system it is in the fact that people are not equally served according to *where* they live. When it comes to medical care, and especially emergency medical care, people are disadvantaged by the size of the community in which they live. In essence, the larger the community in which you live, the better off you are in regard to health care. When we claim that health care is *universal*, and equally available to all citizens, that should apply to people *wherever they live*. The system is only universal if all citizens are served equally regardless of the size of the community in which they live.

Cutbacks to medicine have been happening all across the country. Many of these cutbacks have occurred by closing smaller local health care facilities or hospitals, or else by cutting back on the "level" of care, or hours of emergency care, provided. Such cutbacks are in direct contrast to the principles of Medicare, which is intended to serve people equally. If you happen to live in an area or community where health care has been cut, your *access* to health care has been significantly reduced. Cutting back on health care so that its quality depends more and more on the location of people is equivalent to cutting back on the universality of Medicare.

The quantity and quality of health care service corresponds with the hierarchies of communities in which we live. Depending on their size, cities, towns, and villages will all receive different levels of health care and, as was the case with educational facilities, there will be "have-not" communities when it comes to health care as well. Furthermore, unlike those communities that are disadvantaged educationally by their size, we cannot make up the difference in health care through a program of tax deductions. Getting a break on your taxes because you live thirty kilometres from the nearest hospital is not going to be of much advantage to you while you are in the midst of a medical emergency. Geographical discrimination is creeping into Medicare and the only solution to it, is to try to provide more equal care to citizens regardless of where they happen to live.

Medicare is also being attacked in regard to its ability to provide highly specialized medical care and service. More and more we hear stories of Canadians travelling to the United States to receive sophisticated health care that is not available in Canada. Certain highly specialized kinds of medical operations and treatments are only available in the United States and those who can afford it, take advantage of those services. In spite of political denials that Medicare is not a "two-tier" system, we hear cynics who claim that indeed there is a two-tiered health care system in Canada. The first tier is said to be standard Canadian health care, while the second tier is said to be health care in the United States for those who can afford it. These and other related issues will be addressed in greater detail below. Prior to that, we will look at some basic facts and figures about the medical community in Canada.

**How Big is the Doctors' Bill?**

How much does it cost to pay for Medicare? According to Canada Health Information Resources the total amount spent on health care in Canada in 1996 was $75.3 billion dollars. This is equivalent to $2,513 for every person in Canada. Add this up for the number of people in your household and you will see where all of those tax dollars go. The biggest portion of those dollars goes to hospitals, while doctors' salaries are second, and drugs are third. There were 55,243 physicians in Canada in 1997. Of those 27,135 were specialists. As of 1997 there was one physician for every 541 people. According to Statistics Canada, physicians' 1996 salaries place them among the group having the highest average earnings (for which employment income data are available):

- Judges $126,246
- Specialist Physicians and Surgeons $123,976

- General Practitioners and Family Physicians   $107,620
- Dentists                                       $102,433

Is the distribution of doctors among the Canadian provinces a "fair" one? It is interesting to examine the variation in the number of doctors across the country. Figure 11.1 shows the number of physicians according to the provinces. It can be seen that Quebec and British Columbia lead the country in the number of doctors per person while Prince Edward Island and the Northwest Territories are last on the list.

It is useful to compare this list with Figure 11.2 which shows the *spending* on health services in the provinces per person. There the Northwest Territories and the Yukon lead the way in expenditures per person, while Quebec and Nova Scotia trail the list. The interesting contrast is that while Quebec has the largest number of doctors per person, it also spends nearly the least per person on health care. At the same time, the Northwest Territories, while having the fewest number of doctors per person, spends the most on health care. One conclusion to be drawn, not surprisingly, is that it costs a lot to keep doctors working in the north.

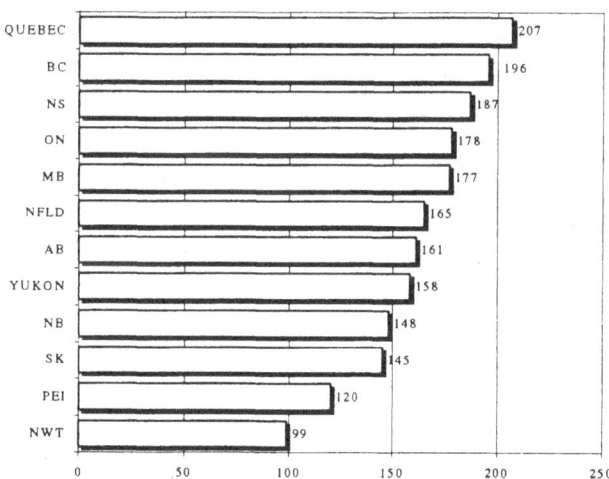

Source: Canadian Institute for Health Information, 1997.

**Figure 11.1 Number of Physicians per 100,000 Population, 1996-1997**

What about sex discrimination in health care? Is there balance among the sexes in medicine? Not quite. A disturbing pattern occurs in the gender balance of physicians in Canada. Figure 11.3 shows the number of physicians by age-group and gender as of 1997. The pattern shows quite an obvious gender bias as one moves from left to right across the figure. In the age ranges 30-39, 40-49, 50-59, and 60-69 one can see that there are far more male than female doctors in each age group, and that the discrimination gets worse as the age of the groups increases. It is only in the 20-29 age group that the pattern has reversed itself and we see slightly more female than male physicians. It is unfortunate that the pattern has taken so long to become more balanced. It can be seen that it will take many more years, about forty in fact, before gender equity is achieved in the profession. Currently, 75 percent of all practising doctors are male and only 25 percent are female.

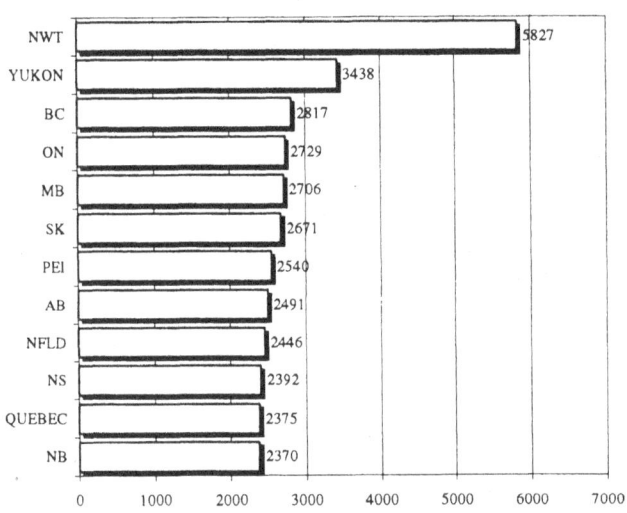

Source: Canadian Institute for Health Information, 1998.

**Figure 11.2 Total Health Expenditure by Province, 1998 - Dollars Per Person**

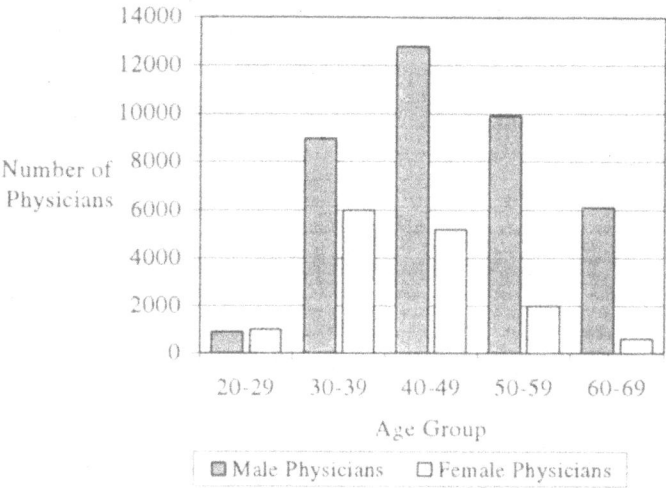

Source: Canadian Institute for Health Information, 1997.

**Figure 11.3 Number of Physicians by Age-Group and Gender, Canada, 1997**

## Community Size and Health Care

There is a one-to-one correspondence between the hierarchy of communities and the hierarchy of medical services, both within cities and in rural areas. Within the city there is a two or three level health care system, depending on the size of the city. A moderately sized city will usually have a two level system, consisting of a larger number of medical clinics scattered around suburban areas, together with one or several hospitals which tend to be centrally located. A very large city will have a system of the same kind as just described, but in addition it will also typically have the more specialized care and services of a large research hospital/medical centre that is associated with a university. Figure 11.4 suggests the hierarchy of medical treatment in the typical large Canadian city.

The travel patterns of users is virtually the same as that described in Chapter 8 for grocery shoppers. For minor medical problems and emergencies, most people need only travel to the neighbourhood medical clinic, while for more serious matters a trip to a larger hospital is required.

The downtown location for many urban hospitals makes them equally accessible to all urban residents. It should be noted that many residents living near the downtown use the hospital emergency department in the same way that the suburbanite uses the local medical clinic.

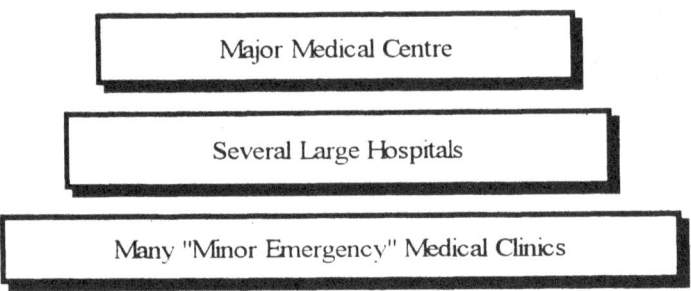

**Figure 11.4 Medical Hierarchy within a Major City**

In rural areas there exists a similar hierarchical pattern of medical services, except that the distances to be travelled are greater. Small towns will tend to have medical clinics, smaller cities will have limited care hospitals, larger cities will have full service hospitals, and at the top level, rural residents will use the same major medical centres as do city residents (see Figure 11.5). In every case, as the "level" of the care required rises, so too does the amount of travel for rural patients. The more specialized the care, the greater the distance. Figure 11.6 shows the likely travel pattern of patients "upwards" in a map of the hierarchy of communities as they are referred to higher levels of medical care.

In all cases, the medical systems exhibit the characteristics of a hierarchy. Small clinics outnumber hospitals, while hospitals outnumber major medical centres. And at every level of the system, be it urban or rural, the amount of travel required increases as the level of medical care increases. In these ways the patterns are identical to those for shoppers and students discussed earlier. Once again we see an instance of where a hierarchy shapes and influences the day-to-day activities of people.

Why does the medical hierarchy exist? Why do we see these patterns? The answer is to be found in the number of occurrences of various types of medical cases and emergencies. For example, lots of people get small cuts that require a few stitches, but only rarely do people get burned severely. In the former case, a large number of medical clinics are required to look after such "minor emergencies." In the latter case, very specialized, high level treatment is required, but only occasionally, so fewer burn treatment facilities are needed. Similarly, people get the flu or a cold quite commonly, so more treatment facilities for such illnesses are required. For rarer problems, such as those requiring a CAT scan, fewer occurrences mean that fewer treatment facilities are needed. The geography of travel for health care is just like shopping for groceries. People need bread and milk quite often, and so acquire them at the nearby convenience store, whereas when it comes to buying more specialized groceries, a longer trip is made, less often, to the larger grocery store.

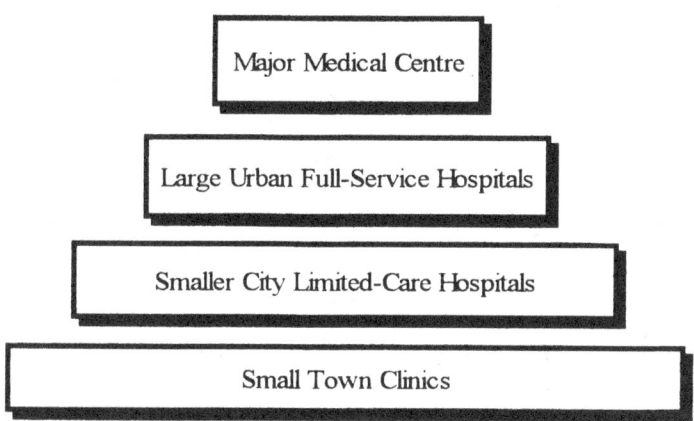

**Figure 11.5 Medical Hierarchy in a Rural Area**

In all of the examples above the key idea is that *economies of scale* are achieved in providing medical care. In other words, facilities are designed to use resources as efficiently as possible. We do not build burn treatment facilities in every small hospital or medical clinic because they would go unused most of the time. Similarly, we do not build a major hospital in every small town because that would be a waste of resources. At the same time, neither do we build a single emergency clinic to serve an entire city. Instead of being underused, it would be so crowded as to be ineffective. So in general the numbers and sizes of medical facilities in a city or rural area *evolve* in response to the demands that are placed on them. It is not a perfect system, but it does use resources very efficiently.

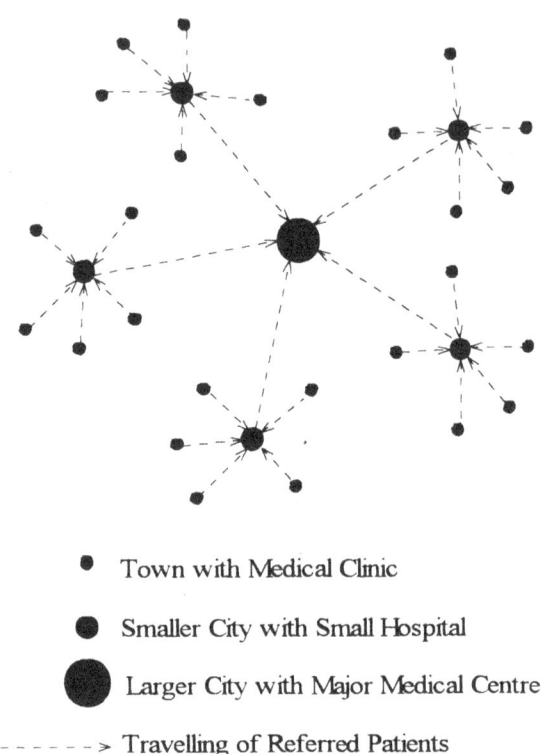

- Town with Medical Clinic
- Smaller City with Small Hospital
- Larger City with Major Medical Centre
- - - - - > Travelling of Referred Patients

**Figure 11.6  Map of Medical Hierarchy in an Area Surrounding a City**

### Erosion at the Bottom of the Medical System

The problems with the medical system start to come about when budget cuts are made and administrators start to "tinker" with the naturally efficient systems that tend to evolve on their own over many years. Attempts are made to make cuts to medical systems to make them more efficient without appreciating that they have already probably advanced to a state of natural efficiency. Reducing the number of beds or number of doctors will not change the natural rates at which accidents and disease occur. Administrators try to adjust medical systems that have literally been designed over dozens of years to serve the population in an area. To suddenly reduce the number of beds or cut the hours of emergency service is to ignore the *medical history* of the area being served.

Some of the cuts that are being made to health care in Canada occur at the lowest levels of the medical hierarchy. It is easier politically to close or curtail a smaller local or regional hospital than it is to cut back at a highly visible urban one. As such cuts take place they change the "fairness" of the Medicare system. People in smaller cities, towns and rural areas are being asked to pay more than their "fair share" with respect to the reduction of medical service. More importantly, residents of smaller cities, towns and rural areas are being asked to pay with their personal safety. As emergency medical treatment gets farther away distance-wise, or as hours of emergency treatment are cut back, residents of "have-not" communities are being placed more and more at risk from the dangers of lack of access to emergency care.

What's the solution? The answer is to stop the erosion of medical care at the "bottom" of the hierarchy of communities. People should have fair and equal access to emergency medical care and steps should be taken to ensure that there is a greater degree of fairness to the delivery of medical care. When access to emergency facilities is not adequate, greater steps should be taken to ensure equality of treatment. This may mean, for example, putting more emergency response teams in place in sparsely populated areas, building new "emergency clinics" in rural areas, or providing more widespread air ambulance services in areas where it is warranted. The bottom line is that it is possible to establish guidelines for the provision of emergency care and then to try to meet those guidelines wherever it is reasonable to do so. Can we not ensure that most Canadians are within a certain number of minutes or kilometres of emergency care? The exact numbers are up to the specialists, but is this not at least a laudable goal to work towards?

It is important to remember too that emergency, rural medical care can be important to everyone. When people are travelling between cities by automobile, or other means, they "temporarily" become residents of rural areas. The question is then whether emergency facilities are adequate for the majority of people in this situation. If you have an accident, or medical emergency on the highway, would you not prefer that emergency assistance be only minutes away?

The decline of small towns and villages was discussed earlier. It is an inevitable fact of economic life that many small communities will continue to lose population. As they do, it seems certain that it will be less easy to provide them with local, day-to-day health care. The population base just will not be adequate to support it. But does that mean that we should abandon the idea of trying to provide those people with *emergency* medical care by whatever means possible? Is it not the nature of Medicare to provide all citizens with some *minimum* level of assistance, wherever they happen to live?

As we have seen, there is a reason for the existence of the hierarchy of communities. It provides people with access to goods and services regardless of where they live. The medical hierarchy mirrors the community hierarchy, and it too serves the purpose of providing people with ready access to health care. People should not expect every little town or small city hospital to maintain a *full* range of services, because that would not be very efficient. But at the same time people have come to expect a certain level of health care availability at the local level. Governments, by their cutbacks, are trying to force the burden of extra travel on to the backs of medical consumers. This is little more than a type of hidden taxation, in the sense that the extra cost of travel to fewer medical facilities is being born by the consumer. More important is the *emotional cost* of family members being widely separated from their loved-ones at the same time that they endure the emotional trauma of sickness and hospital care.

If the principles of Medicare are to be upheld, then there is some base level of healthcare that should be provided locally, regardless of costs. Standards for that local level of healthcare should be devised and adhered to across Canada.

At the same time we should recognize that there is a certain "unfairness" to the geography of the system of medical care. Those who live in "have-not" communities, especially when it comes to more specialized healthcare, pay an extra price in travel costs, time, and inconvenience as a result of their location. When it is necessary to receive specialized treatment or other specialized medical procedures, it is essential for them to travel "upward" through the hierarchy of communities.

**Calgary - The Best Place in Canada to Have a Stroke**

A good example of a health district making an extra effort to provide emergency health care of the type described comes from Calgary. Brad Evenson reports in the February 1999 *National Post* that a revolutionary new drug for the treatment of strokes is being widely used in the United States, but gets limited use in Canada. The drug has been approved for use in the United States but is only used in Canada in a few teaching hospitals. Patients or their families have to give special consent to use it. This is in spite of the fact that 50,000 Canadians have strokes each year. Evenson reports that Canadian doctors are frustrated with Health Canada's "glacial" efforts to approve the new drug.

Previously doctors could do little for patients suffering a stroke, so strokes were not even treated as emergencies. The *National Post* reports that the use of the new clot-busting drug TPA, or Activase, in the United States has revolutionized the treatment of strokes which are now coming to be called "brain attacks" (like heart attacks) in order to recognize their urgency. The problem with TPA is that it is only effective in busting clots if the stroke patient receives it within three hours of the attack. As a result, in the United States strokes are starting to be treated like any other major emergency, where time is of the essence.

Evenson reports on the situation in Florida:

> A new study from the University of Florida shows that the same emergency helicopter system that transports automobile accident victims in rural areas also can get stroke patients to hospital emergency rooms in time to receive effective drug therapy.

The situation has lagged behind in Canada, however, due to the failure of Health Canada to approve of TPA. The exception is in southern Alberta where the significance of the new method of treatment has been recognized:

> "In Canada, Calgary is the only centre equipped to deal with 'brain attacks' on a regional scale, with ambulance attendants and 911 operators trained to get stroke patients quickly to Foothills Hospital. Ontario's Heart and Stroke Foundation estimates only a quarter of the province's hospitals are equipped to handle a stroke emergency.

Dr. Alasdair Buchan, one of the proponents of the use of TPA, had to persuade the Mayor of Calgary to have the ambulance priority list recognize strokes as a top-level emergency.

The TPA program in Calgary represents the kind of emergency medical system that we should be striving to create everywhere in Canada. With the more widespread use of emergency helicopter systems, most Canadian citizens could be "just minutes" away from a hospital emergency room.

The rate of recovery from stroke in Calgary has tripled in two years.

## How Far to the Nearest Doctor?

Just how far from the doctor's office do most Canadians live? Statistics Canada did a study in 1993 in an attempt to answer this question. Using information on the location of physicians and patients, the study was able to measure how far it is to the nearest physician for most people in Canada. What they found out was that:

> At least 90% of Canadians in the 25 census metropolitan areas (at least 100,000 residents) live less than 5 km from the nearest physician. This increased to 99% for centres with a population of 1 million or more. Outside urban centres, however, only 56% of Canadians live within 5 km of a physician.

The implications of this statement are important. It says that since most Canadians live in cities (the "25 census metropolitan areas"), that most of them, in fact ninety percent of them, live within five kilometres of a doctor. The down-side is that *outside cities* only 56 percent of Canadians live within five kilometres of a doctor. The study supports the argument that was made above, that is, that Canadians living in small communities and rural areas are underserved by doctors. The study tells us that outside of cities, 44 percent of Canadians live farther than five kilometres from a doctor. Most of the time, most of those people are living at risk. In the event of a life-threatening emergency they may be too far away from potentially life-saving medical care.

A further finding of the study, having to do with specialist care, also has important implications for Canadians who live in "have-not" areas. In particular the study found that "The 23% of Canadians living in nonurban areas must travel further for specialist care, since *only 3% of specialists practise outside of urban areas*." Isn't that interesting. Only three percent of all specialists in Canada are not practising in cities. That really says a lot about the geography of health care in Canada — 97 percent of all specialists work in the 25 largest cities. Clearly this puts those people living in those 25 cities at a definite advantage when it comes to obtaining specialized medical care. Meanwhile, one-quarter of Canadians living in rural areas, or smaller towns and cities, must travel greater distances to receive the same health care that other Canadians receive locally.

There is another important conclusion of the study as well. It found that "In some cases the lack of a vehicle or public transportation compounds access problems facing patients who are some distance from a physician. Statistics Canada reported that no vehicles were available in 24% of households in rural areas that had an annual income of less than $15,000." The last part of this statement has shocking implications in the context of the promise of the universality of health care. It shows that one-quarter of lower income families in rural areas do not even have a car available when they need to make a routine visit to the doctor. Compare this to the lower-income family in the city that can use public transit, or a taxi, to obtain medical care. Clearly there are a significant number of

Canadians who, because they are poor or live in the "wrong place," are outside of the boundaries of care that Medicare is supposed to provide.

## The Medical "Brain Drain" to the United States?

Chapter 9 indicated that there is a supposed "brain drain" of science and technology graduates from Canada to the United States. Identical concerns are raised by some over the problem of graduates of our medical schools heading south, once they get their "paid for in Canada" education. It is claimed that large numbers of medical school graduates head to the United States once they have received their M.D. degree. One proponent of this line of thought is the Canadian Medical Association (CMA). It is in the Association's own best interest to promote this argument.

The numbers seem to be startling. Table 11.1 shows the number of doctors that have moved abroad as compared to the number that have returned from abroad, and the resulting net loss. The CMA supplies this table as part of their 1998 "Submission to Parliament" in an article provocatively entitled "Canadian Physicians and the Brain Drain." Several interesting patterns are said to emerge. It can be seen that the number of doctors moving abroad, in the second column, increased between 1991 and 1996. The *CMA News* reports that the majority of those doctors leaving, move to the United States. If the last *row* of the table is examined it can be seen that in 1996, 731 doctors moved away while 218 returned from abroad. This means there was a net loss of over 500 trained medical doctors in just one year. The *CMA News* indicates that the number of doctors who left in 1996 "equals the output of approximately five Canadian medical schools."

**Table 11.1 Migration of Active Canadian Physicians, 1991-1996**

| Year | Moving Abroad | Returning from Abroad | Net Loss |
| --- | --- | --- | --- |
| 1991 | 479 | 256 | 223 |
| 1992 | 689 | 259 | 430 |
| 1993 | 635 | 282 | 353 |
| 1994 | 777 | 309 | 468 |
| 1995 | 674 | 256 | 418 |
| 1996 | 731 | 218 | 513 |

Source: Canadian Medical Association, "*Canadian Physicians and the Brain Drain*', 1998.

No doubt the United States is a magnet to some Canadian doctors. However it appears that the CMA may be misleading in some of the statements it makes. The CMA wants more funding for medicine, and so tries to make it appear that all of the movers are young graduates. When one reads that the number of doctors who left equals the output of five medical schools, the automatic conclusion one draws is that those movers were the young graduates of those medical schools. What the CMA does not tell us is the *ages* of those 513 doctors that left. In other words, does it include doctors *of all ages*? If so, it will count senior doctors who are continuing to practice, while retiring to Arizona. It would not be surprising if the number of senior doctors moving to warm climates was increasing a little each year. These figures should not be taken too seriously until we are able to see the ages of the doctors who are leaving.

In any case, the truth of the matter is that the loss of doctors to out-migration is but a small portion of the total number of doctors. It was said above that Canada has 55,243 doctors. If 513 of them leave in a year, that represents less than one percent of the total. Surely that is an insignificant number compared to the over 99 percent who choose to stay in Canada.

In fact, if anything, the numbers are quite surprising. Given the relatively high incomes of doctors, and their freedom to be able to practise anywhere they like, would you not think that doctors would be leaving *in droves* for the warmer climate of the southern United States? Yet the vast majority of them choose to stay at home. The conclusion to be drawn from Table 11.1 is that Canada is *very attractive* to most doctors because very few of them move away.

The Canadian Medical Association evidently uses these figures to appeal for more funding from the government. In a 1998 speech to the House of Commons Finance Committee, the CMA president, Victor Dirnfeld, used Table 11.1 and the "output of five medical schools" as an argument in a pitch for more support. The text of his speech suggests that Ottawa must restore the cash transfers, the implication being that this will stop the supposed brain drain. In the same article he is quoted as saying "Physicians, in their frustration, because of their inability to practise their profession are leaving Canada for the United States." These provocative assertions fail to mention that 99.1 percent of practising physicians are staying right at home in Canada. Moreover, the Canadian Institute for Health Information reported that by 1997, the number of physicians leaving the country had actually dropped by ten percent.

A better picture of the medical profession can be gained by looking at some other numbers. On December 16, 1997 the Canadian Institute for Health Information (CIHI) indicated that in 1996 the total number of physicians in all of Canada decreased by only 48. That's a change of *under one-tenth of one percent.* A decrease of 48 in a pool of 55,243 is insignificant. Does the CMA report this to parliament? At the same time the number of specialists in the country increased in the same year by 350. So the number of highly trained doctors is even increasing. The CIHI reports that the number of general and family practitioners is about 51 percent, while the proportion of specialists is about 51 percent. These proportions, it was said, have remained unchanged for some twenty years now. These kinds of numbers throw cold water on the arguments put forth by the CMA. There appears to be no significant brain drain of Canadian doctors to the United States.

More importantly, what has not even been mentioned is the supply of foreign-trained physicians that move into Canada every year. We saw above that the total number of physicians in Canada is staying just about exactly the same from year to year. That means that in spite of the fact that we are losing about 500 doctors to the United States, we must also be gaining about 500 doctors from other sources. The implication is that the supply of doctors is being maintained, either through graduates from medical schools, or else through the supply of doctors immigrating to Canada in any year. In any case, there seems to be no need to raise the alarm about a shortage of doctors in Canada.

## Health Care Funding in the United States and Canada

There is nothing quite like the sight of the Space Shuttle as it takes off from Cape Canaveral. In an intriguing mixture of power and beauty it blasts into space as the world's ultimate tribute to the majesty of technology. More than anything, the shuttle symbolizes the global dominance and superiority of the United States as the world's most powerful country. Canada participates in the program. It *specializes* in the production of the Canadarm which moves the payload into and out of the shuttle's cargo bay. It is appropriate that Canada participates in the program and it is expected that we can only do so by specializing in one small part of it. Is there any Canadian who realistically believes that Canada should try to maintain its own, independent space program? Could we afford it? The answer is obviously no.

The same argument that applies to the space program, should apply to the medical health research field. Many Canadians in the field of medical research expect Canada to compete with the United States in that field. Given the size of the United States, such a competition is out of the question. Just as with the space shuttle, Canada is just not big enough to do some of the things that the United States can do. The best alternative, like the Canadarm, is to specialize — to fund just a few things, but do them better than anyone else in the world. That is how Canada should be looking to make its contribution to medical science.

As Canadians we have a huge neighbour to our south that is, in fact, ten times larger than we are. Given the sheer scale of the United States, we should expect it to be able to do, and be able to afford, many things that are simply out of the reach of a smaller country like ours. An excellent example of the ability of the United States to do extraordinary things is evidenced in the existence of NASA and the space program. Similarly, the United States military is a huge and enormous enterprise. It is unimaginable for Canada to be able to afford such massive and expensive endeavours. For the United States, such things are well within the realm of possibility.

The same argument that applies to NASA and the United States military should be applied to the relationship between medical research in Canada and the United States as well. Medical research is very expensive. Yet the United States exists on a scale where extremely large amounts of money can de directed towards medical research — far more than could ever be imagined in Canada. It is possible to accomplish grand things with a population, and tax base, of more than 300,000,000 people.

In Canada, the medical community, and the CMA, decries the paucity of spending on medical research in Canada. Although it is agreed that funding to research has been cut to the bone over many years of budget cuts, Canadian medical researchers should never expect to see levels of funding comparable to those that their American counterparts receive. It is simply beyond the scale of Canada to be able to support research on so massive a scale, as does the United States.

Consider an example of the difference in the sheer magnitude of scale between the two countries. *The Globe and Mail*, in a report comparing medical research in Canada and the United States, presented information on the budget of a single, mega-sized cancer centre in Texas as compared to the budgets of Canada's major cancer institutions. It was reported in July 1998 that the M. D. Anderson Cancer Center in Houston, Texas spends $170 million dollars (Canadian) a year on cancer research. Compare this to the National Cancer Institute of Canada a *national* institution, which spends $48 million a year, Canada-wide. Or, compare this to one of Canada's major cancer research hospitals, the Princess Margaret in Toronto, that spends $20 million dollars a year (see Figure 11.7). How can Canada possibly compete, when a single hospital in the United States has a bigger research budget than Canada's national cancer research institute and one of Canada's major research hospitals combined? The dollar amounts in the United States are simply staggering.

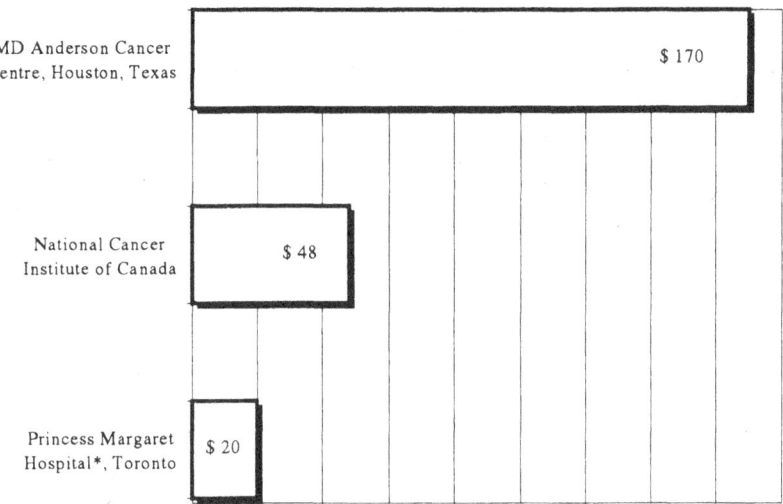

*Figures for Princess Margaret Hospital reflect 1997 budgets, prior to its merger on January 1, 1998 with the Toronto Hospital

Source: *Globe and Mail*, July 11, 1998.

**Figure 11.7  1997 Budgets for Cancer Research (millions)**

In fact, because M. D. Anderson functions in the competitive environment of the United States, it needs to advertise its services to drum up more business. *The Globe and Mail* reports that M. D. Anderson "spends more on its marketing department — $2 million (U.S.) — than the National Cancer Institute of Canada spends on clinical trials of new cancer therapies."

As a further point of comparison, consider the size of funding for research projects in Canada and the United States. Figure 11.8 shows the average level of funding for single research projects by Canada's Medical Research Council (MRC), the National Cancer Institute of Canada, and the United States National Institutes of Health (NIH). It can be seen that NIH grants are nearly three times larger on average than MRC grants. So not only are the *totals* spent on medical research larger in the United States than Canada, but the amounts spent on individual projects are also much larger.

Where Canada does lag behind, is in terms of its basic research funding. Even though we should perhaps not aspire to the level of research set by the United States, we should nevertheless pay "our fair share" towards the cost of medical research. Canada should have medical research

214  *Hierarchical Organization in Society*

funded to a level that is appropriate to the size and international stature of the country. A reasonable approach is to at least have Canadian medical research funding on par with the other members of a comparable group of countries, that is, the G7 countries. In addition to Canada, these include France, Germany, Italy, Japan, the United Kingdom, and the United States. Table 11.2 shows funding for medical research in United States dollars per person for five of the seven G7 countries. Clearly Canada lags way behind comparable nations in its commitment to spending on health research and development. These funding levels are nothing short of atrocious.

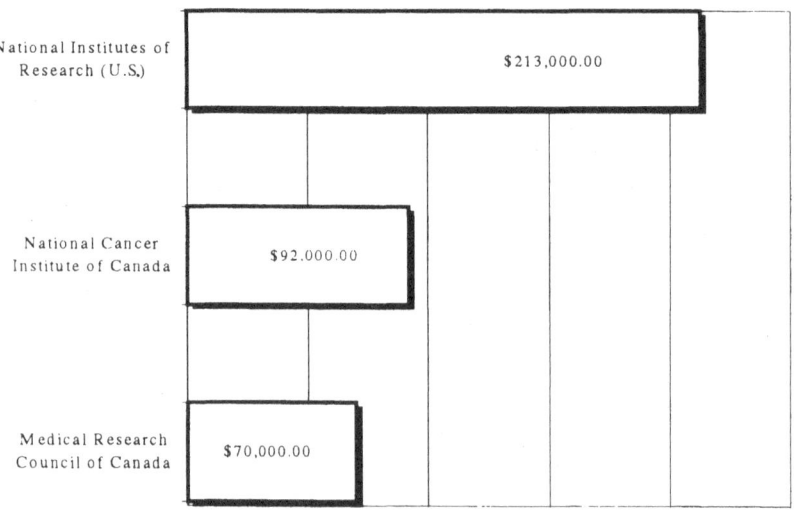

Source: *Globe and Mail*, July 25, 1998.

**Figure 11.8  Average Budget of Research Projects in Canada and the U.S.**

In the 1999 Federal Budget, a new initiative, the Canadian Institutes of Health Research was set up as a way of giving medical and health research in Canada a much needed boost. The new institute adds several millions of dollars a year to medical research in Canada, and should help the country regain its place as a well-known international contributor to medical and health science.

## Table 11.2 Health Spending - Select G-7 Countries, 1994

| Country | $ Per Capita (U.S.) |
|---|---|
| United Kingdom | 78 |
| France | 63 |
| United States | 59 |
| Japan | 35 |
| Canada | 22 |

Source: Canadian Medical Association, 'Canadian Physicians and the Brain Drain', 1998.

## Should the United States Provide a Second Tier of Health Care for Canadians?

A bone of contention among Canadians is the issue of Canadian patients seeking medical care in the United States. As Canadian governments whittle away at medical spending, the problem of Canadian patients heading south in search of better or more sophisticated medical care has become more acute. There is no way of knowing exactly how many Canadians seek out health treatment in the United States, but Sean Fine of the *Globe and Mail* reports in 1998 that there were a total of 650 patients being treated at the "big three" institutes in the United States. Those include the University of Texas, M.D. Anderson Cancer Center in Houston, the Mayo Clinic in Rochester, Minnesota, and the Memorial Sloan-Kettering Cancer Center in New York. There is more to this problem than just patient travel, however. Instead it is indicative of a broader issue which is the relationship between the United States and Canada when it comes to sophisticated health care research.

This book has argued several times that in many ways, Canada and the United States are both parts of a unified economic hierarchy. This has become especially true with the advent of the Free Trade Agreement (FTA) and the North American Free Trade Agreement (NAFTA). The point has been made that the two countries' urban systems, transportation systems, sports leagues, etc., are all parts of a single hierarchical system. The boundary between Canada and the United States has become a much less significant barrier to the flow of goods and people between the two countries. The question that remains to be addressed is how Canada and the United States should divvy-up medical treatment and high level patient care.

As the Canada-United States border becomes more permeable, presumably increased numbers of Canadians will head south for specialized medical care. The number of such trips is apparently bolstered a great deal by the existence of the Internet and other information sources. As Canadians get ill, they seek out information on the Internet, and nowadays this leads them more and more to sources of help in the United States. Sean Fine sums up the situation in a 1998 *Globe and Mail* article:

> Borders are falling in health care, and information is becoming a vital currency. Cancer patients and their families now have access to truckloads of it — through the Internet, new support groups and information services, such as a national toll-free line. Instead of simply heeding the advice of their doctors, they come waving printouts of research studies mined from the Internet.

At the same time, United States hospitals and medical centres operate on a "for profit" basis so they are anxious to have the extra business that a Canadian clientele provides. The problem comes when we try to reconcile this approach to medical treatment with the principles of Medicare that says all Canadians should be treated equally. When wealthier Canadians can afford better or more advanced health care in the United States, the ideals of Medicare are eroded. We end up with a two-tiered system of medicine, in which only the wealthy can afford the second, American tier.

What is the solution to this problem? First, it is necessary to make the point strongly that the problem is not going to go away — it is only going to get worse. Patients have more information than ever before. The border is more open than ever before. American hospitals and medical centres are soliciting the business of Canadians. Canadians are getting older and in need of greater health care. And the number of people who can afford treatment in the United States is on the rise.

Moreover, in addition to these factors, an important point to be emphasized is that, with levels of medical research funding being what they are in Canada, the country will never be able to compete with the United States in high-end medical research and treatment. The massive budgets in the United States enable medical specialists there to work on the cutting edge of medical research and surgery. And it is just this type of aggressive treatment and research that desperate Canadians are seeking out. When it comes to medical research, Canada and the United States represent a single, hierarchical system. Most of the cutting-edge research that comes out of this system will of necessity emanate from centres within the United States. Stated another way, Canada just does not have the population base to support a M. D. Anderson, a Mayo Clinic, or Sloan-Kettering Institute. These huge institutions draw patients and funding from all over the world.

The integration of the American and Canadian economies has been emphasized throughout this book. In Chapter 3 on corporate hierarchies, in Chapter 5 on communities, in Chapter 6 on transportation, and Chapter 9 on migration, a constant theme has been that the border is falling and that continental thinking is the way of the future. The same reasoning needs to apply to medicine. As we have seen in the present chapter, most medical treatment takes place in urban centres. As a consequence, as higher levels of treatment are sought after, patients will ascend through the hierarchy of cities, regardless of national borders. The medical hierarchy is a transnational one that exists in the system of cities in Canada and the United States. Drawing an artificial boundary, and telling Canadians who are desperately seeking life-saving medical treatment in the United States, that they cannot cross that boundary is not only despicable, it is downright cruel.

There are two alternatives. One is to maintain the status quo and let wealthy Canadians continue to seek out and pay for specialized treatment in the United States. Such an approach will serve only to reinforce and solidify the notion that the United States provides a second tier of health care to Canadians, but only for those that can afford it. This approach flies in the face of the principles of Medicare. The other alternative is to recognize that the United States will always be able to supply leading edge medical care and treatment, and to agree that all Canadians should be allowed access to it. This approach implies that Medicare will pay the bills for those Canadians that find it necessary to seek out specialized medical help in the United States. Although provisions are currently made for Canadians to receive limited medical care in the United States, they do not cover highly specialized or aggressive treatments or surgical procedures. What is needed then is a way for all Canadians to avail themselves of high level medical care in the United States at no personal cost. Probably the only way in which the expenses of this approach will not spiral out of control is to have a new regulatory body in place that decides which specialized procedures will be covered by Medicare, and which will not.

Regardless of what such a treatment system might cost in day-to-day expenses, it is still very cheap when one realizes that *the United States is paying for all of the costs of the basic research and infrastructure*. The very existence of the huge medical research community in the United States provides Canadians with literally the best medical research in the world right at their doorstep. Yet, all the Americans ask us to pay is a user fee. That sounds like the best deal in the world. What other country is better able to take advantage of having a neighbour that is so close and that can, at the same time, provide world-class medical care at a bargain price?

## References

Abraham, C. and Fine, S., 'Canada's cancer system slips to second best', *Globe and Mail*, July 25, 1998.
Abraham, C. and Fine S., 'Frontier spirit lures Canadian doctors', *Globe and Mail*, July 11, 1998.
Canadian Institute for Health Information, 'Active civilian physicians and physicians per 100,000 population by type of physician and province, Canada, 1996 and 1997', Southam Medical Database.
Canadian Institute for Health Information, 'Number of physicians by age-group and gender, Canada, 1997', Southam Medical Database.
Canadian Institute for Health Information, 'Physician supply and migration numbers for Canada released', December 16, 1997.
Canadian Institute for Health Information, 'Fewer Canadian physicians leaving country, 1997 figures', August 25, 1998.
Canadian Institute for Health Information, 'Canada to spend more on health care in 1998 says Canadian Institute for Health Information', November 19, 1998.
Canadian Medical Association, 'How far away is the nearest physician?', July 15, 1997.
Canadian Medical Association, 'Canadian physicians and the brain drain', June 9, 1998.
Canadian Medical Association Journal, 'Projected physician supply', June 2, 1998.
Canadian Medical Association News, 'CMA brings concerns on brain drain and research funding to Parliament Hill', July 14, 1998.
Canadian Medical Association Submissions to Parliament, 'Canadian Physicians and the Brain Drain', June 9, 1998.
Evenson, B., 'Clot-busting stroke drug saving lives', *National Post*, February 8, 1999.
Statistics Canada, 'Brain drain or brain gain? What do the data say?', October 1, 1998.
Statistics Canada, 'Employment Income Data', *The Daily*, May 12, 1998.

# Index

Abitibi Consolidated Inc., 40, 41
Activase, 207
Air Canada, 6, 38, 41
Air France, 108
Airbus, 106, 108
Airdrie, 167
Albany, 94
Alberta, 13, 26, 89, 92, 103, 160, 177, 207
Albuquerque, 94
Alcan Aluminum Ltd., 40, 41, 42
Allianz AG, 44
American Airlines, 113
Amoco Canada Petroleum Co., 41
Anchor Stores, 144, 152
Argentina Gold Corp., 46
Asea Brown Boveri Ltd. (ABB), 61
AT&T, 44
Atlanta, 94, 95, 96, 105
Aurora, 41
Austin, 94
Automobile, 8, 12, 13, 75, 84, 118, 121, 123, 125, 126, 127, 129, 130, 132, 133, 134, 135, 136, 205, 207
AXA, 44

Bakersfield, 94
Bank of Montreal, 40
Bank of Nova Scotia, 40
Bankers Trust Corp., 12, 45
Barrick Gold Corp., 40, 46
Bay Networks Inc., 52
BC Telecom Inc., 52
BCE, 40
Bell Canada, 42
Birmingham, 94
Blainville, 167
Boeing, 44, 107, 108
Bombardier, 40, 41
Bonsall, Thomas, 108
*Boom, Bust and Echo*, 66, 117, 128
Boston, 94, 95, 96

Brain Drain, 12, 13, 159, 169, 170, 171, 172, 173, 209, 210, 211, 215
Brain Gain, 13, 172, 173
Brandon, 195
British Airways, 108
British Columbia, 13, 88, 89, 90, 92, 100, 104, 160, 177, 184, 199
British Petroleum p.l.c, 44
Buchan, Alasdair, 207
Buffalo, 94
Burger King, 34
Burlington, 41

C. D. Howe Institute, 173
Calgary, 40, 41, 91, 92, 94, 97, 104, 105, 164, 166, 171, 182, 186, 190, 206, 207
California, 13, 136
Canada, 6, 8, 9, 10, 11, 13, 31, 39, 42, 45, 48, 53, 65, 66, 67, 68, 75, 76, 79, 83, 85, 86, 87, 88, 89, 90, 91, 92, 93, 95, 96, 99, 104, 105, 108, 109, 110, 111, 112, 113, 114, 120, 132, 133, 149, 153, 154, 158, 159, 161, 164, 165, 168, 169, 170, 171, 172, 173, 174, 175, 176, 177, 178, 184, 185, 186, 190, 191, 195, 197, 198, 200, 206, 207, 208, 209, 210, 211, 212, 213, 214, 215, 216, 217
airlines in, 6
airport hierarchy, 106
bank mergers, 95
busiest airports, 105
corporate change, 50
educational system, 66
farm economy, 47
integration with the United States, 159
magnitude of farming, 87
number of farms in, 86
population growth, 66
provincial population sizes, 89

219

## 220  *Hierarchical Organization in Society*

structure of corporations in, 38
top fifty corporations, 40
total population, 1996, 88
*Canada Highlights*, 86, 88
Canada Pension Plan, 10
Canada Safeway, 41
Canada, Mexico, and the United States economic ties, 99
Canadian Advanced Technology Association (CATA), 171
Canadian Cities
   new flows, 191
   percentage rates of growth, 166
Canadian Corporate Hierarchy
   based on the TSE, 39
Canadian Football League (CFL), 12
Canadian Imperial Bank of Commerce, 40
Canadian Institute for Health Information, 199, 200, 201, 210
Canadian Institutes of Health Research, 214
Canadian Medical Association, 209, 210, 215
Canadian Metropolitan Areas
   by population and rank, 91
Canadian Municipalities
   fastest rates of growth, 167
Canadian National Railway, 40, 41, 114
Canadian Occidental Petroleum Ltd., 40
Canadian Pacific, 40, 41
Canadian Tire Corp., 40, 41
*Canadian Transit Handbook*, 127
Canadian Ultramar, 41
Canadian-American Hierarchy of Cities, 97
Canmore, 165, 167
Cape Canaveral, 211
CBC, 190
Census Metropolitan Areas (CMA's), 92
Census of Agriculture, 86, 88
Central Okanagan, 167
Champy, James, 57, 62, 63
Charlotte, 94
Charlottetown, 105
Chemainus, 100, 104
Chicago, 94, 96, 105
Chicoutimi, 91, 164, 165, 166
China, 83, 88, 113, 168, 174, 175
Chrysler, 12, 44
Chrysler Canada, 40
Cincinnati, 94

Cleveland, 94
*CMA News*, 209
CN Tower, 37, 95
CNN, 95
*CNN Financial Network*, 154
Coca-Cola, 14, 38, 95
Coca-Cola Canada, 38
Cochrane, 167
Collector Street, 118
Columbus, 94
Communities
   future of, 79
   map of, 81
Community Size
   and health care, 201
Concorde, 108
Continental and International Migration among cities, 165
Continentalization, 11, 48, 76, 99, 100, 111, 112, 114, 159
Coopetition, 32, 152
Corporate Headquarters, 31, 169
Corporate hierarchies
   types
      of corporations, 38
      within corporations, 38
Corporate Ladder, 1, 54
Courtenay, 167
Cranbrook, 195
Credit Suisse Group, 44
CTV, 190

Daewoo Group, 44
Dai-ichi Mutual Life Insurance, 44
Daimler-Benz AG, 44
Dallas, 94, 95, 96
Dayton, 94
de Geus, Arie, 59
Delayering, 61
Delta Air Lines, 113
Denver, 94, 154
Detroit, 94, 95, 96
Deutsche Bank AG, 12, 45
DeVoretz, Don, 173
Dirnfeld, Victor
   CMA president, 210
Division of Labour, 54, 55, 57, 63
Division of Management, 57, 63
Dixon, Guy, 52
Dofasco Inc., 40
Dorval, 41, 104, 105

*Index* 221

E.I. du Pont de Nemours and Co., 45
Economies of EMU and U.S.
   comparison, 53
Economies of Scale, 45, 46, 70, 72, 81,
   103, 203
Edmonton, 91, 92, 94, 104, 105, 126,
   164, 166, 186, 190
EdperBrascan, 41
Education
   educational bussing pattern, 73
Educational Hierarchy, 68
   in rural areas, 72
   map of, 74
   tree diagram of, 74
Educational System, 4, 11, 29, 65, 66,
   67, 68, 69, 70, 73, 75, 99, 159
   hierarchies within, 77
El Paso, 94
Elementary and Secondary Schools
   enrollment in, 66
Elementary Schools, 70, 71, 73
Elf Aquitaine, 45
Emergency Medical Care, 205
Empire, 41
Entertainment
   travelling, 194
Etobicoke, 41
Euro, 51, 52, 53, 96
Europe
   automobile dealerships in, 13
European Monetary Union (EMU), 51
Evenson, Brad, 206
Excel Communications Inc., 47
Exxon, 12, 44, 46, 50, 53

Fads, 195, 196
Farm Income and Value in Canada, 88
Farm Numbers and Size in Canada, 86
Farmer's Market, 194
Fellegi, Ivan, 172
Fiat, 44
Fidelity Company, 6
*Financial Post*, 12, 13, 34, 39, 40, 53,
   111, 113, 136
Fine, Sean, 215, 216
Florenceville, 41
Foot, David, 66, 67, 117, 128
*Forbes ASAP*, 56, 59
Ford Motor Company, 32, 40, 42, 44,
   49, 54, 56, 57
Ford, Henry, 55, 56, 132

*Fortune Magazine*, 42
Fredericton, 105
Free Trade, 11, 76, 77, 93, 112, 113,
   174, 179
Free Trade Agreement, 11, 48, 111, 114,
   169, 171, 172, 215
Fresno, 94

G7 countries, 214
Gananoque, 100, 102, 104
Gander, 105
General Electric, 44, 50, 53
General Motors, 14, 32, 40, 42, 44, 46,
   54, 56, 57, 61, 80
Global 500, 42
Global Free Trade, 112
Global Top 50, 42, 44
Globalization, 46, 47, 48, 99, 112, 174
*Globe and Mail*, 45, 49, 52, 106, 113,
   169, 212, 213, 214, 215, 216
Grain
   shipment of, 100, 101
Grand Rapids, 94
Greensboro, 94
Greenspon, Edward, 172
Greenville, 94

Halifax, 91, 104, 105, 111, 164, 166, 182
Hamilton, 41, 91, 92, 94, 164, 166, 186
Hammer, Michael, 57, 62
Harrisburg, 94
Hartford, 94
Hartman, John, 132
Hazard, H., 127
Health Canada, 206, 207
Health Care
   second tier, 215
   sex discrimination in, 199
Health Care Funding
   in the United States and Canada, 211
Health Care in Canada, 198, 205, 208
Health Expenditure
   by province 1998, 200
Health Spending
   G-7 countries, 215
Heimler, Peter, 61
Hewlett-Packard, 45
Hierarchical Pattern of Communities, 73
Hierarchies
   importance of, 10
   processes in, 20
Hierarchy

# 222  Hierarchical Organization in Society

air traffic, 104, 106
airline, 6
American and Canadian cities, 168
Americanadian, 93
at different scales, 26
Canadian urban, 93
Canadian urban and the NHL, 186
Canadian-American cities and the NFL, 187
cities, towns and villages, 7
community migration, 162
competitive/cooperative, 32
corporate
    Canadian and global, 38
corporate ladder, 1
definition, 1
democratic/autocratic, 28
diffusion in, 31
direction of information flow, 30
dynamic/static, 27
educational, 68
fast food, 36
formal/informal, 29
funcional/nonfunctional, 34
hardware stores, 4
human body, 14
in nature, 25
information flow, 18
international corporate, 43
medical, in a rural area, 203
medical, within a major city, 202
national transportation, 103, 104, 119
of Canadian communities, 90
of provincial populations, 90
of roads in the city, 146
open/closed, 28
physical form
    dimensionality, 33
    maturity, 34
    symmetry, 32
poltical/benign, 29
private/public, 31
properties
    communications, 18
    physical, 17
public transit, 120
retail, in countryside, 147
retail, in the city, 143
road classification, 111
rural retail, impacts of, 148
rural shopping, map of, 149
self-organizing, 30

shopping mall, 153
shopping, in rural area, 147
street address, 9
structured/unstructured, 27
transportation, ongoing changes, 108
types
    bottom-heavy, 21
    narrow-waisted, 22
    normal, 20
    top-heavy, 24
    unbalanced/nonsymmetrical, 33
    typical within school, 5
urban shopping, 143
warehouse
    map of, 84
within hierarchy, 24
Hierarchy of Communities
changing face of, 85
corporate hierarchies within, 84
map of, 83
treelike, 83
Hitachi, 44
Hockey, 11, 14, 18, 134, 182, 183, 184, 185, 186
    American Hockey League (AHL), 182, 184, 185
    Canadian Hockey League (CHL), 182, 184, 185
    International Hockey League (IHL), 182, 184, 185
    minor, 183
    National Hockey League (NHL), 182, 184, 185, 186
    Ontario Hockey League (OHL), 182, 184
    Quebec Major Junior Hockey League (QMJHL), 182, 184
    Western Hockey League (WHL), 182, 184
Honda, 44
Honda Canada, 41
Honolulu, 94
Houston, 94, 95, 96, 212, 215
Hudson's Bay Co., 41

IBM, 14, 41, 44, 50, 53
Illinois Central Railway, 114
Imasco Ltd., 40, 41, 42
Immigrants, 67, 172, 176, 177, 178
Immigration
    provinces with the highest, 178
Imperial Oil, 41

Index 223

Inco, 40, 41
Indianapolis, 94
Information Technology (IT), 169, 170, 171
*Intermetropolitan Migration in Canada.*, 162
Internet, 19, 27, 188, 191, 216
Itochu Corporation, 44

Jacksonville, 94
Jim Pattison Group, 41
Johnston, David C., 106
Just-in-Time Inventory Management, 102, 110

Kamloops, 182, 189
Kanata, 165, 167
Kansas, 94, 114
Kelowna, 105
Kersell, John, 61
KFC, 34
Kingston, 100, 101, 102, 195
Knoxville, 94
Koperski, Krzysztof, 27
Kroo, Ilan, 107

La Plaine, 167
Ladysmith, 167
Laidlaw Inc., 40, 41
Las Vegas, 94
Lavaltrie, 167
Light Rapid Transit (LRT), 121
Location, 75, 146
*Location Strategies for Retail and Service Firms*, 152
London, 46, 91, 105, 108, 162, 164, 166, 168, 172
Los Angeles, 94, 96, 195
Louisville, 94

M. D. Anderson Cancer Center, 212
MacMillan Bloedel Ltd., 40, 41
Magna International Inc., 40, 41
Malls
  flow of traffic, 154
Manitoba, 89, 160, 184
Maple Leaf Foods, 41
*Market Centers and Retail Location*, 141
Markham, 41
Martin, Paul
  Finance Minister, 169
Marubeni Corporation, 44

Mass Transit Flows
  map of, 122
Masson-Angers, 167
Mass-Transit, 130
Matsushita Electric Industrial Co. 44
McCain Foods, 41
McDonald's, 34
Medical Research Council of Canada, 213
Medicare, 173, 197, 198, 205, 206, 209, 216, 217
  costs of, 198
  geographical discrimination, 198
Medicine
  cutbacks, 197
Memphis, 94
Mercedes-Benz, 12
Mergers
  top five canadian 1998, 52
Mergers and Acquisitions, 38, 45, 46, 47, 48, 87, 95
Metro-Richelieu, 41
Mexico, 96
Miami, 94, 95, 96
Microsoft, 14, 50
Migration, 157, 158, 160, 175, 209
  among Canadian cities, 163
  and education, 161
  costs of, 157
  from Canada to rest of world, 173
  from rest of world to Canada, 175
  hierarchy of, 161
  of active Canadian physicians 1991-1996, 209
Millennium Round, 113
Milwaukee, 94
Ministry of Transportation
  Annual Report 1997, 99, 108, 109
Minneapolis, 94
Mirabel, 104, 105
Mitsubishi, 44
Mitsui & Co. 41, 43, 44
Mobil Oil, 12, 41, 44, 46
Mobility
  corporate, 12
  human, 12
Mode of Transport, 101
Moncton, 105
Montreal, 31, 40, 41, 87, 91, 92, 93, 94, 95, 96, 111, 164, 166, 168, 169, 170, 177, 186, 187, 190
Moore Corp., 41

## 224 *Hierarchical Organization in Society*

Nanaimo, 167
Nashville, 94
National Cancer Institute of Canada, 212, 213
National Football League (NFL), 12, 186, 187, 188
National Institutes of Health (NIH), 213
*National Post*, 46, 47, 114, 206, 207
National Transportation Hierarchy, 104, 118
Nestl, 44
Net Interprovincial Migration 1991-1996, 160
Net Migration, 159
   Canadian cities, 1996-1997, 164
New Brunswick, 89, 160
New Geography, 174
New Orleans, 94
New York, 12, 13, 39, 45, 46, 49, 94, 96, 108, 168, 169, 194, 195, 215
New York Stock Exchange (NYSE), 39
Newfoundland, 13, 88, 89, 159, 160, 192
Newspapers
   by community size, 190
Nippon Life Insurance, 44
Nippon Telegraph & Telephone, 44
Nissan Motor, 44
Nissho Iwai Corporation, 44
Noranda, 41
Norfolk, 94
North American Free Trade Agreement, 11, 48, 169, 215
Northern Telecom Ltd, 52
Northwest Airlines, 113
Northwest Territories, 89, 160, 199
Notre-Dame-de-l'Ile-Perrot, 167
Nova Corp., 41, 52
Nova Scotia, 89, 160, 199

Oakville, 40
Oklahoma, 94
Olive, David, 12, 113
Omaha, 94
Onex Corp., 41
Ontario, 8, 13, 37, 61, 89, 90, 91, 92, 100, 104, 160, 162, 164, 172, 177, 191, 207
Orlando, 94
Oshawa, 40, 91, 92, 164, 166
Ottawa, 8, 9, 91, 92, 93, 104, 105, 164, 166, 186, 190, 210
Ottawa-Hull, 91, 92, 94, 164, 166, 186

Parksville, 167
PepsiCo Inc., 52
Personal Information, 192
Peters, Tom, 56, 59
Petro-Canada, 41
Philadelphia, 94, 96
Philip Morris Companies, 44
Phoenix, 94, 186
Physicians
   by age group and gender 1997, 201
   number of per 100,000 population, 1996-1997, 199
Pittsburgh, 94
Pizza Hut, 34
PolyGram, 51, 52
Portland, 94, 171
Potash Corp. of Saskatchewan, 41
Power Corp. of Canada, 41
Prince Edward Island, 89, 160, 199
Prince George, 105
Princess Margaret Hospital, 212, 213
*Profit 100 Magazine*, 48
Providence, 94
Provigo, 41
Public Transit, 69, 120, 121, 123, 125, 126, 128, 129, 130, 134, 208
Public Transport, 129

Qualicum Beach, 167
Quality of Life, 129, 134, 173, 182, 192
Quebec, 89, 91, 92, 94, 104, 105, 160, 161, 164, 166, 177, 186, 199
Quebecor, 41

Radio, 191
Raleigh, 94
Ravenstein, E.G., 161
*Reengineering Management*, 62
*Reengineering the Corporation*, 54, 57, 62
Regina, 41, 91, 105, 164, 166
Reguly, Eric, 45, 49
Research Projects
   average budget of in Canada and the US, 214
Retail Hierarchy
   map of in the city, 145
Retail Strategies, 151
Revenue Canada, 10, 75
Richmond, 94
*Ride & Drive*, 108

# Index 225

Road Improvement
  endless cycle, 121
Rochester, 94
Royal Bank, 38
Royal Dutch/Shell Group, 44, 50
Rural Communities
  in decline, 150

Sacramento, 94
Saint John, 91, 105, 164, 165, 166
Saint-Colomban, 167
Sainte-Catherine, 167
Saint-Emile, 167
Saint-Jean-Chrysostome, 167
Saint-Lin, 167
Salaries, 198
  dentists, 199
  general practitioners and family physicians, 199
  judges, 198
  physicians and surgeons, 198
Salt Lake City, 94
Samuel, Peter, 136
San Antonio, 94
San Diego, 94, 136
San Diego Association of Governments, 136
San Francisco, 94, 96
Saskatchewan, 89, 160
Saskatchewan Wheat Pool, 41
Saskatoon, 41, 65, 91, 105, 164, 166
Scarborough, 41
Schachter, Harvey, 48
Scranton, 94
Seagram Co. Ltd., 40, 42, 51, 52
Sears Canada, 41
Sears, Roebuck, 45
Seattle, 94, 96
Secondary Schools, 65, 71, 73
Shell Canada., 41
Shopping and Travel, 141
Siemens AG, 44
Sloan, Alfred P., 56, 57, 215, 216
Smith, Adam, 54, 55, 57, 62
Snowbirds, 169
Sony, 44
Specialized Goods, 3, 147, 148, 149, 175
Sports and Hockey, 181
St. John's, 91, 105, 164, 166, 195
St. Louis, 94
State Farm Insurance, 45

Statistics Canada, 10, 66, 67, 86, 88, 89, 91, 92, 94, 105, 159, 160, 161, 163, 164, 166, 167, 172, 173, 177, 178, 198, 207, 208
Stelco, 41
Stellarton, 41
Street Hierarchy
  journal across town, map of, 119
Stroke
  in Calgary, 207
Sudbury, 91, 105, 164, 166
Sumitomo Corporation, 44
Sumitomo Life Insurance, 45
Sunbirds, 169
Super Malls, 154
Syracuse, 94

Taco Bell, 34
Tampa, 94
Teaming, 61
*Technology.com*, 169, 170, 172
Teleglobe Inc., 47
Telus Corp., 52
Texaco, 44
*The Daily*, 89, 91, 94, 160, 164, 166, 167
*The Financial Post*, 39, 40, 96
*The Geography of Urban Transportation*, 122, 125
The Oshawa Group, 41
The Thomson Corp., 41
*The Top 10 of Everything 1999*, 178
*The Wealth of Nations*, 54
Thunder Bay, 91, 105, 164, 166
Tierney, Christine, 13
Tokyo Electric Power Co, 45
Tomen Corporation, 45
Toronto, 11, 12, 31, 37, 38, 40, 41, 48, 87, 91, 92, 93, 94, 95, 96, 100, 101, 102, 104, 105, 110, 117, 128, 136, 153, 162, 164, 166, 168, 169, 172, 177, 186, 187, 189, 190, 192, 195, 212, 213
  Skydome, 12
Toronto 35 Index, 38
Toronto Stock Exchange (TSE), 38, 39
Toshiba, 45
Toyota, 44
Trading Partners
  world's top 10 biggest 1995, 113
Traffic, 8, 104, 105, 111, 120, 121, 123, 130, 131, 136, 153
Traffic and Development

endless cycle of, 131
TransCanada Pipelines, 40, 52
Transport
    most popular types, 109
Transportation, 99, 100, 103, 109, 118, 123, 129
    within hierarchies, 100
Transportation Association of Canada, 132, 134, 135
Tricon Global Restaurants, 34
Tropicanca Products Inc., 52
TSE 35, 39, 40
TSE 100, 38
TSE 300, 38, 39
Tucson, 94
Tulsa, 94
Turner Broadcasting, 95

U.S. Bureau of the Census, 94
Unilever N.V./Unilever p.l.c., 44
United States, 11, 12, 13, 45, 51, 52, 53, 76, 89, 90, 93, 95, 96, 99, 105, 111, 112, 113, 114, 159, 161, 169, 170, 171, 172, 173, 174, 184, 185, 186, 188, 198, 206, 207, 209, 210, 211, 212, 213, 215, 216, 217
    automobile dealerships in, 13
    farm economy, 47
    free trade agreement with, 11
United States Postal Service, 44
University Endowment Area, 167
Urban Hierarchy
    map of travel in, 101

size of flows, map of, 102
Urban Transit Systems, 119, 120, 122
Uruguay Round, 113

Val-des-Monts, 167
Vancouver, 41, 46, 91, 92, 93, 94, 100, 101, 102, 103, 104, 105, 111, 164, 166, 177, 186, 190, 195
Vanderkamp, J., 162
Varennes, 167
Veba AG, 45
Victoria, 91, 100, 101, 103, 105, 164, 166
Volkswagen AG, 44
Volvo, 49

Wal-Mart Stores, 44
Wasaga Beach, 165, 167
Washington, 13, 94, 96, 184
Wendy's, 34
West Edmonton Mall, 153
West Palm Beach, 94
Westcoast Energy, 41
Weston, George, 40
Whistler, 165, 167
Whitehorse, 105
Windsor, 40, 91, 162, 164, 166, 172, 195
Winnipeg, 91, 92, 94, 104, 105, 164, 166, 186

Yellowknife, 105
Yorkdale Mall, 153
Yukon, 89, 160, 199